A Brief History of
COCAINE

Second Edition

A Brief History of
COCAINE

From Inca Monarchs to Cali Cartels: 500 Years of Cocaine Dealing

Second Edition

Steven B. Karch, M.D.

Taylor & Francis
Taylor & Francis Group

Boca Raton   London   New York

A CRC title, part of the Taylor & Francis imprint, a member of the
Taylor & Francis Group, the academic division of T&F Informa plc.

Published in 2006 by
CRC Press
Taylor & Francis Group
6000 Broken Sound Parkway NW, Suite 300
Boca Raton, FL 33487-2742

International Standard Book Number-10: 0-8493-9775-8 (Hardcover)
International Standard Book Number-13: 978-0-8493-9775-2 (Hardcover)
Library of Congress Card Number 2005050214

Library of Congress Cataloging-in-Publication Data

Karch, Steven B.
    A brief history of cocaine / Steven B. Karch.-- 2nd ed.
        p. cm.
    Includes bibliographical references and index.
    ISBN 0-8493-9775-8 (alk. paper)
    1. Cocaine--History. I. Title.

QP801.C68K369 2005
362.29'8'09--dc22   2005050214

Taylor & Francis Group
is the Academic Division of T&F Informa plc.

Visit the Taylor & Francis Web site at
http://www.taylorandfrancis.com

and the CRC Press Web site at
http://www.crcpress.com

Preface to the First Edition

In 1986, I was a visiting fellow in Margaret Billingham's cardiac pathology laboratory at Stanford University. I was studying the cellular changes that occur in the heart during cardiac arrest. It seemed to me that if we could characterize the changes that occurred at the microscopic level, we might be able to understand what was happening to the patient's entire system and devise better treatments. While reviewing sections of heart from a group of cardiac arrest victims, I noticed some peculiar changes and asked Professor Billingham about them. She explained that the changes that I identified were characteristically associated with stress, and with high levels of adrenaline, i.e., the stress hormone.

A few weeks later, I saw the same peculiar changes in the heart of a young San Francisco housewife who had collapsed and died, while using cocaine. She had no known medical problems; however, she and her husband had been "experimenting" with cocaine for about a year. When I examined her heart, I noticed that it was enlarged, and its walls were thickened. I also noticed an unusual, gritty feeling when cutting into the heart. I processed several portions of the heart for examination under microscope. One week later, when I finally had time to look at the sections, I was astonished to see how badly scarred the heart was.

Although not particularly interested or knowledgeable about the medical complications of drug abuse, I knew that cocaine affected stress hormones, and I wondered whether some abnormality having to do with high levels of adrenaline might have been responsible for the woman's death. I contacted the San Francisco Medical Examiner, Dr. Boyd Stephens, and asked him if I could review any similar cases that had occurred in his jurisdiction. He invited me to come and take a look.

We found 30 similar cases that occurred over a 2-year period. We compared the appearance of the cocaine users' hearts to those of a control group. There was no question that the same stress hormone-related changes were present in the cocaine users' hearts and were absent in the controls. A paper was soon written by the members of our group and quickly accepted by *Human Pathology*. The paper received quite a bit of attention, partially because of the death of Len Bias, an extremely talented young basketball player. Bias died while using cocaine a few weeks after our paper was published. His heart showed the same changes we saw and described.

Months later, while looking for a book in the stacks at Stanford's Lane Library, I found a copy of *Der Kokainismus*, a book published in Germany in 1926. Written by Hans Maier, a Swiss author and psychiatrist, it chronicled the medical and social history of cocaine-related disease. A chapter on the medical consequences of chronic cocaine abuse contained illustrations made by two Italian pathologists, Eugenio Bravetta and Giuseppe Invernizzi, in 1922. The illustrations depicted the changes they observed in the hearts of experimental animals, and in a man who died as a consequence of chronic cocaine abuse. I was astonished to notice that the illustrations showed exactly the same changes our group had observed in San Francisco.

Our original observations were not quite as original as we thought they were. I was concerned lest anyone think we appropriated the work of other earlier researchers and passed it off as our own. And so I started to write a letter to the journal that published our paper, with the intention of acknowledging the earlier work of Bravetta and Invernizzi and pointing out that we had not been aware that other researchers had ever looked at the problem. But after reading more of Professor Maier's book, I became fascinated with the story of cocaine abuse at the turn of the century and started reading more of the old literature. The Stanford medical library has a complete collection of medical journals dating from the mid-1880s. It did not take a great deal of research to find that not only had the pathology of cocaine-related heart disease been studied, but also that cocaine-related heart attacks and strokes were reported in large numbers, long before the turn of the century.

What started out as a letter acknowledging the work of the earlier researchers turned into a short history of the medical problems associated with cocaine use [The history of cocaine toxicity, *Human Pathology*, 20 (11), 1037–1039, 1989). The paper is still occasionally quoted, but even while writing it I wondered how much of the problem of cocaine abuse had already been solved by earlier researchers whose work was now completely ignored, just because it was published a long time ago, in another language. It turns out, quite a bit.

I discovered that not only has past medical research been ignored, but also that there is extensive literature dealing with many other aspects of the cocaine problem, all written before World War II, with much of it written before World War I. Earlier researchers did not just confine their attention to the medical complications of cocaine abuse, they also analyzed the agriculture, botany, chemistry, and political science of coca. Much of what I read sounded like it could have been written today.

In particular, neither the language nor the proposals of politicians wrestling with ways to control the spread of cocaine in the 1920s differed in any important respects from what is being said and proposed today. The only real difference between political leaders then and now is that political leaders at the turn of the century did not have to speak in 15-second sound bites and did not have 75 years of experience to guide them. I hope that with the publication of this book some of that information will become more accessible and perhaps even used.

Steven B. Karch, M.D.
Berkeley, California

Preface to the Second Edition

In the Afterword to the first edition of this book, I quoted Sir Edward Grey, the British Foreign Minister, who in 1910 wrote to the American Ambassador warning that the "spread of morphia and the cocaine habit, is becoming an evil more serious and more deadly than opium smoking, and this evil is certain to increase." I observed that Grey's warning was certainly prophetic, and that it was unlikely that even Grey could have predicted just how much worse the situation would become. I also discussed the possibility that deciphering the DNA codes for cocaine production, manufacturing copies of the DNA instructions and inserting them in some innocuous plants, such as corn or soybeans, would not be that hard to do. At the time, I had no inkling that my words might have been as prophetic as those of Grey.

On August 5, 2004, John Walters, the head of the U.S. Office of National Drug Control Policy (ONDCP), told narcotics officers attending a conference in Bogota, Colombia, that in 2003, 440 tons of cocaine were seized in Latin America, the United States, the United Kingdom, and Europe. He said this number represented 40% of the estimated flow of cocaine to the United States, the United Kingdom, and Europe. He added that "In the next 12 months, we will see changes in availability of the drug — probably first lower purity, followed by higher prices." The higher prices have still not materialized.

If Walters' numbers were correct, and 440 tons amounts to only 40% of the world's total cocaine production, then total world production is 1100 tons, roughly twice the number repeatedly suggested by officials of both the United States government and by the United Nations. Where did the other 600 tons of cocaine come from?

According to official reports, the acreage devoted to coca cultivation in Colombia fell to 250,000 hectares in 2004, roughly the same acreage devoted to Colombian coca in the previous 3 years. Herbicide fumigation destroyed 136,555 hectares in 2004 compared to a paltry 43,246 in 1999. If you subtract the amount fumigated from the amount grown in 1999, 122,500 hectares of coca remain. If you subtract the amount fumigated today, 136,555 hectares, from the 250,555 hectares planted, 114,000 hectares of viable coca are still growing. In other words, Plan Colombia has succeeded, but only to a very limited degree. Despite all of the expenditures and the huge area defoliated, output has dropped by only 8500 hectares since 1999, from 122,500 to 114,000 (these numbers are based on a March 25, 2005, press release from the Office of the Drug Czar). By any standard, the program has failed.

It is not just that defoliation is ineffective; there is another explanation for the apparent failure of the program. In late August of 2004, newspapers began reporting that Colombian authorities suspect that a hybridized, if not genetically engineered, coca is now being planted. The plants are said to be taller (coca shrubs are usually 5 feet high), herbicide resistant, and have a higher cocaine content. A toxicologist who advises Colombia's antinarcotics police told reporters that the new "super plants," some 7 to 12 feet tall, were seen in the Sierra Nevada mountains in northern Colombia, and in La Macarena, a savannah and jungle-covered region in central Colombia. Similar sightings are alleged in other areas, including in Putumayo state in southern Colombia, where locals call the new varieties White Bolivian and Black Bolivian.

These reports have yet to be independently confirmed. Whether or not any super plants are really being grown, there is plenty of evidence from our own government laboratories that Andean growers are hybridizing their plants to improve yield. According to a report by U.S. government researchers, the use of DNA profiling methods showed that nearly one-third of the samples collected from illicit coca fields in Colombia from 1997 to 2001 were genetically altered; whether in the laboratory or by crossbreeding is impossible to say. But if Monsanto can manufacture Roundup Ready® soybeans, can Roundup Ready coca be far behind?

In his Bogota speech, Walters said he believes fumigation remains an important and effective option, but he also indicated that money spent on spraying could be used elsewhere: "We need to make sure other areas are well-funded, such as interdiction." Was Walters' speech an implicit admission that eradication is no longer working? Only time and drug prices will tell.

Steven B. Karch, M.D.
Berkeley, California

Acknowledgments, First Edition

John Taylor, the military historian at the National Archives, United Kingdom, gave me invaluable help. Until I met him, I had never heard of "Purple," let alone "The Red Intercepts," and I knew nothing about navigating my way through the miles of documents that Taylor seems to know by heart. In England, Cheryl Piggott, the former archivist at Kew Gardens, was kind enough to ferret out workbooks and correspondence, mostly uncataloged, describing the early days of the coca business. Dr. J. T. Omtzigt, from the Gerechtelijk Laboratorium in the Netherlands, uncovered much of the material about the Colonial Development Bank and the Cocaine Producers Cartel, and was even kind enough to translate it and portions of Marcel de Kort's thesis, for me. Dr. Kari Blaho, at the University of Tennessee, found the material on Harvey Wiley's plan to police America's soda fountains. Thanks also to Joe Bono, of the U.S. Drug Enforcement Administration's special testing lab, for finding a way to get me a copy of *La Coca De Java* — no easy task as there appears to be only two in the United States. Professor Rudolph Steiner, of the Political Science Department at Stanford, who actually attended the Tokyo War Crimes Trials, and who knows more about them than anyone else, took the time to read the chapters on Japan and point me in the right direction when I began to wander. I hope his account of the trial is finished soon. Eva Rigney helped with some of the German translations. Bill Keach, a reference librarian with the Providence Public Libraries, was able to supply the references and unearth obscure statistics, faster than I ever thought possible. Without his help, this book would have taken even longer to write and would not have been nearly as accurate. Sara Morabito read all of the versions and always had helpful comments to make, even though we do not always agree politically. Fellow 1 K flyer Richard G. McCracken also provided encouragement and much appreciated help with the final manuscript.

My thanks also to Professor Paul Gootenberg and the Russel Sage Foundation for inviting me to participate in their workshop on cocaine. Some of the thoughts we shared helped make this a better book. Hardwin Mead and Roger Winkle continue to make their own unique contributions. Thanks also to Professor Rob Sprinkle in the School of Public Affairs at the University of

Maryland. Because he took the time and trouble to read and review my first attempts, this final version is much improved. And thanks go to my wife, Donna, who not only was patient with me during the process, but who also helped wade through the miles of documents we reviewed. It is a good thing we both like old books.

Acknowledgments, Second Edition

Bill Keach is now with the Cape Fear Community College, Wilmington, NC, but he is still my favorite fact checker. Sara Morabito is still my proofreader, Hardwin Mead and Roger Winkle continue to make their own unique contributions, and Donna's help remains as invaluable as ever. Sadly, Sylvester, my other proofreader, and severest critic, is no longer with the program.

The Author

Steven B. Karch, M.D. earned his undergraduate degree from Brown University in Providence, Rhode Island, and attended graduate school in anatomy and cell biology at Stanford University, Palo Alto, California. He earned his M.D. degree from Tulane University School of Medicine in New Orleans, Louisiana, did postgraduate training in neuropathology at the Royal London Hospital, and in Cardiac Pathology at Stanford University.

Dr. Karch is the author of nearly 100 papers and book chapters, most having to do with the effects of drug abuse on the heart. He has published seven books (*Karch's Pathology of Drug Abuse*, 1st, 2nd, and 3rd editions), *Drug Abuse Handbook, A Brief History of Cocaine, The Consumer's Guide to Herbal Medicine*, and *A History of Cocaine: The Mystery of Coca Java and the Kew Plant*, an account of the Southeast Asian cocaine industry in the early 1900s. He is currently at work on the second edition of the *Drug Abuse Handbook* and is completing another book on the death of Napoleon.

Dr. Karch is a fellow of the American Academy of Forensic Sciences, the Society of Forensic Toxicologists (SOFT), the National Association of Medical Examiners (NAME), the Royal Society of Medicine in London, The Forensic Science Society in the U.K., and is a member of The International Association of Forensic Toxicologists (TIAFT).

Dr. Karch helped to prepare the case against Britain's most prolific serial killer, Dr. Harold Shipman. He has testified on drug related matters in courts around the world, and has a special interest in alleged cases of euthanasia, and in cases where mothers are accused of murdering their children either by breast feeding or by *in utero* administration of abused drugs. In addition to his other commitments, Dr. Karch lectures frequently on the investigation of drug-related deaths. He and his wife Donna live in Berkeley, California.

Dedication, First Edition

For my Uncle Stanley Shlosman on his 85th. Governor Long may have had the first word, but you had the last, and I'm glad. And for Sara Morabito, the best proofreader a son-in-law could ask for.

Dedication, Second Edition

To the memory of Dr. Boyd Stephenson, a good teacher and better friend who will be sorely missed. And to my wife Donna, of course.

Table of Contents

Introduction

Experience and history teach us this: that nations and governments have never learned a thing from history, or acted in accordance with anything they might have learned from it.

G.W.F. Hegel, Lectures on the Philosophy of World History, Introduction, 1840

Reality Check[*]

A reality check, or at least some sort of status report, should probably precede any serious discussion of the cocaine problem. How bad is the situation? The short answer is that things are "not good." Intensive eradication efforts in Colombia, Peru, and Bolivia caused growers and traffickers to seek new areas to cultivate, with the national parks of Colombia providing the latest attractive refuge. Traffickers are also using advanced technology to obtain better yields and improve harvests by neutralizing the effects of aerial spraying, by recycling chemical precursors that are increasingly scarce because of international controls, and by growing pesticide-resistant plants with greater yields. Destroying half the acreage has little effect if the yield of the remaining half can be doubled. The U.S. Department of State reports that in 2002, 144,000 hectares of coca were under cultivation (roughly 550 square miles) in Colombia, sufficient to produce 680 metric tons of finished cocaine.

Cocaine produced in Colombia, Bolivia, and Peru arrives in the United States via two main routes. It is estimated that 75% of all cocaine produced is destined for the United States, and that more than 60% of all cocaine leaving Latin America transits the Caribbean corridor, mostly by sea and also by private and commercial aircraft. Cocaine is also shipped to the U.S. using land routes across Mexico. The pattern of current seizures suggests that

---

[*] Much of this Introduction is reprinted from my book *A History of Coca, The Mystery of Coca Java and the Kew Plant*, Royal Society of Medicine Press, London, with kind permission.

Central America is serving as a storage region for cocaine that is later dispatched via the Caribbean.

Colombian mobsters control wholesale level cocaine distribution in the northeastern United Sates. Mexican organizations now control wholesale cocaine distribution throughout the West and Midwest. According to Interpol, the waterways in South America are used not only for delivering cocaine to the United States. They are now also being used to transport chemical precursors needed to make cocaine back to South America.

Cocaine destined for European countries travels via Africa. The drug is shipped mainly by use of the postal services and, increasingly, by use of sea containers. Nigerian criminal organizations operate widely in the African continent, and they control the sub-Saharan drug markets, though most of the drug making its way to Africa is transshipped back to Europe. The markets for cocaine in southwest and southeast Asia remain small, perhaps because of competition by local amphetamine manufacturers.

Approximately 520 tons of cocaine entered the United States in 2002. Prices vary, but a kilogram of cocaine sells for approximately $25,000. In Great Britain, it can fetch up to twice as much. Massive expenditures of money and manpower by governments on both sides of the Atlantic have led to the confiscation of hundreds of tons of cocaine. In 2003, more than 60 tons of cocaine were confiscated in the Eastern Pacific Ocean and Caribbean alone, and that figure was probably over 100 tons in 2004. Yet there has been no noticeable decline in price or purity of cocaine on either side of the Atlantic.

Since Plan Colombia — a funding package originally designed to address the war on drugs —became law in 2000, the United States sent more than $2.4 billion to Colombia. In fiscal year 2004, $553 million was provided in military aid alone. In 2002, the wholesale price (kilogram quantities) in the United States ranged between $15,000 and $30,000 per kilogram, and it is estimated that 520 tons of cocaine were produced. Assuming a mid-range value of $20,000 per kilogram, then something like $10 billon changed hands at the wholesale level. At the street level, the amount expended was, of course, much higher. The U.S. Drug Enforcement Administration (DEA) believes that half-gram-sized "rocks" of crack cocaine sell for between $10 and $20. One ton contains 1,016,000 grams, enough to make 2,032,000 half-gram rocks of cocaine. If 520 tons of cocaine were sold, its net value on the street would have been $16 billion. The statistics speak for themselves.

Why Is There a Cocaine Trade?

The revelation that Sinn Fein was, for a fee, giving bomb-making lessons to South American terrorists should have surprised no one. Sinn Fein's expansion into vocational education follows naturally from the two basic principles of the drug trade: globalization and terrorism.

Most Third World countries, where the raw materials for illicit drug making are produced, lack the ability to control what goes on within their borders. Drug producers in Colombia command resources far in excess of those controlled by Colombia's central government, even when that government is heavily subsidized by the United States. In effect, the drug cartels operate as governments within governments, equally well prepared to export drugs, or terror, for profit.

Drug cartels around the world function autonomously, partly because of the unequal resources they command and partly because the republics of Colombia and Peru (or Lebanon, or Afghanistan) lack legitimacy. Citizens of drug-producing countries seldom hold either their government or its policies in high regard. One direct consequence is that governments not deemed legitimate by their subjects must ultimately govern by repression, not by consent.

Repressive governments, like those of the former Soviet Union or the current government of Cuba, are invariably administered by large bureaucracies. The larger the bureaucracy, the less it is respected. The less the bureaucracy is respected, the greater the opportunities for corruption. The Sicilian mafia's relationship to the Italian government is one good example, and the recently ascended Russian mafia is another.

Illicit drug trade is nurtured by the existence of large, incompetent bureaucracies. Low-paid customs inspectors are inclined to turn a blind eye when offered 10 times their yearly wages. The more highly paid the bureaucrats, the larger the bribe. Witness the succession of Mexican generals charged with drug dealing. As bureaucracies become thoroughly corrupted, their members metamorphose, becoming drug dealers themselves. The army generals in Myanmar now effectively control the world's largest methamphetamine factories, as well as an estimated 81,000 hectares of opium poppies, producing more than 810 tons of opium (which is less than one-third the yield per acre achieved in Afghanistan).

Throughout recorded history, central governments have regularly behaved as if they were criminal cartels, using drug revenues to fund expansionist goals. The salaries of the Kwangtung occupation army were paid, in large part, by revenues generated by the state-run opium monopoly, and other funding schemes generated cash by the sale of war bonds guaranteed by narcotic sales. Prosecutors at The International Military Tribunal for the Far East successfully argued that these actions constituted a crime against humanity.

Japan's approach to financing its occupation of China was neither new nor novel. Nearly five centuries before Emperor Hirohito ascended the

Chrysanthemum throne, King Philip of Spain taxed coca sales in his new world possessions. The revenues were used to help pay his army of conquistadors and an even larger army of government administrators. Taliban and al-Qaida operatives may not have known how the Kwangtung army raised funds, but there is no question that they used profits from heroin and opium sales to fund their jihad.

A Catechism for Drug Warriors

The cocaine trade was globalized almost from its beginning. The first cocaine cartel was formed in Switzerland, not Colombia, and it was comprised of international pharmaceutical companies intent on manipulating the market for legally sold narcotics. How is it then, that when elected officials and appointed bureaucrats attempt to deal with the problems and issues generated by the illicit drug trade, they act as if cocaine was some sort of newly minted menace?

Institutional ignorance of what has gone before almost guarantees that any newly proposed solutions were previously tried and found wanting. Governments planning antidrug crusades, and it matters not at all which government, which century, or which drug, always propose the same limited set of four approaches: crop substitution, crop suppression, enhanced efforts at interdiction, and more international cooperation. All four approaches have repeatedly failed.

The failure of international cooperation to restrain the drug trade is illustrated by the behavior of the Japanese government during the period just before World War II. Japan was signatory to every international drug control treaty and attended every meeting of the League of Nation's Opium Committee, up until the start of World War II. While Yosuke Matsuoka, the Japanese representative to the League, was attending conferences on drug control in Geneva, other Japanese Foreign Ministry employees were resolving a trade dispute between Mitsui and Mitsubishi. A bidding war over limited supplies of opium was narrowly averted when diplomats of the Japanese Foreign Office negotiated a compromise giving Mitsui the rights to sell narcotics in the south of China, and Mitsubishi the rights to sell in the north of China. Fifty years later, is there any reason to suppose that any wartime government, badly in need of cash, will not behave in exactly the same way today? Hardly. In fact, the latest drug intelligence reports suggest that, in an attempt to revive its failed economy and support its massive army, North Korea entered the highly competitive business of growing poppies and refining heroin.

Attempts at interdiction, the third option, usually focus on the disruption of drug distribution networks. The idea is not new. King Philip of Spain's Casa de Contratación was a semiautonomous agency that was founded in 1503 to regulate trade with the New World. Only Spanish ships were allowed to carry commerce to the New World, and they were only allowed to dock in Cartagena, in what is now Colombia, Puerto Bello in Panama, and Vera Cruz in Mexico. The goods they carried had to be Spanish made, and it was required that they carry the stamp of the Casa de Contratación. It did not take long for the other countries in Europe to build a thriving business, smuggling restricted goods into and out of the Spanish colonies. Coca leaves were just one of many different items smuggled back to Europe. These are the same operating principles underlying the current key role of certain Caribbean islands in the transshipment of cocaine from South America to the United States and Europe.

The problem with interdiction is that no matter how many resources are dedicated to the process, drug producers can dedicate more. The lopsided nature of this contest is nicely illustrated by figures from the U.S. National Institute of Justice, a research branch of the U.S. Department of Justice. According to that agency, in the year 2000, the United States spent $1.5 billion on international interdiction efforts. The dollar amount equates to the approximate street value of 16 metric tons of cocaine. With a net value of at least $100 million U.S. dollars a ton, is it any wonder that Mexican drug cartels can, and do, lose that much cocaine in a few shipments, with no discernable effect either on the amount of cocaine on the streets or on the amount of money accruing to the cartels?

Just after World War II, officials at the League of Nations estimated that total world cocaine production amounted to less than 10 tons per year. The U.S. State Department recently estimated that in the year 2000, total South American cocaine production was approximately 700 tons, giving the total cocaine produced for that year a value in excess of 70 billion dollars. Increased interdiction is easily countered by increased production. With revenues in excess of 70 billion dollars, illicit cocaine producers almost certainly write off any losses as negligible operating expenses. Legitimate governments, on the other hand, cannot dismiss an expense of $1.5 billion as negligible, especially when the expenditure leaves hundreds of tons of cocaine in the pipeline.

Even if interdiction and international cooperation do not work, there is always crop substitution and crop suppression. As a practical matter, replacing coca with some other crop would not be difficult. In most parts of the world, coffee will grow just as well as coca, and coffee is simpler and easier to grow. But prices for coffee fluctuate wildly on world markets, and even when prices are high, return to the local growers never approaches the return provided by coca. Indigenous peoples choose coca as a cash crop because it gives them the most income.

The Second Marqués de Cañete, Spanish viceroy in Peru from 1555 to 1560, was the first to confront this reality. After the Spanish Conquest of Peru, supplying coca to laborers in the silver and mercury mines became a very lucrative undertaking. So lucrative, in fact, that farmers stopped growing other crops, and basic foodstuffs were in short supply. Cañete issued decrees limiting the total acreage that could be devoted to coca and even created financial incentives to encourage the substitution of food crops for coca. The measures proved to be ineffective.

What about crop suppression? Many different chemical agents are now being sprayed on South American hillsides and, occasionally on the South American people. Tebuthiuron was used in the late 1990s, but it persists in the soil, and concerns about groundwater contamination led to a search for alternatives. Tebuthiuron was then replaced with glyphosate (Roundup Ultra™), fortified with Cosmo-Flux™, a product of Britain's Imperial Chemical Industries. Precise figures are difficult to come by, but more than 30,000 hectares of land were sprayed in Colombia's Putamaya province alone. Nonetheless, the program seems to have been less successful than the U.S. government might have hoped.

On August 5, 2004, the U.S government first began dropping hints of its dissatisfaction. Speaking in Bogota, John P. Walters, director of the U.S. Office of National Drug Control Policy (ONDCP), told narcotics officers attending a conference there that "Aerial spraying is a major component of Colombia's strategy for fighting the drug trade and is the program with the single greatest potential for disrupting the production of cocaine before it enters the supply train to the United States. Spray operations have the potential to cause collapse of the cocaine industry if the spraying is intensive, effective, and persistent. Replanting coca is expensive for farmers, in terms of both labor inputs and opportunity costs (coca seedlings typically take a year to begin bearing harvestable leaf). According to estimates by the Institute for Defense Analyses, eradicating 200,000 hectares of coca would cost farmers $300 million — costs significant enough to cause growers to conclude cultivation is uneconomical."

Actually, costs for Plan Colombia now exceed $3 billion, but why quibble? Walters conceded that despite the impressive success claimed, "Thus far we have not seen a change of availability in the United States." He added, that "Seizing cocaine, destroying coca crops, and locking up drug traffichers in Colombia has little impact on the flow of cocaine on U.S. streets," and he also indicated that money spent on spraying could be used elsewhere. According to Walters, "We need to make sure other areas are well-funded, such as interdiction." When asked why street prices in the United States had yet to increase, he suggested that drug traffickers still have tons of cocaine stored along transport routes, and that they have been drawing upon this stock to keep prices low. He maintained that once the current stock is depleted, drug prices will go up, and availability will decrease. That was more than a year ago.

Just a month later, on September 16, 2004, the U.S. Senate Appropriations Committee approved President George W. Bush's request for $731 million to fund the "Andean Counter-Drug Initiative" (ACI) account, which includes antidrug, military, and economic aid for Colombia and six of its neighbors. The bill (S.2812) specifically holds back 80% of funds for herbicides, pending certification on the environmental and health effects of fumigation (which clearly will not be forthcoming), and provides payments for legal crops destroyed by spraying. It also holds back funding for fumigation in Colombia's national parks, at least until Secretary of State Condoleezza Rice is willing to certify that the spraying of Colombia's national parks (where the increasingly sophisticated coca growers are now planting their fields) is in accordance with Colombian laws and that there are no effective alternatives to reduce drug cultivation in these areas.

While the relative merits and toxicities of different herbicides can be debated, what is not debatable is that poisoning the crops has not proven to be an effective cure, or else the government would be pursuing the approach more aggressively. Would the invention of better herbicides solve the problem? The answer is clearly no. Deforestation is only a viable option if the area of destruction has some reasonable limit. As the documents reproduced in this book clearly show, coca will grow almost anywhere.

The authors of the U.S. strategic plan for controlling drug production in Colombia appear to be as unaware of historical precedent as they are of coca agronomics. In the early 1900s, more coca was grown in Java than in South America. If, for whatever reason, it became impossible to grow coca in Colombia or Peru, business would move eastward — or perhaps to Africa. Coca was once grown commercially in Nigeria, and for a while, coca produced more revenue for that country than rubber. Until just 4 years ago, the U.S. government operated a research coca plantation that flourished on the Hawaiian island of Kauai.

There is, of course, another possible explanation for the apparent failure of these crop eradication programs. In the summer of 2004, newspapers in South America, and a few in the United States, began to report that Colombian authorities suspect that hybridized, if not genetically engineered, coca has been introduced in that country. The plants are said to be taller (coca shrubs are usually 5 feet high), herbicide resistant, and higher in cocaine content than traditional Colombian coca. These plants were sighted in the Sierra Nevada mountain range in northern Colombia, and in La Macarena, a savannah and jungle-covered region in central Colombia. Similar sightings are alleged in other areas, including Putumayo state in southern Colombia, where locals call the new varieties White Bolivian and Black Bolivian. These reports have yet to be independently confirmed. The plants described seem to possess most of the features seen in the coca grown in Indonesia and Taiwan in the early 1900s. Readers of the first edition of this book will recall that there was much debate about the origins of the plants grown in Java, but there was no debate about their very high cocaine content and their resistance to pests. Could it be that Colombians have somehow resurrected the old Java coca, or engineered a plant variety much like it? It is too early to say for certain, but the evidence points in that direction.

The cocaine industry was globalized from the beginning. During the early years of cocaine globalization, motives were mixed. Cocaine was, after all, the first effective local anesthetic. Before cocaine, surgical procedures were, of necessity, limited to those that could be performed in a matter of seconds. After the discovery of cocaine's ability to anesthetize, a variety of technically feasible, but previously unthinkable, surgical procedures were undertaken. Subsequently, the demand for cocaine became great. But then, so too were the profits to be made by the drug companies. Or, as the British naturalist and Amazon explorer Clements Markham put it, "the distribution of valuable products of the vegetable kingdom amongst the nations of the earth — their introduction from countries where they are indigenous into distant lands…is one of the greatest benefits that civilization has conferred upon mankind." Governments are not the only entities privy to this knowledge. The cocaine cartels know it also.

The Inca and Spanish Conquests

1

When Amerigo Vespucci finally reached the coast of Venezuela in 1499, one of the first images to greet his eyes was a group of people chewing coca leaves:

> We descried an island in the sea that lay about fifteen leagues from the coast [and there we found] the most bestial and ugly people we had ever seen. And all of them had their cheeks full of a green herb that they chewed constantly like beasts, so that they could barely speak; and each one carried about his neck two gourds, one of them full of that herb that they had in their mouths and the other of a white powder that looked like pulverised plaster, and from time to time, they dipped a stick into the powder after wetting it in the mouth, and put the stick in the mouth, an end on each cheek, in order to apply powder to the herb that they chewed; they did this very frequently. We were amazed at this thing and could not understand its secret.

Venezuela is not now a coca producer, but coca has always grown there naturally, and what Vespucci witnessed was the widespread custom of chewing the tough coca leaves, along with lime made from roasted seashells (the process helps liberate the cocaine from the leaves). The practice has not changed in the last 500 years.

The same method as that witnessed by Vespucci is illustrated on a 2500-year-old pot recently found in northern Peru. The pot was an artifact of the ancient Moche tribe, created before they were absorbed by the Incas. In 1997, tomb excavations revealed the graves of two Moche warrior-priests. The warriors wore gold masks, and their bodies were decorated with finely crafted copper and gold ornaments. All around them lay sacrificial victims, presumably

1

household servants, who were murdered at the time the two priests were buried. Alongside the victims were containers for coca leaves and shells to hold the lime.

Other archaeological finds confirm the importance and complexity of the Moche's coca-chewing rituals; usually, though not always, they were associated with war and sacrifice. In Colombia, the Quimbaya, another tribe overrun by the Incas, observed nearly the same customs, but they used fine gold containers to store the lime that was chewed with the leaf. Coca leaves were found in graves, dating from long before the Moche, in southwest Ecuador and northern Chile. The oldest of these graves is more than 4000 years old. In Chile, traces of cocaine were found in the hair of mummified corpses, shown by radiocarbon dating, to be at least 1500 years old. As anyone subject to drug testing already knows, once drugs like cocaine are deposited in the hair shaft, the drug remains a part of the hair indefinitely, even long after death.

The great Inca Empire eventually assimilated all of the earlier cultures in the Andes, but details about them remain sketchy. What we do know about the Inca is largely thanks to their Spanish conquerors. Cieza de Leon, a Spaniard who reached the Americas as a 14-year-old soldier, wrote the first serious account of Andean coca. De Leon settled in what is now Colombia and spent 4 years traveling through Bolivia and Peru, keeping a record of what he saw. Garcilaso de la Vega, the son of an Inca princess and a Spanish nobleman, also recorded detailed observations. de la Vega's *The Royal Commentaries of the Incas*, first published in 1609, was followed by a second book, *The General History of Peru*, printed in 1617. Both books were translated into English many times. A translation was even produced by Clements Markham, a British government agent who, in the mid-1800s, helped England establish coca and quinine plantations around the world. All of the Spanish writers tell remarkably similar stories.

At its peak, the Inca Empire was comprised of at least 100 different ethnic groups, with a population of some 12 million people. The Empire stretched 2500 miles North to South, and 200 miles from East to West. The Incas imposed their own culture on their new subjects but did not completely stamp out native traditions. The word "coca," in fact, is derived from the language of one of the conquered tribes — the Aymara of Bolivia. It is their word for tree.

The origins of coca are embedded in Inca legend (see Figure 1.1). The Spanish Viceroy Toledo wrote the following:

> Among the natives there was a legend that before the coca tree was as it is now there was a beautiful woman, and because she lived a loose life they killed her and cut her in two. From her body grew the bush that they call Mama-coca, and from that time they

MANCO CCAPAC AND MAMA OCLLO HUACO.   [*After Rivero and Tschudi.*]

Figure 1.1   Drawings of Mama Coca, taken from Mortimer's text, which, in turn, was adapted from a drawing of Jakob Joham Tschudi's *Reisen in Peru 1818–1889*. The ancient accounts vary, but it was Mama Coca who gave cocaine to man.

> began to eat it. They carried it in a small bag and it was forbidden to open the bag and eat it until after they had had relations with a woman, in memory of that woman. For this reason they call it coca.

It appears that then, as now, using coca was associated with sex, but it took the Incas some time to find out about it. Coca did not grow well within the original boundaries of the Inca Empire, but as their Empire expanded ever eastward, the Incas found a better climate for mass cultivation. The plant grows most vigorously in hot damp forest clearings, though the most desirable leaves, those with the best taste, come from plants grown on drier hillsides. The Incas created new plantations on the eastern slopes of the

Andes and greatly expanded production within that region. No matter in
what part of the Empire the coca was grown, all of the harvest had to be
turned over to the royal coca collectors, who, in turn, delivered the leaves
the Emperor and his family. The Royal family then dispensed the coca leaves
as they pleased.

Garcilasa de la Vega described how Yahuar Huacac, the Seventh Inca
King, kept "a little purse called a *chuspa*, for his personal use…slung from
his left shoulder to his right side, to keep his coca leaves in." de la Vega added:

> The use of coca was nothing like so widespread then as it is today
> [mid-sixteenth century], but was the exclusive privilege of the king
> who occasionally offered a few leaves as a mark of favor to this or
> that prince or curaca [chief] in his immediate circle.

Not all scholars accept de la Vega's version. There is considerable evidence
that coca played an important part in the religious life of every Inca, not just
the lives of royalty and priests. Indian folklore, not to mention many accounts
by Spanish colonials, strongly suggests that coca was chewed by all members
of that society.

Why did the Incas chew coca? Coca must have seemed like a miraculous
drug. Coca leaves contain cocaine, and cocaine eliminates feelings of hunger
and thirst. Better still, it produces an exhilarating sense of well-being, and it
is not hard to see how the ability to produce these feelings might induce some
sort of religious reverence. The drug's effects probably also explain why coca
leaves were offered in ritual sacrifices to the gods, especially Pachamama, the
earth goddess (also translated as Mother Earth, Mother Time, or Mother
Universe). To this day, South American Indians make offerings to the same
goddess, in the hope that she will favor their crops or bless their houses.
Images and statues of Inca gods usually show the gods with one cheek filled
with coca leaves.

Priests were allowed to chew coca during rituals, and the victims of these
rituals were permitted the same pleasure. Sacrificial victims were well supplied with coca first — before being strangled with an iron collar or having
their necks broken with a stone or, worst of all, having their still-beating
hearts torn out, following a ritual similar to that regularly employed for
sacrificing sheep and goats.

The bodies of several freeze-dried children, victims of another type of
sacrifice, were uncovered in 1996. The bodies were found in the Peruvian
mountains, at an altitude of over 18,000 feet, at a site known as Mount Sara
Sara. Children were placed in an earthen cave, covered with a stone slab,
which was, in turn, covered with successive layers of earth and stones piled
5 feet high. The soil acted as insulation, maintaining the living grave at a

constant temperature all year round, and keeping out bacteria and larger predators. Bags of coca leaves have always been found in such graves, presumably to help ease the deceased on their way to the afterlife. No doubt following the same line of thought, the dead had coca leaves placed on their tongues to facilitate passage to the underworld.

It was presumed that coca leaves had magical powers, and they were, accordingly, used for divination. The Incas believed that fire provided contact with the spirits. Flames were blown to a red heat with hollow tubes, after which the *yacarca* (shaman) would put himself into a trance by chewing coca. He would then summon the spirits to speak, which they did, probably with the aid of some ventriloquism. Shamans also claimed to be able to see the shape of the future in the rising smoke of burning coca leaves. Smoke from coca leaves was used to purify the places inhabited by evil spirits and to drive out the spirits of diseases.

The Incas were obviously aware that chewing coca leaves made the tongue numb, and this may have led them to believe that the same leaves would help slow the process of decomposition, for they used a tincture of coca in the process of mummification. According to Spanish historians, the mummified corpses of important ancestors were paraded during great rituals "in litters…with diadems on their heads. A pavilion was erected for them…and the dead kings were placed in these in order, seated on their thrones and surrounded by pages and women with fly whisks in their hands, who ministered to them with as much respect as if they had been alive."

The Incas employed coca for other purposes, some practical and some hedonistic. One of the earliest accounts describing both was written by Nicholas Monardes, a Spanish doctor who never visited the New World but who, in 1569, published a treatise on New World plants and their medicinal uses. His book is perhaps most famous for containing the first account of tobacco. After noting that the Indians held coca in reverence, many of them even named their children "Coca," Monardes provided a description of how the natives preserved coca leaves. First, they roasted cockle- or clamshells, then ground them down, and then chewed the ash with coca leaves, forming little pellets that were then set out to dry in the sun. The pellets were used whenever the Indians had to make long journeys, when they were likely to be forced to do without food or water for days. The second purpose Monardes mentioned was "if they wanted to be happy at home." In other words, if they wanted to "become intoxicated," they would chew coca leaves mixed with tobacco. In a later English translation of Monardes' book, John Frampton states: "Surely it is a thyng of great consideration, to see how the Indians are so desirous to bee deprived of their wittes, and be without understanding." Proving, thereby, that even the earliest Amazon explorers and writers knew that coca leaf was mind altering and potentially addictive.

Still other accounts describe young women, spectators at athletic competitions, giving the runners coca to make them race faster. Cieza de Leon wrote:

> In Peru, in all its extent, it was the custom, as is, to carry this coca in the mouth and from morning until they retire to sleep they carry it without emptying it from their mouths. And when I enquired of certain Indians why they keep their mouths ever filled with that herb (the which they eat not neither do they more than carry it between their teeth), they say that they have little sense of hunger and feel great vigor and strength.

These observations probably gave rise to the notion of coca/cocaine being a performance-enhancing drug, a recurring theme still heard today.

Pizarro's army entirely conquered the Incas by 1539, but Spanish settlers began arriving in Peru even before the conquest was complete. They were given tracts of land, called *repartimientos*, and the lands came complete with enslaved Indians to work them. Initially, the Conquistadors took little interest in coca, except, perhaps, when used in place of money, and did nothing to interfere with the Indians' practice of growing and chewing coca. But as restrictions on the availability of coca loosened, and finally disappeared, coca chewing became ever more popular, and it did not take the Spanish too long to realize that coca had immense commercial value. As a result, more land was given over to growing coca. So much money was involved, that in 1539, the Bishop of Cuzco began to tithe coca, taking a tenth of the value of each crop. Coca production in Peru expanded so rapidly that, within a few years, there was a temporary glut of leaf on the market, and price competition forced a drop in the earnings of Spanish coca producers. Indians were forced to do longer stints working the hot and humid plantations.

The death rate for the *repartimientos* was appallingly high. Workers quickly succumbed to a succession of horrible diseases that attacked the lungs, caused anemia, and made them less resistant to a painful parasitic disease (*mal de los Andes*) that rotted the nose, lips, and throat. Just which parasite caused the disease has never been precisely identified, but there would have been no shortage from which to choose in the area. Between one-third and one-half of the annual quota of coca workers died as a result of their 5-month service. Those who survived returned to their villages "so sick and weak that they never recuperate," wrote King Philip II of Spain. But not all the Spanish were without conscience, and as one observer put it: "down there, there is one disease worse than all the rest: the unrestrained greed of the Spaniards."

In 1545, huge silver deposits were discovered at Potosí, Bolivia, and a year later at Zacatecas. Silver soon replaced gold as the New World's most important export. The Crown cut taxes on silver-mining revenues, in the hope of encouraging investors to commit large sums of money needed to develop the new mines. The incentives worked. From 1546 to 1601, the mines surrounding Potosí produced more than half of the world's silver supply. Once the silver reached Spain, it was either sold on the open market as a luxury item or used to pay off the heavy debts that were incurred by the Crown. There was only one problem: the mines at Potosí were at 13,780 feet above sea level.

Living conditions at Potosí were appalling. Nothing grew in the sparse soil and thin air. Everything required for normal, day-to-day living, not to mention whatever was needed to run a mining operation, had to be brought up by pack train. Often, the packs were carried on the backs of Indian porters. Conditions in the mines were intolerably cold and damp, and the mortality rate among the workers was, if anything, higher than that among those forced to grow coca.

To assure a steady supply of workers at the mines, and of porters to supply the miners, the Spanish Viceroy established a system of forced labor. Up to one-seventh of the inhabitants of any given region could be called for temporary work outside their community. Most of them were sent to the mines, as imported African slaves did not survive the high altitude. In 1550, a Spanish friar described the mine as "a mouth of hell, into which a great mass of people enter every year and are sacrificed by the greed of the Spaniards to their 'God.'" Convicted criminals would not have to undergo such appalling conditions as these, he said. The miners were ill housed, poorly fed, and forced to work in dangerous conditions, but they were kept well supplied with coca leaves.

So much money could be made selling coca in Potosí that many merchants were attracted to the business. Indian workers at Potosí spent nearly twice as much on coca leaves as they did on food and clothing. Coca leaves, bought for a few pesos in Cuzco, could be sold for ten to eleven pesos in Potosí. A street in Potosí was even named after the coca merchants. There was a coca producers' lobby at the court, and its leader estimated that at least 2000 Spaniards were involved in the coca trade.

Shipments from Cuzco, the coca-producing hub, to Potosí required hundreds of pack animals and porters to carry thousands of baskets of coca leaves. The value of one such shipment was 7500 pesos, equivalent to 34 kg of gold, making annual shipments worth more than 4500 kg of gold. In Potosí, where normal produce was taxed at a rate of 2%, coca was taxed at 5%. The Bishop of Cuzco profited handsomely by organizing coca deliveries to the mines. Tax laws were revised to permit landowners to make their tax payments in coca leaves. The coca economy boomed.

The Spanish clergy had its doubts. Most, but far from all, churchmen opposed coca chewing. The Catholic Church assumed that coca chewing was linked to religious belief, and that these beliefs would almost certainly undermine Catholicism. An ecclesiastical council was convened in Lima, Peru, in 1551. The bishops urged the government to outlaw the use of coca, condemning it for "strengthening the wicked in their delusions," and concluding that it was "an object without benefit, created for the superstition and abuse by the Indians."

The colonial government, for its part, probably agreed with them, but for different reasons. Coca was indelibly linked with Inca tradition and probably linked with any remaining notions any of the native peoples might have had about overthrowing the colonial government. In the end, the civilian government opposed the Church's position and did nothing to limit the supply of coca. Opponents waged a long, and not totally unsuccessful, campaign against the practice and succeeded in forcing the government to draw up reforms designed to protect the rights of Indians working in the mines and at coca plantations. Though attempts at an outright ban on coca growing failed, the Marqués de Cañete, fearing for the health of the Indians, used his position as the second Spanish Viceroy (from 1555 to 1560) to promulgate land reform measures limiting the number of acres devoted to coca cultivation. He also limited the number of days Indians could be forced to work on the plantations to 24, and he passed other regulations to ensure that the workers were provided with daily rations of maize.

De Cañete even created financial incentives designed to encourage the substitution of food crops for coca (a constantly recurring theme in this history), but the Peruvian government's attempts were in vain. The colonial government was short of cash, and taxes on drugs provided revenue. The Spaniards, including King Philip II, genuinely believed that without coca to chew, the silver miners would be unable to work. And Philip II was constantly being lobbied by Spanish colonial producers. As Juan Matienzo, lobbyist for the coca growers, wrote in a letter to King Philip II in 1566: "The cultivation and trade of coca is a very important enterprise and of the greatest significance."

When the second council of Lima was convened in 1569, a strong argument was advanced that the only way to solve the coca problem was to eradicate coca, because "Coca is a thing without benefit and...takes the lives of many," and "Coca is a plant that the devil invented for the total destruction of the natives." Four hundred years later, in 1961, Peru signed the United Nations (UN) Single Convention on Narcotic Drugs. Under the terms of the convention, coca chewing by the people of the Andes was to be completely eradicated by 1986. In 2005, the UN's convention remains in effect, and the people of the Andes are still growing coca, and still chewing it, and there is still a great deal of money to be made from selling it.

"Joyfulle News"

2

So far as colonial Spanish administrators and the Casa de Contratación were concerned, silver was the ideal export. Gold was more profitable, but after the first round of plunder, gold took more work to acquire. Silver was as compact as gold, easy to ship, and worth enough in Europe to make the expense of the trans-Atlantic crossing worthwhile. Tobacco and sugar met the same criteria: sufficient demand in Europe and sufficient availability in Peru. Coca was not a candidate for export mainly because there was no demand for it in Europe. The reason nobody wanted to buy coca was that they had never heard of it.

The lack of demand for coca was a problem of Spain's own making. During the 16th century and most of the 17th century, Spain prevented mention of coca from ever reaching Europe. The Spanish imposed an embargo on all news about the New World. What gave Spain the right to control all New World trade? It was God's will, of course. Or at least it was the will of God's representative on earth, the Pope. The kings of Portugal and Spain, with the blessings of Spanish-born Pope Alexander VI, divided Africa and South America between themselves.

The division was made formal in a decree issued by the Vatican Chancery, called a Papal Bull (the name is from the Latin *bulla* describing the boiled appearance of the seal affixed to the decree). The Bull was issued when Christopher Columbus returned from his first voyage (Bull *Inter caetera*). The Pope decreed that Spain and Portugal should divide the non-Christian world into two parts: one controlled by Spain and the other by Portugal. Division was to be along a north–south line located 100 leagues west of Cape Verde (in other words, between 48° and 49° west of Greenwich). Given that the Pope was Spanish, it should shock no one to learn that the entire New World was turned over to Spain.

Portugal did not do badly either — it was awarded all of Africa and India. Still, King John III of Portugal was not happy, and he wanted the terms of the division to be renegotiated. He opened back-channel negotiations with King Ferdinand V and Queen Isabella, and finally worked out a new agreement that was signed in Tordesillas (a mid-sized town about 150 km northeast of Madrid) on June 7, 1494. A circular line of demarcation passing 370° west of the Cape Verde Islands was substituted for the original line drawn by the Pope. It was suggested that the geographical knowledge of those negotiating the treaty was so primitive that the Portuguese did not realize they had acquired Brazil. They probably did not much care either, because the treaty had more to do with navigation rights than land ownership. Arab merchants, who extracted heavy fees for rights of passage, controlled trade routes between India and China. The Portuguese were looking for a better way to get to China, and they were sure they found it.

Spain was concerned about more than navigation rights. The Spanish Crown was not keen on sharing its knowledge of the New World (especially its knowledge of where gold and silver were to be found), and they certainly did not want to advertise the amount of plunder that was being brought home. The last thing Spain wanted was to have other seafaring nations, including England, France, and the Netherlands, landing explorers in New World territories. The treaty signed at Tordesillas allowed Spain to maintain its embargo, and the embargo included knowledge. Anything written about the New World was subject to rigid censorship by the King, by the Holy Office of the Inquisition, by the Council of the Indies, and by the Casa de Contratación ("house of hiring").

The Casa was a semiautonomous agency founded in 1503. Within a few years of its founding, the Casa de Contratación came to control nearly every aspect of the colonization process. Bureaucrats working for the Casa decided which ships could sail to the New World, what the ships could carry, and who could sail on them. The Casa licensed ships, inspected cargoes, and collected taxes. It advised the King on trade and functioned as a sort of trade court. It made sure that no undesirables (Jews or Arabs) were allowed to set foot in the new territories. But mostly what it did, or tried to do, was to make sure that Spain maintained a strict monopoly on New World trade. Ships heading for New World ports had to fly a Spanish flag, could only call at certain ports, and were only allowed to carry goods made in Spain. Goods traveling in the other direction, including written accounts of what was happening in Spain's colonies, could enter only through Seville, and these accounts were subject to strict censorship. This censorship regime extended to the Jesuit missionaries who accompanied the explorers. Nonetheless, the missionaries faithfully documented the histories of the native peoples in great detail, down to, and including, surveys of coca production and descriptions of how coca was used.

Three individuals, in particular, wrote accurate accounts of coca cultivation and coca-chewing rituals. The explorer Amerigo Vespucci wrote the first account in 1505. Thirty years later, Portuguese-born Gonzalo Fernandez de Oviedo y Valdes (1478–1557) published another detailed account. But the best known of all the early reports was written by a man who never visited the New World, Nicholas Monardes (1493–1588). Monardes was born and raised in Seville but studied medicine and botany in Alcala. During most of the 16th century, Alcala was the premier medical center in Spain, and probably in all of Europe.

Monardes received his medical degree on April 19, 1533, and returned to Seville, where he married, fathered seven children, wrote seven books, maintained a busy medical practice, and earned a great deal of money (partly from sensible real estate investments and partly from the slave trade), before dying of a stroke on October 12, 1588. One of Monardes' books was devoted to the plants and medical practices of the New World. The first volume was published in Seville in 1569 and the second in 1571. Monardes' book was annotated and translated into Latin by a professor of medicine at Leiden, Holland. The translator was a famous physician and botanist in his own right, named Charles de L'Ecluse (1526–1609), known better to botanists by his Latinized name, Clasius. Early in his career, Clasius traveled widely, and he even visited Seville in January of 1565. Whether he actually met Monardes during this visit is debated, but there can be no doubt that he left Seville with a copy of Monardes' book as a souvenir; he inscribed his name and the date on the fly leaf of the first volume, which can still be seen in the library at Cambridge University.

According to one popular account (there is no cooperating evidence), Clasius translated Monardes' book from Spanish into Latin at the end of a visit to England. The ferry to Holland from Gravesend was delayed by weather, and Clasius happened to be carrying his copy of Monardes' book. Clasius was an extraordinary man. He was fluent in Latin, Greek, Flemish, French, Spanish, and Italian, and in 1587, he became the professor of botany at the University of Leiden. Despite his academic brilliance, he is probably best remembered for having introduced the tulip. In spite of Clasius' translation, the Latin version of Monardes' book was not widely read. However, 22 years later it became a bestseller, when John Frampton translated it into English. Frampton was a merchant living in Cadiz until 1567, when he was captured and tortured by the Inquisition. In his introduction to his translation, Frampton explained that he was now retired, with time on his hands and nothing much better to do, and so had translated Clasius' Latin version into English.

Frampton also gave the book a new title, calling it *"Joyfulle News Out of the New Founde Worlde, Wherein Is Declared the Virtues of Herbs, Treez, Oyales, Plantes and Stones"* (Figure 2.1). It contained accurate descriptions of the coca plant, and of the way that the leaves of the plant were used. Monardes

Figure 2.1 Nicholas Monardes, a Spanish doctor, never visited the New World, but in 1569, he published a treatise on New World plants and their medicinal uses. His book is perhaps most famous for containing the first account of tobacco. After noting that the Indians held coca in reverence, many even named their children "Coca," Monardes provided a description of how the natives preserved coca leaves. First, they roasted cockle- or clamshells, then ground them down, and then chewed the ash with coca leaves, forming little pellets that were then set out to dry in the sun. The page illustrated is from the first English translation of Monardes by John Frampton, published in 1577. (From the original text, New York Public Library, with permission.)

also discussed the potential for coca toxicity. He even mused about why people would want to use the drug in the first place. He wrote, "Surely it is a thyung of greate consideration, to see how the Indians are so desirous to bee deprived of their wittes, and be without understanding." Frampton's translation contained illustrations, some more detailed than Monardes' original drawings, suggesting either that Frampton had a remarkably fine eye for botanical details, or that he may have, at some point, seen the real plants. Even though Monardes had never been to the New World, he had his own botanical garden, where he cultivated native and exotic plants. He would have had access to ships returning from the New World, and nothing would have prevented him from growing New World plants, like coca, in his garden.

The printing of Frampton's translation might also explain how a contemporary of John Milton's, Abraham Cowley (1616–1667), came to write a poem about coca leaf. Cowley, whose poetry is not as well remembered as that of John Milton, was mainly a dramatist and satirist. He studied medicine at Oxford and, along with his friend, Christopher Wren, helped found the British Royal Society. In all probability, Cowley was a spy for the Royalists opposing Cromwell. He was a secretary to Lord Jermyn, the secretary of Queen Henrietta Maria. Cowley spent 12 years living with the exiled Queen in Paris, translating coded messages, and accompanying Lord Jermyn on "dangerous journeys." Cowley's poem, "A Legend of Coca," appeared in a collection of poems about plants that was published in 1662 (*A. Covleii Plantarum Libri Duo*). The last paragraph of the poem begins "Nor Coca only useful art at Home, A famous Merchandize thou art become." Perhaps Cowley had access to a private source, but there really was very little of the "merchandise" for sale in Europe.

More than 250 years elapsed between Frampton's translation of Monardes' book and the appearance of another English-language publication about coca. The new work was a paper by Sir William Hooker, and it included the first picture of coca to appear in the popular English press. The article appeared in the *Companion to the Botanical Magazine* for 1836, a semiofficial publication of Kew Gardens (United Kingdom), which was edited by Hooker. For his model, Hooker used a specimen that was sent to Kew by a botanist named James Matthews. According to Matthews, the plant was collected in the neighborhood of Chincheros, Peru, an area that lies about halfway between Cuzco in the south and Lima in the north. The actual origin of this plant was to later become a source of controversy. As will become clear shortly, the origin of this plant remains a cause for concern for those charged with eradicating coca. Hooker's drawing is shown in Figure 3.1, Chapter 3.

Botanists in France had their chance to see real coca plants nearly 100 years before Hooker, but only by accident. The French Academy of Science sponsored an expedition to the New World in 1735. The purpose of the expedition was to settle an argument between Isaac Newton, who maintained that the earth had the shape of an oblate spheroid (slightly flattened at the poles), and Jacques Cassini, the Royal Astronomer of France, who maintained that the earth was a prolate spheroid (slightly constricted at the equator). The debate soon came to be perceived as a matter of national honor. To settle the debate, the French Academy decided to send simultaneous expeditions to the Arctic and the equator, where an arc of the meridian could actually be measured and the controversy resolved.

Figure 2.2 Abraham Cowley. Cowley, whose poetry is not quite as well remembered as that of John Milton, was mainly a dramatist and satirist. He studied medicine at Oxford and, along with his friend, Christopher Wren, helped found the British Royal Society. In all probability, Cowley was also a spy for the Royalists opposing Cromwell. He was a secretary to the secretary of Queen Henrietta Maria, Lord Jermyn. Cowley spent 12 years living with the exiled Queen in Paris, translating coded messages, and accompanying Lord Jermyn on "dangerous journeys." Cowley's poem, "A Legend of Coca," appeared in a collection of poems about plants that was published in 1662 (*A. Covleii Plantarum Libri Duo*). The last paragraph of the poem begins "Nor Coca only useful art at Home, A famous Merchandize thou art become." The existence of the poem suggests that Cowley had ready access to coca, probably when he was living in France.

The Academy's expedition to the equator sailed on May 16, 1735. It was headed by Charles Marie de la Condamine (1701–1774), a mathematician and friend of Voltaire, who was also a supporter of Newton's theories. Other crew members on the expedition included a watchmaker, a draftsman, a mathematician, the nephew of the treasurer of the Academy (who appears to have had no scientific qualifications), and a botanist named Joseph de

Jussieu (1704–1779). In addition to being a botanist, de Jussieu was a competent physician, engineer, and mathematician.

When he completed his mission of 9 years, la Condamine returned to France. The first leg of the return home involved a trip down the length of the Amazon in a two-man canoe. The trip to Pará, on the Atlantic, took 4 months, long enough for la Condamine to acquire samples of two of the Amazon's three botanical prizes, rubber and quinine. la Condamine arrived back in Paris in the spring of 1745. Thanks to the efforts of the ship's botanist, de Jussieu, samples of coca followed a few years later.

Botanist de Jussieu decided not to return home. He stayed in the Amazon and worked as a physician, and he continued to collect and classify botanical specimens. It is said that from 1747 to 1750 he managed to collect an enormous number of previously unseen botanical specimens. Unfortunately, all of the specimens, and his notes, were lost due to a shipping mishap.

According to one account, the samples that de Jussieu collected were packed in crates, and the crates were taken to the pier to await loading. Thieves, thinking that the crates contained something valuable, broke into them. When they found only plants, they were so angry that they tossed the crates into the water, where they promptly sank. De Jussieu did not take the loss well and suffered a nervous breakdown, though at some point he obviously recovered. In 1750, he managed to successfully ship samples of coca back to his uncle, Antoine, in Paris, who was then a demonstrator and professor at the Jardin du Roi, Paris. Along with the dried coca plants, de Jussieu sent seeds of fragrant heliotrope that, because of its intense fragrance, quickly became popular in Europe. Antoine donated the plant specimens to the Museum of Natural History in Paris, where they were eventually examined by all of the pioneers of modern botany, including by Carl von Linnaeus, and later, by Lamarck. The plant illustrated in Lamarck's encyclopedia, which was published in 1786, appears to be identical to other plants that eventually found their way to Hooker's office at Kew, in 1835.

There is no doubt that the plant used for a model by Hooker and the plant illustrated by Lamarck were the same plants, but it is also clear that the particular variety of coca plant illustrated was not the kind of coca plant commonly chewed by the Indians. It also was not the same variety eventually sold by traders when an export market for coca finally developed. This discrepancy proved to be a major factor in the development of the cocaine industry.

Botanists, Naturalists, and Pedestrians

3

Botanists

Even though the Spanish never fully appreciated the export value of coca, and certainly never took measures to capitalize on it, botanists in London did. To be fair, it took the discovery of quinine, and another two centuries, before British scientists realized there was money to be made growing coca. The idea originated among botanists working at the Royal Botanical Gardens at Kew, in the United Kingdom. Today, the gardens are known mainly for their beauty and collections of exotic flowers, as well as for their extensive research programs, but they were once an important resource for the economic exploitation of New World discoveries. Located on the south bank of the Thames River in Surrey, six miles by road west–southwest of Hyde Park Corner, the first Kew Gardens occupied only 11 acres. Lord Capel of Tewkesbury established the gardens in 1721, mainly to provide his kitchen with vegetables. Capel's Gardens consisted of little more than some pretty ornamental plants and a few vegetables. That changed when the gardens became the property of the Princess Dowager, widow of Frederick, Prince of Wales. The Princess also had an interest in pretty plants, but knew little, and cared less, about the science of botany. Fortunately, King George III did.

George III may have had periods of "madness," but he was sane enough to accept advice from his friend, Sir Joseph Banks, the botanist who accompanied Captain James Cook on his first voyage. Banks served for 42 years as the President of the Royal Society, and it was obvious to Banks that some of the plants being discovered in the new colonies were worth money. Banks convinced King George III to make Kew Gardens a repository for exotic new plant life from the colonies, and to use Kew as a training center for young botanists, who could then go out and collect more new specimens. The King agreed. One of the botanists selected had the misfortune to accompany Captain William Bligh, and to die from exposure when Bligh and his party were set adrift in their longboat. Other Kew agents were more successful and brought thousands of exotic specimens back to England. Unfortunately, before the economic potential of any of these new plants could be exploited, work on the gardens abruptly halted. Kew's fortunes and England's economy both suffered setbacks when King George III died in January 1820. Banks died in June of the same year, and succeeding administrators did not share the vision of either man.

Without the King's support and Banks' expertise, little happened at Kew Gardens until 1841. In that year, a government-appointed committee recommended that the original plans for Kew Gardens, as envisioned by Sir Banks and King George, should be revived. Sir William Hooker (1785–1865) was appointed as director of the gardens (Figure 3.1.). Hooker immediately ordered the construction of a giant new herbarium and, at the same time, initiated an exhaustive survey of plant life across the English Empire. Under Hooker's leadership, Kew Gardens expanded to occupy over 300 acres. Hooker sent Kew-trained botanists and gardeners around the world, and he

Figure 3.1   Sir William Hooker (1785–1865). Appointed in 1841 as Kew's first official director, he built Palm House, the Museums of Economic Botany, the Herbarium, and the Library, and commissioned Richard Spruce, among others, to collect plants of possible economic value in the Amazon. From *A History of Cocaine*, Royal Society of Medicine Press, 2003. With permission.

contracted with other independent explorers who made their livings by cataloguing newly discovered plants and sending them back to England for analysis and cultivation. Any plant that appeared to have the faintest economic potential was propagated and fostered. Kew scientists, under Hooker's leadership, were the real inventors of "economic botany."

Discounting Bank's early experiments with the importation of flax and spinach from New Zealand, and Captain Bligh's disastrous attempt at transporting breadfruit from the South Pacific to the West Indies (both ventures lost money), Hooker nonetheless persisted in his attempts to secure a stable supply of quinine, and his efforts ultimately led to Kew and its scientists trying to change the world by applying the principles of economic botany. Unfortunately for Kew, and for Hooker, the organized attempt at finding quinine failed, but the magnitude of the failure was not initially apparent— it was only recognized years later. There was, however, a positive result: the mechanism had been put in place to develop coca as a cash crop.

In 1852, the British Foreign Office sent letters of inquiry to its South American Counsels instructing them to identify possible sources of cinchona tree seeds for planting in the British Colonies. Nothing came of the request, and eventually, Hooker decided to mount an organized effort to procure a supply. A team of scientists was appointed, headed by Clements Markham (1838–1916), who later founded the Royal Geographic Society and sponsored Robert F. Scott's expedition to the South Pole. Markham's team included Amazon explorer Richard Spruce (Figure 3.2), who was already collecting South American plants under a contract with Kew.

Markham went to Peru in 1860 and brought living cinchona plants back to Kew. After allowing the plants to recover for a few months, Markham took the seedlings to India, where they were planted at Nilghiri Hills, a steep plateau in Southwest Madras. Unfortunately, Markham had come back with the wrong seeds. By 1900, more than a million of the wrong cinchona trees were growing in India and Ceylon, and they all had to be ripped out. It was not that they were the wrong trees entirely, it was just that they did not contain enough quinine to make the venture commercially viable. The seeds sent back by Spruce, which he collected at enormous risk to life and limb, were not any better. But Markham's failure was not apparent for many years, and initially his venture seemed to be a success. Scientists at Kew used the acquisition of quinine as a role model and sought other projects — plants from which they might extract useful medicines, or foodstuffs that might feed the masses. Coca seemed a likely candidate. The problem was deciding which kind of coca to grow.

The plant that Hooker used for a model in 1836 was collected in the neighborhood of Chincheros, Peru, an area that lies about halfway between Cuzco in the south and Lima in the north (Figure 3.3). But, the seeds from

Figure 3.2   Richard Spruce (1817–1893). Spruce worked as a contract collector for Kew Gardens, under the direction of William Hooker, then director. A specimen of coca collected by Hooker near the junction of the Rio Negro and Amazon rivers may have been the original source of the high-yielding "Coca Java."

that plant were not those used for the project. Instead, coca seeds from a commercial variety of coca collected somewhere in the Huánuco Valley were used. Huánuco is located just to the south of Cuzco, Peru, nearly 200 miles from where the first Kew specimens were collected. They arrived at Kew in 1869. The Huánuco seeds were continuously cultivated at Kew for at least 40 years, and seeds from these plants were shipped to botanical research stations around the British Empire.

Kew sent samples to its affiliated botanical gardens and experimental agricultural stations in India, Africa, Ceylon, Malaya, and even Jamaica. But Kew never sent samples to Java, which was just as well for the Dutch growers. In an almost exact replay of the quinine disaster, the variety of coca seeds distributed from Kew contained only a fraction of the cocaine found in the variety grown in Java. The source for the Java variety was never clearly

Figure 3.3 Coca leaves. After hearing rumors about coca for several centuries, Englishmen finally got to see an accurate rendering in 1835. This illustration was drawn by Sir William Hooker, then the Director of Kew gardens. Hooker's drawing appeared in the *Companion to the Botanical Magazine* (1, 161–175, 1835). It accompanied Hooker's translation of a German naturalist's account of life on the Amazon. For his model, Hooker used a specimen collected in the neighborhood of Chincheros, Peru. It was sent back to Kew by a botanist named James Matthews. It later became apparent that this was not the best variety for producing cocaine.

identified. The seeds were obtained from a trading company called Herman Linden and Company, in Ghent, Belgium, but how the seeds came to be in Ghent still remains a mystery.

There was, however, at least one more Kew plant, and it was sent to Kew by Richard Spruce, in 1851. Spruce was collecting specimens near Manaus, Brazil, before Hooker reassigned him to the search for quinine. At the time,

Spruce was collecting plants along the banks of the Rio Negro River, hundreds of miles from where the variety of coca grown at Kew was collected, and thousands of miles from where the specimens from Joseph de Jussieu were originally collected. According to Spruce's notebooks, "In January 1851 I saw ipadú prepared and used on the small river Jauauarí near the mouth of the Rio Negro and I sent a quantity to Kew for analysis."

Published descriptions of the plants grown in Java match those of specimens collected by Richard Spruce. The unique feature of Coca Java, and presumably of the plants found by Spruce in 1851, was that they contained an enormous amount of cocaine. When processed correctly, they were capable of yielding more than twice as much cocaine as that from leaves cultivated in South America, or leaves grown at any of Kew's branches in English colonies around the world. More than any other single factor, the high cocaine content of the Java plant made Indonesia the world's premier coca producer, and also made possible the later development of Japan's illegal drug trade. Thus, appearance of the leaves and type of plant being grown were of utmost importance, because scientists at the time were unable to directly determine the cocaine content of the leaves. All coca is not created equal. Analytic techniques in the mid-1800s were just not that sophisticated, and, in any case, no one had enough leaf to analyze.

That was certainly the problem faced by the Kew botanists, as only a handful of coca plants were ever grown there at any one time. It was also a problem for scientists elsewhere in Europe, because coca leaf could only be grown there in greenhouses. Given the state of analytic chemistry at that time, many pounds of dried leaves would have been needed in order to carry out any type of successful analysis. The relative shortage of raw material probably explains why initial advances in the field of cocaine chemistry were made in Germany, and not in England. German chemists had an edge, because German naturalists supplied them with enough coca leaf to analyze.

Naturalists

German naturalist Johan von Tschudi made several trips to Peru. His primary interest was the classification of animal life, but he also recorded observations on cinchona (quinine-containing trees), balsam, and coca. One of his books is filled with anecdotes about coca. His general impression was that using coca "may even be very conducive to health," but one of his anecdotes in particular seems to have struck an especially responsive chord among Europeans. He described the behavior of an Indian laborer named Hatum Humang. During 5 days and nights of nearly continuous work, Hatum Humang ate almost no solid food but chewed 14 g of coca leaf every 3 hours.

Hatum Humang's story was picked up and repeated in dozens of European newspapers and medical journals. It confirmed the suspicions of many European scientists that coca had miraculous powers.

In 1857, just before he was to return to Germany, von Tschudi visited Enrique Pizzi, a professor of chemistry and pharmacology who taught at the University of La Paz. Von Tschudi convinced Pizzi to try isolating coca's active principle. Pizzi accepted the challenge, and eventually gave von Tschudi a sample of purified cocaine to take home.

When von Tschudi returned to Göttingen, he immediately went to the laboratory of his friend, Fredrich Wöhler, chairman of the chemistry department at Göttingen. Wöhler (1800–1882) was not just any ordinary organic chemist. He, and his sometime friend and collaborator, Justus von Liebig (1803–1873), practically laid the foundations of modern organic chemistry. In 1825, when he was a chemistry instructor at the Berlin Trade School, Wöhler synthesized urea, the first organic compound to be prepared from inorganic materials. Wöhler was appointed chairman of chemistry at Göttingen in 1836, and remained there for the rest of his career. He trained literally thousands of students and made the University of Göttingen a major center for the study of chemistry. It was only natural that von Tschudi should take the sample to Wöhler to analyze.

Wöhler gave the sample to his graduate student, Albert Niemann (1834–1861), who analyzed it and found that it contained only gypsum. It remains an unanswered question whether Pizzi or Niemann was inept, but obviously someone made a mistake. Thirty years after the mix-up, Pizzi's successor, Clemente Torretti, wrote a letter to the *American Druggist* magazine, claiming that he found the original isolates prepared by Pizzi, tested them, and found that they contained cocaine. By that time, of course, Niemann already published a technique for the isolation of cocaine from coca leaf.

A few months after the plaster-of-paris debacle, Wöhler got another chance to find the active principle in coca. Austrian Archduke Ferdinand decided to send the frigate *Novara* (Figure 3.4) on an around-the-world cruise. Having men-of-war circumnavigate the globe was something of a craze during the mid-1800s, and Austria was not immune. However, the voyage of the *Novara* was more than an expensive way to show the colors; it was also a training cruise for young naval officers and, at the same time, a scientific mission to relatively unexplored regions of South America and the Pacific. The peaceful intent of the voyage was clear from the way that the 6-year-old, 165-foot-long, 2600-ton *Novara* was refitted. One-third of the cannons were removed, the ship's gunroom was converted into a library and reading room, and more staterooms were added. A distilling apparatus, manufactured by Rocher et Nantes, was fixed on the gun deck. It could supply enough drinking water, so it was unnecessary to store large amounts of water.

Figure 3.4   The German frigate Novara in Sydney harbor. Sailing on board was a friend of Germany's greatest chemist. When the Novara reached South America, Carl von Scherzer (1821–1903) got off and managed to collect 40 lb of coca leaves and sent them back to Germany for analysis. From the website of Michael Organ, M.D., with permission.

Having so much freshwater was an unheard of luxury for ships of the line, and so was the installation of crew showers on the deck and forecastle.

The German Imperial Academy of Science nominated two of the crew members, while the Navy selected the remainder of the scientific team. In addition to the naval cadets, the crew included a botanist, a zoologist, an artist, and a "flower gatherer." Carl von Scherzer (1821–1903) was one of those selected by the Imperial Academy. Just before the *Novara* sailed for Trieste on March 15, 1857, Wöhler contacted von Scherzer and asked for his help. If Wöhler was going to identify the active principle of coca, he needed a real supply of coca leaves, not just a handful. Wöhler estimated that he would need at least 50 or 60 lb of leaf. Von Scherzer promised he would try, and he did.

The *Novara* was recalled to Austria before it could reach Peru, so von Scherzer left the expedition at Valparaiso, on Chile's northern coast, and made his own way north to Lima. He wrote a book about his travels, but the book makes no mention of where he purchased the coca leaves. He did, however, manage to acquire 60 pounds of leaves. Von Scherzer packed half of the leaves in his luggage and made arrangements with two Austrian merchants living in Lima to forward the rest of them back to Germany. He then continued his journey overland to Panama, where he booked passage home. He delivered the leaves to Wöhler in September of 1859. Wöhler, again, gave them to Albert Niemann to analyze.

The analysis proved to be the basis for Niemann's doctoral thesis, which he successfully defended in 1860, the same year that Abraham Lincoln was elected president of the United States. Niemann began his thesis by acknowledging von Scherzer's efforts. He then went on to discuss the similarity of coca to other plant-derived stimulants, such as coffee, tea, and tobacco. He pointed out that all of these chemicals appear to be used for roughly the same purpose, i.e., to provide energy and stamina. The rest of the document consists of a description of the techniques he used to isolate what he called "cocaina." Except for the scale of operations, the method devised by Niemann was not very different from the process used in clandestine jungle laboratories today.

Other than the fact that Niemann earned his doctorate by isolating cocaine from coca leaves, and that he carried out the work under Wöhler's guidance, not much is known about him. His thesis was reprinted in a number of journals, and readers in the United States were able to see it in 1861, when the *American Journal of Pharmacy* printed an abridged translation. Niemann died shortly after his thesis was published. The cause is not known. His discovery was greeted with modest enthusiasm, but 10 years went by before anyone bothered to confirm his observation that cocaine crystals made the tongue numb, and almost a quarter of a century elapsed before Karl Koller discovered that cocaine was an effective local anesthetic.

The lack of interest in cocaine chemistry is more apparent than real. There was no cocaine available with which to experiment. Very little leaf was being imported into Europe, and the technique devised by Niemann was, for those days, both cumbersome and unreliable. Physicians wanting to experiment with coca leaves, or with refined cocaine, were never entirely sure what they were actually administering. Products billed as cocaine were frequently found to be inert. Leaves, claimed to be fresh from Peru, were often in transit for such a long time that they contained too little cocaine to matter.

But other factors, still undefined, must have been involved. Had there been a demand for cocaine, chemists and drug manufacturers would have supplied it. Merck began producing cocaine just 18 months after Niemann published his method for extracting it from coca, but Merck's average production amounted to less than a quarter of a pound per year. Merck chemists certainly could have produced more, a fact that was clearly proven within a few years, when cocaine's local anesthetic properties were discovered. Less than 2 years after Koller's announcement that the use of cocaine drops permitted painless eye surgery, Merck was manufacturing cocaine by the ton.

Pedestrians

For nearly a quarter of a century, from 1860 when Niemann's thesis was published, until Koller's paper on cocaine's anesthetic effects was read at the Ophthalmology Congress at Heidelberg in 1884, coca and cocaine remained curiosities. What little interest there was centered almost entirely on coca's alleged abilities to enhance performance, increase endurance, and act as a "substance d'épargne," an agent that would allow individuals to go without food. This preoccupation with strength and endurance was partly the result of press coverage; stories about coca-induced feats of strength and endurance, such as those of Hatum Humang's, made fascinating reading. But the biggest moving force in reviving interest was the teachings of one particular scientist: Justus von Liebig (1803–1874).

Von Liebig was a brilliant chemist, born in Darmstadt, Germany, just after the turn of the century. He became chairman of the chemistry department in Munich in 1852, as well as president of the German Academy of Sciences. Von Liebig was the author of at least 317 separate papers and books, the founder of the *Annals of Chemistry* (still published today), and the editor of an encyclopedia of chemistry. Perhaps, more importantly, he was the first famous entrepreneur scientist. He exploited his reputation, and the growing respect with which the public viewed science, to make money; von Liebig invented the bouillon cube.

Von Liebig believed, quite incorrectly, that the energy required for muscles to contract was produced by oxidizing (burning up) portions of the muscle. In order to maintain the ability to work, destroyed muscle had to be constantly replenished. He was convinced that the only way that could be accomplished was to ingest nitrogen-containing compounds in amounts equal to the amount destroyed. Carbohydrates and fats, he thought, were used only to generate heat and to support respiration. In 1847, von Liebig published a paper describing the components of a rational diet. One component was a meat extract, called extractum carnis. It amounted to little more than what we today call bouillon. Bouillon was soon being sold as a cure-all under the name, "Liebig's extract of meat." Advertisements made outrageous claims for the product, and von Liebig, who got a percentage of sales for lending his name to the product, made an outrageous amount of money.

In his early years, von Liebig was a friend of, and collaborator with, Fredrich Wöhler. Probably as a result of his closeness with Wöhler, von Liebig knew about coca and was interested in its effects. He even gave some coca to his students and studied the effects it had on them. Given the rumors about coca's effects on performance, Liebig must have been fascinated by the possibilities, and would certainly have communicated this interest to his students.

By the late 1870s, other physiologists, including many of his own students, began to reject von Liebig's theories. But even though von Liebig's theories about performance were in decline, people still believed that particular substances could have profound and immediate effects on performance. Both the scientific community and the popular press remained fascinated with coca's effects on strength and endurance. It is hardly surprising then, that the first reported case of sports "doping" involved athletes chewing coca leaves. The first known athlete to cheat by using drugs was a racewalker from the United States.

Racewalking was an English invention. During the 16th and 17th centuries, wealthy travelers employed "footmen" to run, or at least walk quickly, at the sides of their coaches. The footmen would run ahead of the coaches to make arrangements for food and lodging. Eventually, those riding in the coaches began wagering on which footman could get to the next inn the fastest. The practice slowly morphed into formal race competitions, where professional "pedestrians" competed for large sums of money.

These competitions were mostly without rules. By custom, footmen had to keep pace with the owners' coaches, without actually breaking into a run. By the second half of the 18th century, another twist was added to the competitions. Instead of racing against each other, pedestrians competed against the clock. The usual goal was to cover 100 miles in less than 24 hours. Winners ("survivors" might be a better term) were called "Centurions."

Watching one person walk for 24 hours must have been a boring pastime. To improve ratings, other racewalkers were added to the mix, usually to see which athlete could complete the 100 miles sooner, or, if that goal could not be attained, at least to determine who could stay on his feet the longest. Some of the races were on closed courses, and others went from town to town. There were large prizes for the winners and large profits for local bookmakers taking bets on the competitors.

In the mid-1800s, the racewalking craze took root in the United States, attracting large numbers of spectators and generating even larger purses, sometimes amounting to more than $10,000, which, at the time, amounted to an enormous amount of money. The leading pedestrian in the United States was a man named Edward Payson Weston (1839–1899), who, in addition to being a racewalker, was a reporter for the New York *Herald*. Weston is pictured in Figure 3.5.

The Veteran Pedestrian, Edward Payson Weston
Near Rochester, N. Y.

Figure 3.5 Edward Payson Weston. In 1876, Weston sailed to England and defeated the English ultramarathon champion in an indoor, 105-mile race. A furor ensued when Weston disclosed that he was chewing coca leaf much of the time. Photo postcard from the collection of vintageviews.org. With permission.

In 1876, Weston sailed to England to challenge England's racewalking champion. The challenge took the form of a 24-hour, 115-mile, ultramarathon. The race began on the evening of February 8, 1876, at the Royal Agricultural Hall on Liverpool Road in Islington, a London suburb. Weston was described as a "spare" man, 37 years old, 5 feet 7.5 inches high, and weighing "a little under" 140 pounds. Weston's English opponent was a faster walker but lacked Weston's endurance. Foot pain caused the Englishman to quit 14 hours into the race after he had covered only 65.5 miles. When examined immediately afterwards, he did not look well. His pulse and temperature were elevated, his blood pressure was too low, and his feet were extensively blistered.

Weston, however, kept walking through the heat, despite foot blisters that caused him to pause briefly after 17 hours. After a short rest, he continued walking until the full 24 hours elapsed, and he had covered 109.5 miles. During the race, Weston fortified himself with liquids, primarily tea and coffee, along with egg yolks and Liebig extract. He also chewed coca leaf during much of the race. When reporters found out that Weston was chewing coca leaf, it caused a furor. The results of the race, however, were never disputed. In a letter to the *British Medical Journal*, Weston admitted he was using coca but said that he did not believe it helped him. In fact, he claimed, it made him sleepy.

The connection between coca and performance was so widely accepted, that racewalkers were still relying on coca 10 years after Weston's victory. In 1885, Dr. Palmer, a coca advocate from Louisville, Kentucky, published a description of another race. This race involved six female "pedestrianists" who were to run 350 miles in 7 days. Dr. Palmer stopped in on Day Six of the race and noticed one contestant, a 120-pound, 17-year-old woman named "L.C.," who appeared to be imminently in danger of collapse. Palmer, being the solicitous doctor that he was, administered a glass of Fraser's Wine of Coca, which the woman drank, stating afterwards that it tasted "elegant." She did not win the race, but she finished the 350 miles in just under 7 days, even though someone had stolen her bottle of coca wine, and in spite of the fact that she had fallen and sprained her ankle.

Weston and the women "pedestrianists" were not the first, the only, or the most prominent, to study coca's effects on performance. Sir Robert Christison (1797–1882), president of the Scottish Medical Association and Professor of Materia Medica at Edinburgh (a combination of medicinal chemistry and botany), experimented on some of his students in 1870, and on himself in 1875. In the first set of experiments, Christison observed that students who drank coca extract reported increased feelings of well-being. A second set of experiments was conducted with leaves that one of his students, Alexander Bennett, obtained in Paris (see below). In the first experiment, Christison gave coca extracts to students who then took 20- to 30- mile hikes; the students reported they felt no fatigue. Christison was so enthused with these results that on September 15, 1875, he climbed Ben Vorlich, a small (3224 feet) mountain, in Scotland. The climb presented no challenge, and Christison enjoyed himself so much that he increased the dose of coca and repeated the climb again 8 days later. While the height of Ben Vorlich (943 meters) is not all that impressive, Christison's age, 78 years, was. Other researchers published similar reports that same year.

As the reports by Christison and the other researchers clearly showed, coca was still a novelty in the 1870s. For whatever reason, very little coca could be found in either England or the United States. Coca's scarcity, especially in England, is also evident from the medical literature. In 1874, Doctor Sieveking wrote to the *British Medical Journal* that "I have never had the good fortune to meet with any medical man who had a personal acquaintance with it (coca)." He went on to add that he expected it would prove to be "a very valuable restorative." Sieveking's letter prompted responses from several pharmacists saying that they carried the leaves, and others wrote to the journal confirming Sieveking's impressions.

Today, a report describing a patient who died of a cocaine-related heart attack would almost automatically be rejected by medical journals, because cocaine-related heart attacks are so common that another anecdotal report would not be considered worth publishing. However, the same report, had it been submitted in 1975, would surely have been accepted. No one bothers to write or publish an anecdotal medical report unless it is about an uncommon event. In the English literature, at least, from the time of Niemann's discovery until the time of Koller's announcements, all of the reports were anecdotal. The frequency with which drugs are mentioned in the scientific literature is a good indicator of how frequently that particular drug is being used. Coca was hardly ever mentioned, which suggests that it was scarce and not readily available to doctors, let alone the public.

In 1873, Alexander Bennett published his doctoral thesis in the *Edinburgh Medical Journal*. He compared the effects of cocaine, caffeine, and other alkaloids on experimental animals. Bennett complained that in order to find the coca leaves to make cocaine, he had to go to Paris. "In this country," he wrote, "the coca leaves needed are rare, and even in Paris, where they can be obtained, they are very expensive." In 1876, Allan Hamilton, a physician working at a hospital for neurological diseases in New York, wrote a letter to the *British Medical Journal* describing how he felt after he had drunk an extract of coca leaves. Hamilton was able to experiment on himself only because someone had given him a pound of dried coca leaf as a gift. Why was coca leaf available in Paris and not in London? Surprisingly, the explanation had little to do with trends in scientific research. Rather, it was the result of financial considerations, and the efforts of a self-promoting pharmacist/manufacturer named Angelo Mariani.

Celebrity Endorsements

4

The literature of cocaine is more voluminous than valuable, more expectant than exact.

J.T. Brown, 1886

Question: What is your opinion of coca leaf?

J.K. Visalia, California

Answer: The virtues of coca leaves have probably been exaggerated; but in our opinion, nevertheless, they possess very remarkable properties.... Although we have had no personal experience, we consider the reports in their favor sufficient to warrant giving them a trial.

From a letter to the editor of the *Druggists Circular and Chemical Gazette*, September 1876

In the 1880s, the name most often associated with coca belonged neither to Sigmund Freud nor Karl Koller, the man credited with inventing local anesthesia. At the turn of the century, mention of cocaine brought to mind only one name — Angelo Mariani, and his coca-based wine, Vin Mariani.

Mariani (Figure 4.1) was a Corsican, born at Pero-Casevecchie in 1838. He died in 1914 at his villa in Saint-Raphaél, outside of Paris. Mariani's early history is vague, made even vaguer by Mariani's penchant for self-promoting publicity. It can be said, with reasonable certainty, that Mariani worked as an apprentice pharmacist in Paris at Chantrels, a pharmacy located on the Rue de Clichy. Sometime during his apprenticeship years, Mariani moved to another pharmacy in Saint-Germain. He always claimed that he was a certified

Figure 4.1   Angelo Mariani.

pharmacist, and his death certificate supports that claim, but there is no record that he ever passed the examination required for certification.

He first produced a coca wine when he was still working as an assistant at Chantrels Pharmacy in late 1868 or early 1869. Part of his job description was to assist in the preparation of "wine tonics." At the time, medications were often prescribed in the form of wine tonics. Many of the then-popular drugs were foul tasting. The wine made them more palatable, and as a practical matter, most of the medications dissolved more easily in alcohol than in water. A French pharmacopoeia, an early ancestor of the modern *Physicians Desk Reference* (PDR) published in 1844, listed 100 medicinal wines. By 1884, that number had grown to 154.

Mariani read of the miraculous properties of coca and was surprised that no one had yet conceived the idea of combining coca with wine. When a famous actress of the Comédie-Francaise came to Chantrels complaining of depression, Mariani recommend a coca wine. The depressed actress rapidly improved, and she was soon recommending Mariani's mixture to her friends. At some point, and it is not exactly clear when, Mariani decided to leave the pharmacy and go into business for himself. By 1870, Vin Mariani was being sold all over France. Mariani's Paris office was located at 41 Boulevard Hauss-mann. As sales increased, he opened additional branch offices, including one in London and another in New York City.

Although he may have read about it in a short book published in the 1880s, most of what Mariani knew about coca, he probably learned from his cousin, Charles Fauvel. Fauvel, born in Amiens, France, in 1830, was a physician. He was one of the first ear, nose, and throat specialists in Paris, or anywhere else for that matter. Fauvel had a celebrity practice and mainly treated famous singers and opera stars. One of the reasons for Fauvel's success was that his treatment usually produced good results. The reason his results were so good was that he found a way to effectively anesthetize the throat. With adequate anesthesia, it became possible to do more thorough examinations and perform more extensive surgical procedures.

Although Koller later received credit for discovering that cocaine drops could anesthetize the eye, Fauvel observed, almost a quarter of a century earlier, that application of a coca tincture (an alcohol solution in which coca leaves were dissolved) could make throat surgery painless. Surgeons came from the United States and other countries to study Fauvel's techniques, and Sigmund Freud even gave Fauvel credit for his discovery when he published "On Coca." Even so, Fauvel received little recognition, while Mariani, by virtue of his great commercial success, became famous. Mariani was a master at self-promotion, and it is difficult to decide which of his two great inventions he should be remembered for: the discovery of coca wine, or the invention of the modern publicity campaign.

Justus von Liebig may have been the first famous scientist to make money by promoting his own product line, but Mariani was the first to collect celebrity endorsements and use them to sell his own product. Typical Mariani endorsements are shown in Figure 4.4 through Figure 4.7. Mariani's early advertising campaigns were aimed mainly at doctors. He would send the doctors free wine samples, asking that in return they send him an endorsement for his product. By 1902, Mariani had amassed letters of praise from more than 8000 physicians and other happy clients from around the world. Many of these endorsements were then included in other Mariani publications.

Mariani also wrote and printed scientific brochures and monographs, and these too were distributed free of charge to physicians. Not surprisingly, the brochures always contained endorsements, if not from media stars and artists, then from physicians claiming impressive cures. Leaving nothing to chance, Mariani also advertised in the Paris newspapers. Prominent graphic artists, such as Chéret and Robida, were commissioned to produce graphics for those newspaper advertisements. The same artists were paid to draw posters that were displayed around Paris. There was also a line of medallions and plaques, each with a different Vin Mariani endorsement.

Mariani soon found himself challenged by an army of competitors, and product recognition became a problem. Modern winemakers in California, who have sued one another for appropriating the distinctive shapes of their wine bottles, may be surprised to learn that similar scenarios were played out more than a century ago. Mariani had a bottle especially designed for his wine, and he never changed its shape. The Mariani wine bottle was as recognizable then as the Coca-Cola bottle is today. Advertisements in medical journals warned members of the medical profession about the "disappointment and annoyance caused by imitations and substitutions" and advised them to "impress on patients to accept only Mariani Wine."

Mariani liked to be around famous people. He often rented Le Doyen, a well-known Parisian restaurant, and served opulent dinners to members of the Society of French Artists. Art nouveau illustrators, of course, drew menus for these gatherings. A painting of one of these dinners by the artist Grun shows Mariani seated among the famous guests. Mariani also commissioned established writers, paying them to produce stories about the marvelous effects of coca and of his wine. The same artists and writers also volunteered enthusiastic endorsements for Mariani's products.

Some artists even produced lithographed albums of biographical notes, photographs, autographs, and accounts of the many wonderful experiences they had while they were drinking Vin Mariani. According to Joseph Uzanne, Mariani's secretary and publicity director, the artists sent the first letters spontaneously, but eventually it became a cash transaction. From 1891 to 1913, Mariani published a series of albums, each containing 75 profiles. Lalauze, a respected illustrator, lithographed these profiles. Cheaper anthology additions were also produced.

A total of 1086 celebrity portraits was published. The list of celebrities included three popes, sixteen kings and queens, and six presidents of the French Republic. There were also painters, sculptors, composers, actors, politicians, generals, bishops, physicians, and respected scientists. Most of the profiled celebrities were French, but Americans were not totally ignored. Later editions to the series included both the investor Thomas Edison and the actress Sarah Bernhardt. Different celebrities made different kinds of contributions. H.G. Wells drew two small cartoons of himself. In the first, he was slouched and depressed. In the second, a happy-looking Wells is shown drinking Vin Mariani. President William McKinley's secretary, John Addison Porter, wrote to Mariani and thanked him for the case of wine he sent to the White House. Porter assured Mariani that the wine would be used whenever the occasion presented itself. A complete set of these endorsement albums can be still be seen at the British Museum (Figure 4.2).

The celebrity folios were expensive and were designed to reach an influential, if limited, audience. To increase product recognition, Mariani reprinted extracts taken from the folios. He republished biographies of individual celebrities and issued them as bulletins. The bulletins were then inserted in local papers around Paris. These bulletins, or supplements, were similar to the promotions used by supermarkets and department stores today. The supplements were folded into the centers of leading Parisian newspapers

Figure 4.2   A typical endorsement for Vin Mariani, this one featuring the Pope. Hundreds, if not thousands, of members of French and European High Society contributed similar endorsements. This advertisement, with a picture of the Pope, appeared in a London newspaper in 1899. A complete collection can be seen at the British Museum. From the author's private collection.

under the title, *Contemporary Figures*. Each issue was 16 pages long, and measured 32 cm × 23 cm.

The magnitude of Mariani's promotional campaigns is hard to grasp. He printed 800,000 copies of *Contemporary Figures* at a time, and had them inserted into *Le Journal, Le Monde, L'Eclair, Le Figaro*, and half a dozen other major newspapers. Over the 20 years of publication, more than 64 million issues of Mariani's *Contemporary Figures* were distributed. Mariani squeezed additional mileage out of the supplements by taking individual photographs from the albums and reprinting them as postcards. Four different series, each comprised of 30 cards, were printed and sold for 10 cents a card.

Not only did Mariani like to be surrounded by the rich and famous, he also emulated their lifestyle. His dedication to coca was evident everywhere. By the turn of the century, he constructed large greenhouses, filled with thousands of coca plants, on his estate. He also constructed a laboratory, a production plant, and a large art nouveau salon, built of elaborate glass and wrought iron. Images of coca plants were woven into the rugs and curtains, and even the floor tiles and ceiling moldings were decorated with a coca leaf motif. He commissioned Eugène Courbin to paint his office ceiling with an

Figure 4.3 Newspaper advertisment for Vin Mariani. Angelo Mariani was a master at self-promotion, and it is difficult to decide which of his two great inventions he should be remembered for: the popularization of coca wine or the invention of the modern publicity campaign. Vin Mariani was immensely popular. Mariani would send cases of free wine to celebrities, who would then write thank you notes or even endorsements that Mariani collected and published. Thomas Edison and Sarah Bernhardt wrote endorsements, as did Pope Leo, III. President William McKinley's secretary, John Addison Porter, wrote Mariani to thank him. Porter assured Mariani that the wine would be used whenever the occasion required. From the author's private collection.

allegory of "The Goddess Bringing the Coca Branch to Europe." Coca leaves were carved into the chairs and sofas, and rooms were decorated with artificial coca plants in ceramic pots.

In the final analysis, Mariani's advertising innovations were probably more important than his pharmaceutical or winemaking skills. Like the makers of Coca-Cola, Mariani never disclosed the formula for his famous wine, saying only that he used a "fine" Bordeaux and only "the finest coca leaves." Actually, the formula for coca wine was no secret. The French government had set guidelines for its manufacture, and any pharmacist could produce it. The formula was simplicity itself. Sixty grams of ground coca leaves were soaked for 10 hours in 1 liter (2.1 pints) of red or white wine, containing 10% to 15% alcohol.

Figure 4.4 An advertisement for Hall's Coca Wine, one of Mariani's competitors. From the author's private collection.

By modern standards, Vin Mariani did not contain very much cocaine. With an average cocaine content of one-quarter to one-half percent Bolivian leaf (the only kind of leaf available in France at the time), 1 liter of wine would have contained as little as 150 mg, and certainly no more than 300 mg, of cocaine. One ounce of Mariani's tonic would have contained only 6 mg of cocaine, and two glasses would have contained less than 50 mg of cocaine, equivalent to one "line" of snorted cocaine. A 50 mg dose of cocaine is barely enough to produce measurable effects in humans.

Mariani had competitors in England (Figure 4.3), the United States, and France. In 1895, a representative of the Pharmaceutical Society of Lyon complained to the French government when one of its generals ordered a supply of Vin Mariani for his troops in Madagascar. He pointed out that any competent pharmacist could make wines every bit as good as Mariani's and

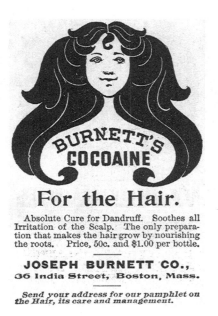

Figure 4.5 Burnett's Cocoaine For the Hair. As soon as cocaine became available in sufficient quantities, snake-oil manufacturers started adding cocaine to all of their product lines. This advertisement is from a Boston newspaper published in the late 1890s. From the author's private collection.

complained that "since the general had not found it necessary to specify any particular non-coca containing brands of Bordeaux or Champagne wine for the troops, it is equally undesirable that he should give one maker a monopoly of the supply of coca wine."

The American brands of coca wine tended to contain more cocaine (4.5 to 10.8 mg/oz) than Vin Mariani. Wyeth & Brothers produced a sherry containing 15.2% alcohol with 4.5 mg of cocaine per ounce, while Metcalf & Company, located at 39 Tremont Street in Boston, offered a Malaga (a kind of sherry) containing nearly 21% alcohol with 9.7 mg of cocaine per ounce. In contrast to Mariani's "fine Bordeaux," H. Caswell & Company used a generic "red wine" that contained nearly as much alcohol as Mariani's and one third more cocaine (11.5 mg) per ounce. In order to stay competitive, Vin Mariani exported to the United States was formulated to contain slightly more cocaine than the variety sold in France (7.2 mg/oz versus 6 mg/oz).

Without refined cocaine to add to the wine, the only way to raise the wine's cocaine content was to soak more leaves in the wine. The problem with this approach was that other compounds, and some of them not particularly tasty, were extracted into the wine as well; thus, the higher the

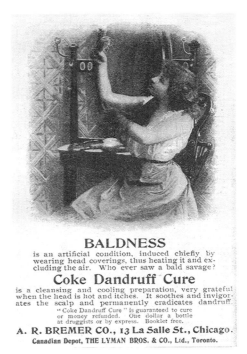

BALDNESS

is an artificial condition, induced chiefly by wearing head coverings, thus heating it and excluding the air. Who ever saw a bald savage?

Coke Dandruff Cure

is a cleansing and cooling preparation, very grateful when the head is hot and itches. It soothes and invigorates the scalp and permanently eradicates dandruff.

"Coke Dandruff Cure" is guaranteed to cure or money refunded. One dollar a bottle at druggists or by express. Booklet free.

A. R. BREMER CO., 13 La Salle St., Chicago.

Canadian Depot, THE LYMAN BROS. & CO., Ltd., Toronto.

Figure 4.6 This advertisement for a cocaine-containing baldness cure was published at approximately the same time as the advertisement for the Burnett's product. From the author's private collection.

cocaine content, the worse the wines tasted. Commercial quantities of refined cocaine did not become available until the late 1880s, about the time that U.S. versions of Vin Mariani came to market. They contained more cocaine than Mariani's formulation, because the U.S. manufacturers were adding pure cocaine to their products, not leaves. Eventually, though, the higher cocaine content of the American wines led to their own undoing, because it helped lead to the passage of the U.S. Pure Food and Drug Act of 1906.

Something similar happened in England. Pharmacists in England were allowed to sell coca wines tax free ("nonexcisable"), provided that the wines contained so much coca leaf extract (at least 30 mg/oz) that they were guaranteed to taste terrible. Wines that contained lesser amounts of extract were considered beverages, not medications, and as such, were taxable. If a pharmacist wanted to sell the good-tasting wines, he had to purchase the equivalent of a liquor license. Enterprising pharmacists got around that law by selling concentrated essences to customers, who could then add the "essence" to their own wines. One popular version of "essence" contained 0.25% cocaine, while other brands contained up to twice as much. When added to

Figure 4.7 Another celebrity endorsement for coca wine — this one from Emile Zola. From the author's private collection.

the customer's own bottle of port wine, for instance, the final product would have been hard to tell from any of the specially brewed coca wine products.

In later years, Mariani ridiculed competitors who simply added refined cocaine to wine. He maintained that other components of the leaf were needed for flavor and character. If not appropriately blended, it was not drinkable. It would be tempting to dismiss Mariani's claim as "spin," or marketing hyperbole, but if the history of the Coca-Cola Company is any indication, Mariani was probably correct. Sometime after 1901, Coca-Cola dropped cocaine from its formula, but continued to add an extract of coca leaves from which the cocaine had been removed. The decocainized leaves, referred to as "Merchandise No. 5," were prepared especially for Coca-Cola at the Shaeffer Chemical Manufacturing Facility in Maywood, New Jersey. Presumably, these decocainized leaves supplied the same desirable flavoring claimed by Mariani.

Mariani's U.S. competitors never really tried to market the good taste of their versions. Instead, they made mostly medical claims, repeating the claims for coca leaf made by European physicians in the 1870s, before purified cocaine was available. Advertisements for Metcalf's Coca Wine were typical. Metcalf's Coca Wine sold for $1 a bottle.

> With stimulating and anodyne properties combined, Metcalf's Coca Wine acts without deliberating, being always uniform and therefore always reliable. For Athletes it is invaluable in imparting energy and resisting fatigue; Public Speakers and Singers find it indispensable as a "Voice Tonic," because being a "tensor" of the vocal chords, it greatly strengthens and increases the volume of the voice; and to the elderly it is a dependable aphrodisiac, superior to any other drug.

Neither Mariani nor any of his competitors could possibly have had any idea how or why their "anodyne" was so stimulating. More than a century passed before that secret was unraveled. In 1990, separate groups of researchers, one in Barcelona and one in Miami, discovered that the combination of alcohol and cocaine does more than make users feel good. It also produces an unusual compound called cocaethylene. When cocaine is consumed in the absence of alcohol, it is broken down into two principal metabolites: one called benzoylecgonine and one called ecgonine methyl ester. In humans, at least, neither of the two metabolites has any stimulant or psychological effects, but cocaethylene does. In fact, cocaethylene produces nearly as much stimulation as does cocaine.

When cocaine and alcohol are consumed together, cocaine's stimulant effects are enhanced and probably prolonged. Vin Mariani drinkers were, in effect, getting more cocaine than either Mariani or his competitors thought they were providing. That may explain why Vin Mariani, and the other cocaine-containing wines, were so popular. The discovery of cocaethylene also explains the puzzling observation that drinking relatively small amounts of coca wine seemed to cause an intense feeling of well-being, out of proportion to the amount of cocaine consumed. And it certainly could explain why the wines were so popular.

Modern cocaine abusers, who surely would never have heard of Vin Mariani, still combine cocaine and alcohol. The practice can be explained as an exercise in empirical pharmacology; users found a way to get a more intense, or at least prolonged, stimulant effect for the same amount of money. The downside to this approach is that using cocaine and alcohol together appears to make cocaine more toxic, not just in terms of behavior, but also in terms of damage to the heart and blood vessels. A systematic study has never been done, but postmortem blood tests disclose the presence of alcohol in more than a third of those dying from cocaine toxicity.

Advertising claims made by Mariani and his competitors are not nearly as outrageous as they seem today and should not be judged too harshly. The claims of the coca winemakers were entirely consistent with the ideas generally held by the medical community at the time. Von Liebig's theory of nutrition, bizarre and flawed as it was, had many adherents in the 1870s and 1880s. There was a general feeling, shared by physicians and their patients, that many ailments were the result of "tissue wasting," and that tissue wasting occurred when certain vital, but uncharacterized, compounds were absent from the diet. Von Liebig believed that nitrogen-containing compounds were the prime suspect. The fact that coca leaves contained nitrogen, albeit in small amounts, made them especially interesting to the medical community. Mariani died in 1914, but his wine lived on, remaining in production until 1954, when its name was changed to Tonique Mariani. It no longer contained any cocaine, but it remained on the market until 1963.

A Cholo of Huarai

5

The writings of naturalists and explorers returning from the Amazon made it seem likely that cocaine, or at least the coca plant, possessed real medicinal value. Following the Napoleonic wars, the pace of exploration in South America noticeably increased, affording a succession of European naturalists the opportunity to explore the Amazon. Two of the earliest were Karl Fredrich Philip von Martius (1794–1868) and Johan Baptist von Spix (1781–1826). They sailed to Buenos Aires, then traveled by land to Chile and north to Ecuador. Von Martius and von Spix, like de la Condamine before, completed their trip by canoeing the Amazon River. The naturalists took botanical specimens back to Europe, but whether or not they shipped back any coca plants is unclear. Von Martius, however, made detailed observations of Indian life, especially on the natives' use of medicinal plants. He was fascinated by the diet of the Indians, noting that they subsisted on only a few spoons of maize and water each day, and never complained, as long as they also had coca leaves to chew on.

Unlike von Martius and von Spix, who spent 3 years in Peru, Johan Jakob von Tschudi's (1818–1889) primary interest was in animal classification. However, he also recorded detailed observations of many plants, including sasparilla, cinchona, balsam, and coca. von Tschudi did not much like the natives, finding them "unsocial and gloomy." He was, however, fascinated by some aspects of their lifestyle, especially their use of coca. Von Tschudi swore that chewing coca leaves could prevent "the difficulty of respiration felt in the rapid ascents of the Cordilleras," a disorder known today as high-altitude pulmonary edema. However, it was an account of his employee, Hatan Humang's, remarkable endurance that fascinated him, and his readers. According to von Tschudi:

> A cholo of Huarai, named Hatan Huamang, was employed by me in very laborious digging. During the five days and nights he was

in my service he never tasted any food, and took only two hours sleep each night. But at intervals of two and a half or three hours he regularly chewed about half an ounce of coca leaves, and he kept an acullio (a wad of leaves) continually in his mouth. I was constantly beside him, and therefore I had the opportunity of closely observing him. The work for which I engaged him being finished, he accompanied me on a two days' journey of twenty-three leagues across the level heights. Though on foot, he kept up with the pace of my mule, and halted only for the chacchar (more coca leaves). On leaving me, he declared he would willingly engage himself again for the same amount of work, and that he would go through it without food, if I would but allow him a sufficient supply of coca. The village priest assured me that this man was sixty-two years of age, and that he had never known him to be ill, a day in his life.

These claims, and a similar one made by others returning from South America, were taken seriously and were firmly lodged in the public's consciousness. Letters to the editors of the *Lancet* and the *British Medical Journal*, from military surgeons and team physicians, described how coca chewing could be used as a way to decrease thirst and increase endurance. In 1877, a Canadian physician described what happened when he gave coca leaves to members of the Toronto Lacrosse Club:

The day was exceedingly hot, the thermometer marking 110°F in the sun. The antagonists of the club were men of sturdy build, of good physique, well trained in the game and, in general, connected with the mechanical trades, or with out-door avocations. In the latter particular they were in strong and apparently unfavorable contrast with the players of the Toronto club, whose occupations were all of a sedentary character. However, at the close of the day, during a short interval of rest between the games, I remarked that the men of the rival club were so thoroughly exhausted that it was with the utmost difficulty they could be roused by their field captain to take part in concluding the game, while the coca chewers were as elastic and apparently as free from fatigue as at the commencement of play.

Given the known effects of cocaine, and ambient temperatures of 110°F, the result is difficult, but not impossible, to believe. At the 1996 Olympic games in Atlanta, Georgia, several Russian athletes were disqualified for using an amphetamine-like drug known as Bromantane. Although structurally different from cocaine, it exerts many of the same physiological effects. The drug was developed by Russian Army chemists searching for agents capable of improving performance in hot and humid climates. Actually, cocaine would probably diminish, rather than enhance, the performance of an athlete competing in a hot environment. But such is the power of suggestion, and the desire for a competitive edge. Once the notion of cocaine-induced performance enhancement became established in the popular press, it persisted. In controlled clinical trials, stimulants do improve athletic performance, but not by very much. Taking cocaine might shave fractions of a second from the sprint times of elite runners. In average people, under average conditions, the effects are immeasurable.

Another group of coca enthusiasts described how chewing coca helped them to climb Mont Blanc in Switzerland. Each of the climbers chewed a total of 5 g of dried coca leaf during the 10 hours required for the climb. They drank no water, no tea, and no coffee, though they did indulge in some wine. According to the climbers, the trip was made in "comparative comfort." And there was, of course, the famous climb of a mountain in Scotland, made by the 78-year-old president of the Scottish Medical Association. He also claimed that chewing coca eliminated feelings of hunger and thirst. Given the quality and type of coca leaf that was available in Europe in 1882, it is unlikely that the Mont Blanc climbers could have ingested much more than 25 mg (0.05% of 5 g) of cocaine, far too little to have produced any measurable physiological effects. But the climbers were so convinced of coca's powers that they would probably have felt the same if the leaves they chewed contained no cocaine. In 1882, the placebo effect was not yet recognized.

Surgeon-Major T. Edmonston Charles of the Indian Army wrote to the *Medical Times and Gazette* and recommended coca for "assuaging thirst during great exertion in hot countries." Charles argued that a particularly famous military disaster in Afghanistan could have been averted if the troops were supplied with coca. This preoccupation with endurance culminated with the publication of a paper from a German author that described what happened when a military surgeon secretly added cocaine to the drinking water of Prussian artillerymen.

The physician was Theodore Aschenbrandt (1855–?). An Austrian, Aschenbrandt studied pharmacology in Würzburg from 1891 to 1892. The director of the pharmacology department at Würzburg, Dr. Michael Rossbach (1842–1894), was interested in cocaine research and had knowledge of the topic. Prior to Aschenbrandt's arrival in Würzburg, Professor Rossbach supervised another student, Vassili von Anrep (1852–1925), who was also interested in cocaine research. Von Anrep wrote a comprehensive review about cocaine's actions and even suggested that cocaine might prove to be a useful anesthetic.

Von Anrep could well have become famous as the inventor of local anesthesia, but he did not capitalize on his findings. He was a good scientist, but he believed that the results of his animal experiments, at least as far as cocaine's anesthetic properties were concerned, were not as clear cut as they could be. Von Anrep had planned to do a series of follow-up experiments in humans, but before he could do them, he returned to his home in St. Petersburg, where he became a professor of pharmacology, allowing Karl Koller, in Vienna, to receive credit for the discovery of local anesthetic in 1884, 14 years later.

Rossbach had tried to convince Aschenbrandt to continue von Anrep's work. He didn't, and he never made any significant discoveries, and never became an academic, but he did eventually contribute to the literature on cocaine. After receiving his degree, Aschenbrandt went into private practice, and he joined the Army Reserve. In 1883, while on summer maneuvers with the Bavarian Artillery, Aschenbrandt was called upon to treat a number of soldiers with heat exhaustion. Aschenbrandt went to the local pharmacy and purchased some cocaine. In the paper he subsequently published, he described the results in six cases. In one of the cases, he reported that when a soldier collapsed on the second day of a forced march, he was given one tablespoon of cocaine-containing solution. According to Aschenbrandt, "he stood up of his own accord and traveled the distance to H., several kilometers, easily and cheerfully and with a pack on his back."

The success of Aschenbrandt's experiment was almost as miraculous as the success of the climbers on Mont Blanc. In reality, cocaine could only make heat exhaustion worse, and Aschenbrandt offered no proof that heat exhaustion was, in fact, the problem. The soldiers in question could simply have been tired, and if that was the case, the cocaine would almost certainly have helped to alleviate their symptoms. Because cocaine makes the heart work harder and raises core body temperature, the latter explanation seems more likely. Aschenbrandt saw what he wanted to see.

Cocaine's alleged ability to promote strength and endurance received most of the attention, but there were other recurring themes in the medical literature. Coca was believed to be an effective remedy for shyness, nervousness, and even stage fright. This claim is particularly strange, because the symptoms of stage fright are the result of high circulating blood levels of stress hormones (the hormones epinephrine and norepinephrine). Coca actually increases the blood levels of those hormones. The modern treatment for those pathologically afraid of public speaking consists of giving drugs called beta-blockers, which counter the effects of the stress hormones.

Another area of interest was the treatment of morphine addiction. Opium was used sparingly in Europe during the Middle Ages, but its popularity increased during the Renaissance. By the dawn of the 19th century, opium addiction was a major problem. By the 1830s, case reports describing "morphia" toxicity were a regular feature in the medical journals. Almost as soon as coca leaf became commercially available, physicians began experimenting with it as a treatment for opium addiction. Given that basically nothing was known about the process of addiction in the late 1800s, the idea of treating opiate addiction with cocaine was not as bizarre as it sounds.

Addicts in the late 1800s differed from today's addicts in two very important respects: (1) they took opium, not morphine, and (2) they took it orally, not by injection. The distinctions may seem academic, but they are not. Opium taken by mouth is partly destroyed in the stomach and partly detoxified before it reaches the brain. This means that the addiction potential is much lower. The oral use of opium had built-in safeguards that made addiction less likely and toxicity harder to produce. The safeguards were partially eliminated when morphine, the active ingredient of opium, was successfully isolated from opium, by Friedrich Wilhelm Sertürner, in 1805. In that year, Sertürner announced that he had isolated an alkaline base in opium that he called morphium. The event marked an important milestone for organic chemistry, and not just for addicts.

Prior to Sertürner's successful experiment, it was universally believed that chemicals isolated from plants could only be acids, and that only metals could be alkali. Sertürner's discovery put an end to those beliefs. More importantly, his discovery rapidly led to the successful isolation of dozens of other potent drugs from plants, all alkali. Quinine and cocaine were just two of the many useful molecules found in plants. As a group, they were referred to as "plant alkaloids." The founder of England's Royal Pharmaceutical Society, Thomas Morton, started to refine and purify morphine in 1821. Merck of Darmstadt began the following year. Morphine's isolation may have marked a chemical milestone, but it was a nonevent for addiction, because the morphine was, like opium, still being taken by mouth.

The first attempts at injecting opium date back to at least the 17th century, and perhaps earlier. Christopher Wren (1632–1723), the architect who rebuilt St. Paul's Cathedral, and who was president of the Royal Society, was also a student of anatomy. In 1664, he helped Thomas Willis (1621–1675) create the illustrations for his famous book on neuroanatomy (the confluence of blood vessels at the base of the brain, the shape of which often determines outcome in cases of stroke and head trauma, was first described by Willis and is still referred to as "The Circle of Willis"). Wren was interested in medical problems long before he became an illustrator for Willis. According to the history of the Royal Society, when Wren was a professor of Astronomy at Gresham College, Oxford, in 1656, he began a series of experiments that involved giving intravenous opium injections to dogs. As the hypodermic syringe was not yet invented, Wren made do by attaching a quill to a small bladder that he filled with an opium solution. All of the experimental animals survived, and Wren was so encouraged by his preliminary results that he decided to repeat the experiment on a man. An ambassador to the Court of St. James offered the services of a "delinquent servant." The servant survived, but things did not go quite as well as they had with the dogs, and Wren abandoned the project. The idea of injecting medications was all but abandoned for the next 150 years.

In the early 1850s, Alexander Wood, a Scottish physician, reasoned that the best way to relieve painful extremity injuries would be to inject morphine directly into the nerves that supplied the painful area. Even in the 1850s, syringes were clumsy affairs, and Wood's experiments were not particularly successful. However, it quickly became apparent to Wood that the morphine he was trying to inject into the nerves was producing effects throughout the body. Wood's findings were published in 1855. "It is truly astonishing," he wrote, "how rapidly it affects the system. If you throw in a large quantity of morphine, you will see the eyes immediately injected and the patient narcotized." Wood carried out a number of experiments, mainly on his wife and himself. He proved that effective pain relief could be achieved by injecting morphine. In the course of his research, Wood managed to addict both his wife and himself. Unfortunately, Wood's wife holds the distinction of being the first woman to die of an injected narcotic drug overdose.

A few years after the publication of Wood's paper, an American physician named Charles Hunter (1834 or 1835–1878), decided to expand upon Wood's original experiments. Hunter found that a small dose of morphine, when given by injection, produced the same effects as a large dose given orally. Wood's observation became widely known just about the time of the U.S. Civil War. By the beginning of the U.S. Civil War, in 1861, commercially manufactured hypodermic syringes were available in America and Europe. The supply of syringes remained limited for much of the war, but by the war's conclusion in 1865, supplies of syringes were abundant, and so was the number of addicts. Addiction was extremely common, and American physicians expended considerable effort finding ways to treat the problem.

Physicians of the time had no idea how morphine relieved pain, much less how it caused addiction. Some misguided theorists even argued that hypodermic injection of morphine was less, rather than more, likely to produce addiction. Because cocaine's effects were so obviously opposite to those of morphine, many physicians concluded that cocaine would be an ideal treatment for morphine addicts. It should come as no surprise that they were encouraged in this belief by the drug companies that manufactured cocaine-containing products, particularly the Parke, Davis & Company of Detroit, Michigan.

George Davis, one of its owners, also owned a medical journal called the *Therapeutic Gazette*. Davis solicited articles from several physicians who claimed to have cured morphine addicts using Parke, Davis' tincture of coca. These articles caught the attention of Sigmund Freud and prompted him to experiment with cocaine.

Genies and Furies 6

The genies that they summoned up to help them turned into furies
bearing misfortune and disaster.

Albert Erlenmeyer
*Describing the events that occurred after Sigmund Freud recommended
cocaine as a treatment for morphine addiction*

Good ideas catch on slowly, but if the history of cocaine is any guide, bad
ideas spread like wildfire. In 1884, Karl Koller assured his place in history,
and helped to usher in the era of modern surgery, when he announced his
discovery that a few drops of cocaine solution could prevent the pain of eye
surgery (Figure 6.1) Koller got all the credit, but he was not the first to make
this observation. A succession of other physicians had already discovered that
cocaine was a local anesthetic, and they wrote about their findings.

In 1855, the *French Archives of Pharmacy* published a paper written by a
chemist named Gaedecke. The paper described the small, needle-like crystals
Gaedecke isolated from coca leaves, which he called "Erythroxyline." There
is no evidence that Samuel Percy of New York City read Gaedecke's paper,
or even heard of him, but just 2 years later, in November of 1857, Percy read
a paper at a meeting of the New York Academy of Medicine that described
how he found crystals that resembled, in every detail, the crystals described
by Gaedecke. Like Gaedecke, Percy named the substance "Erythroxyline" and
suggested that these crystals could be used as an anesthetic. Bearing in mind
that the accepted taxonomic name for the coca plant is Erythroxylon, it may
have been a coincidence that both authors chose the same name. Then again,
maybe it was not.

Albert Niemann repeated Gaedecke's studies and expanded upon them.
In 1860, Niemann isolated the same four-to-six-sided, needle-like crystals
from coca leaf that Gaedecke and Percy described. Niemann also noticed that

Figure 6.1   Karl Koller. This photograph of Koller was taken one year after he announced his discovery that cocaine was an effective anesthetic. Several years later, he was challenged to a duel by an anti-Semitic junior surgeon at the Vienna General Hospital. Koller won the duel, but realized that the future for Jewish doctors in Vienna was not good. He emigrated to New York, where he died in 1944. This photo originally appeared in *Acta Physiology Scandinavian; Supplement*, 299, 3–26, 1967.

when he placed the crystals on his tongue, it made his tongue feel numb. Niemann's discovery attracted a great deal more attention than did Gaedecke's work, probably because Niemann was working in the laboratory of the world's most famous chemist, Friedrich Wöhler (1880–1882).

A start-up German pharmaceutical company, called Merck of Darmstadt, took Niemann's observations seriously. While Niemann was still working as a graduate student under Wöhler, Merck was operating out of one, rather small, factory in Darmstadt. Merck chemists rapidly adopted Niemann's techniques for cocaine isolation and, in 1862, began producing small amounts (less than 50 g per year) of purified cocaine. Because nobody seemed to pay any attention to Niemann's confirmation of Gaedecke's original observations that cocaine was a local anesthetic, it is not exactly clear why the Merck chemists went to all the trouble of producing cocaine in the first place. With no known market for the product, Merck could not have been anticipating much in the way of sales.

A succession of other researchers repeated Gaedecke's and Niemann's experiments, but they never received much recognition either. In 1862, a

Viennese physician named Frederick Schroff tried cocaine on himself. He noticed that, at first, cocaine made him feel cheerful, but he also noticed that those feelings quickly wore off. Schroff reported that he found himself becoming thoroughly depressed after he used the drug. He also observed that, when cocaine crystals were placed on the tip of his tongue, his tongue became numb. He reported his observations in a paper read before the Viennese Medical Society. He advised others not to use cocaine because of the severe depression he had experienced, but it seems that no one paid much attention.

Even less notice was taken of a monograph published by Thomas Moreno y Maiz in 1868. Moreno y Maiz, a former surgeon in the Peruvian army, went to Paris for post graduate training. Both Moreno y Maiz and another Peruvian, Alfredo Bignon, were students of José Casimiro Ulloa, a native of Peru who trained in Paris nearly half a century earlier, during the early 1800s. Ulloa completed his studies, returned home, and founded the local medical society in Lima. He also started a medical journal and did everything he could to promote the adoption of European medical advances in Peru. In his spare time, he fostered research on the coca plant.

While Moreno y Maiz was training in Paris, Bignon stayed home. Bignon, who practiced in Lima. He was a naturalized French citizen and a pharmacist with some training in chemistry. Within a few years of the publication of Sigmund Freud's papers on cocaine, translations became available in South America. It was immediately obvious to local entrepreneurs, including Bignon, that demand for their native crop was about to increase, probably by a great deal.

Bignon developed an original, and fairly simple, way to manufacture crude cocaine. Because the Bignon technique was locally developed, even the Lima Medical Society and two separate official Peruvian Coca Commissions promoted its use. They insisted that Bignon's method was far superior to the techniques being introduced into South America by German pharmaceutical companies, like Merck, which they correctly inferred, was trying to corner the export market for semirefined cocaine. But even by 1900 standards, Bignon's technique was not all that good. It failed to extract all of the valuable cocaine from the leaves, leaving too much to go to waste. By 1886, German companies (including Merck) had taken over the business, exporting their raw product back to Hamburg for further processing.

Moreno y Maiz believed in the experimental scientific approach and was a follower of Claude Bernard (1813–1878), the first person to hold the chair of physiology at the Sorbonne. More than anyone else, Bernard is credited with having introduced scientific method into medicine. He dismissed the "intuitive" conclusions reached by many. He insisted that the only way to prove something was by doing an experiment, and that it did not matter whether the discipline was physics or medicine — the behaviors of electricity and people alike are bound by rules. As a consequence, the experimental studies conducted by Moreno y Maiz were not all that different from ones that would be conducted today. Moreno y Maiz published his results in a book entitled *Recherches Chimiques et Physiologiques sur l'Erythroxylon Coca du Pérou et la Cocaine*. The body of the book contained descriptions of the reactions he observed when he injected frogs with cocaine. The beginning and the end of the book contain the most interesting material.

In the introduction to his book, Moreno y Maiz complained about the high prices and limited supply of coca leaf, and the poor quality of refined cocaine that was for sale in Paris. He finally resorted to buying coca leaf (probably at the market in Hamburg) and then refining the leaves himself. He tried to use the same extraction technique employed by Niemann but found it "difficult and uncertain." In a footnote at the end of the book, Moreno y Maiz wondered, "Could one utilize it as a local anesthetic? One cannot make a decision on the basis of such a limited number of experiments; it must be decided by the future."

Moreno y Maiz was never able to get his hands on enough cocaine to do the experiments he wanted, but at least one person believed he was on the right track. At Fauvel's request, Mariani prepared a special tincture of cocaine that when applied to the throat effectively blocked painful sensations. Visiting American and English physicians observed Fauvel's techniques and adopted the practice. Despite the visitors' enthusiasm, Fauvel's ideas never gained general acceptance, at least not until Freud and Koller publicized his discovery in 1884.

Vassili von Anrep (1852–1925), Michael Rossbach's other famous student, was another cocaine researcher who received almost as little recognition as Moreno y Maiz, but he did prove that Moreno y Maiz's speculations were correct. Von Anrep was born in St. Petersburg, where he attended medical school. He then studied pharmacology in Würzburg, Austria, from 1891 to 1892, under the direction of Michael Rossbach (1842–1894). Von Anrep studied the effects of cocaine on experimental animals and on himself, and his conclusions were unequivocal. The results of all his experiments led him to believe that cocaine could alter mood, and that cocaine could be recommended "as a local anesthetic as well as (a treatment) for melancholics."

When no one paid attention to his findings, von Anrep stopped doing research and changed careers. He returned to Russia and eventually founded the first women's medical school in that country. He also chaired the Russian Red Cross during World War I. Despite his good works, von Anrep was imprisoned at the outbreak of the Russian Revolution and was eventually expelled from the country. He died in Paris, in 1925, without receiving any recognition for his discoveries. Even after Freud cited the works of von Anrep and Moreno y Maiz in *Uber Coca*, the work of these pioneers was completely ignored and remains so today.

The reason Koller became famous, and his predecessors did not, was that his results could be duplicated. When other researchers tried to replicate the works of von Anrep or Moreno y Maiz or even Fauvel, they were unable to do so. The reason they could not conduct successful experiments had to do with the cocaine supply. The cocaine content of stored coca leaves deteriorates markedly with time. Before the 1880s, coca leaves were not shipped to Europe with regularity. And, the quality of the leaves that arrived on the wharves of London, Hamburg, and Amsterdam, was not very good, as often as not they contained hardly any cocaine. Not only was the quality of the raw material unreliable, but also, as Moreno y Maiz observed, Niemann's extraction process was difficult and "unpredictable."

Experimenters failed to get the anticipated responses and were unable to replicate the works of Moreno y Maiz and von Anrep because what they were experimenting with was, often, not cocaine. By 1884, the year before Koller and Freud published their papers, Merck's annual total cocaine production was still less than one pound. Edward Squibb (1819–1900), the founder of what was later to become the E.R. Squibb and Sons (now part of Bristol Meyers Squibb), became so frustrated with the restrictive supplies of coca leaf that he decided to stop selling coca-based products. As far as Squibb was concerned, good coca leaf was unobtainable. When he analyzed the coca-containing products that were then being sold, Squibb found that none contained any cocaine. Squibb suggested that physicians might just as well prescribe caffeine.

The idea is not as insane as it sounds. Caffeine was available and cheap. Squibb believed that caffeine probably had many of the same effects as cocaine. He helpfully supplied a conversion table. According to Squibb's calculations — it is not entirely clear on what he based them — 180 mg of caffeine (roughly the content of three cans of today's Coca-Cola™) exerted the same effects on the body as 2700 mg of cocaine (in today's parlance, the equivalent of 50 to 60 lines of cocaine). Of course, Squibb's notions of equivalency were absurd. But cocaine and caffeine are related alkaloids, and caffeine was, at the time, much simpler to purify than cocaine, and much cheaper. By the time Squibb's paper was first published, consensus was emerging that many of cocaine's effects could also be produced by caffeine. The theory might have taken hold, except that Squibb's paper was published just 2 weeks before reports of Koller's discovery became known in New York City. Subsequent events in 1884 forced Squibb to reconsider his position on cocaine.

In the spring of 1884, Freud published *On Coca*, in which he recommended using cocaine to treat a variety of different conditions, including morphine addiction. In the fall of that same year, Koller discovered that cocaine could be used as a local anesthetic. The reasons that Freud's paper, and Koller's discovery, were taken seriously, while those of earlier workers were not, had more to do with the existence of the Merck chemists in Darmstadt, than with any novel scientific discoveries on the part of Freud or Koller.

Merck was able to supply pure, chemically active cocaine. Given a reliable cocaine supply, it finally became possible for researchers to duplicate each other's findings. Still, things may have turned out differently if the chemistry of alkaloids had been better understood at the time. Freud, for example, might have received credit for the discovery of local anesthesia, or at least could have shared credit with Koller.

Freud suggested to Leopold Königstein (1850–1924), an ophthalmologist friend, that he should try using a cocaine solution to relieve the pain of individuals with eye diseases such as trachoma (a painful eye infection that can result in blindness). Königstein obliged but was appalled to find that the cocaine solution made things worse, not better. Even though pure Merck cocaine was provided, the pharmacist who prepared the eye drops mixed the cocaine with too much acid. The mistake effectively neutralized the anesthetic effects of cocaine and, at the same time, caused great irritation to the patient's eyes.

In July of 1884, Freud published the first in a series of papers on cocaine. The first paper, *On Coca*, became the most famous. It recounted the history of cocaine and what was then known about its chemistry and pharmacology. After reviewing what was known, Freud listed a series of conditions for which, he suggested, treatment with cocaine could be useful. Some of the suggestions were good; several were reasonable; and several were very bad. To Freud's credit, he recommended cocaine as a local anesthetic. Unfortunately, he also recommended cocaine as a treatment for morphine addiction. The latter suggestion was immediately adopted, but Freud's suggestion that cocaine might have some anesthetic value was generally ignored — except by Karl Koller.

Like Squibb's ideas on caffeine, Freud's proposal that morphine addicts could be treated with cocaine was not nearly as absurd as it sounds today. In fact, Freud was not even the first to suggest this approach. In light of medical thinking at the time, Freud's suggestion was reasonable. By the time Freud sat down to write *On Coca*, American physicians already published several papers describing how coca extracts, if not cocaine itself, had proven effective in the treatment of morphine addiction. The idea that stimulants, such as cocaine and caffeine, could be used to antagonize narcotics like opium and morphine was widely accepted. Freud based his suggestion on the existing literature, but, as Albert Erlenmeyer pointed out, it was an idea "expounded by individuals without any truly scientific experience." Had Freud been more experienced, he might have realized that several of the American papers he quoted in his paper were actually little more than paid advertisements for Parke, Davis & Company.

Traditionally, Freud's critics attributed his morphine misadventures to his need for money and his desire to become famous. These suggestions probably contain an element of truth, but they do not explain how Freud was taken in by the cocaine endorsements contained in the *Therapeutic Gazette*, and they do not explain why his recommendations that cocaine could be used as an anesthetic were so halfhearted. The truth will never be known with certainty, but these particular errors of judgment can easily be explained by Freud's lack of training and his lack of clinical experience. At the time, Freud was only 28 years old, and barely out of medical school, when he published *On Coca*.

Medical training in the 1870s was far different than what it is today, and Freud's training was unusual even for his time. Lecturing was the only means of instruction; there was no bedside teaching. Students could graduate from medical school, as Freud did, without ever having examined a patient. In 1873, during his third year of training, Freud became a student in the laboratory of Ernst Wilhelm Ritter von Brücke (1819–1892). He spent 6 years as a researcher in von Brücke's laboratory, where he learned microscopic techniques and studied the comparative neuroanatomy of developing animals. The work addressed no clinical issues and involved no patient contact.

Freud found time to attend an occasional lecture at the medical school, and that was enough to allow him to sit for his examinations and obtain his medical degree. While training with von Brücke, Freud became close friends with one of von Brücke's assistants, a pathologist named Ernst von Fleischl-Marxow. Von Fleischl-Marxow (1846–1891) had become addicted to morphine after having surgery to amputate his thumb. It was Freud's personal knowledge of von Fleischl-Marxow's problems that aroused his interest in treating morphine addiction. In 1882, after Freud met his fiancée, Martha Bernays, he decided to abandon research in favor of clinical medicine. He left the research laboratory and began what today would be called a "rotating internship" at Vienna General Hospital.

Freud spent 2 months on the surgical service of Christian Billroth (1829–1894), the first surgeon to perform gastric surgery, or at least the first to do that sort of surgery and have patients survive with any regularity. Freud's surgical rotation was followed by 9 months in general medicine. In May 1883, Freud transferred to the neurology and psychiatry service, where much of his time was spent, again performing microscopic neuroanatomy. During this interval, Freud published several papers on his neuroanatomic studies. He was still working part time in the research laboratory when he wrote *On Coca* in the summer of 1884. The following year, he was given a teaching appointment at Vienna General Hospital. *On Coca*, which discussed possible clinical applications for cocaine, was written by Freud when he had less than 1 year of general clinical experience, and no experience, whatsoever, with treating the problems of addiction, except, of course, his experiences treating his poor addicted friend, von Fleischl-Marxow.

Freud found the source materials for *On Coca* by consulting a copy of the 1883 edition of the Index Catalog of the Library of the Surgeon-General's Office (known as the Surgeon General's List), the predecessor of today's "Index Medicus," a comprehensive list of published scientific papers. If it was published today, Freud's paper would be described as an editorial review paper: a paper describing the research of others, weighing its importance, and making recommendations for treatment based on the reported studies. But, Freud's paper was not based on placebo-controlled clinical trials, it was based upon unsubstantiated and anecdotal material, actually, paid advertisements. A paper like Freud's would never be published today, because no reputable modern journal would accept a paper based on anecdotal reports. Even more important, no journal would accept a review paper written by a physician with no experience in the field being reviewed.

Even before Freud consulted the Surgeon General's List, he read Theodore Aschenbrandt's article in which it was claimed that cocaine could be used to increase the endurance of soldiers. On April 21, 1884, Freud wrote to his fiancée, Martha Bernays, and told her he had decided to do a study on cocaine. He told her about Aschenbrandt's paper, and that he decided to order some cocaine and try it himself:

> Perhaps others are working at it; perhaps nothing will come of it. But I shall certainly try it, and you know that when one perseveres, sooner or later one succeeds. We do not need more than one such lucky hit to be able to think of setting up house.

The records of Merck Pharmaceuticals show that on April 24, 1884, C. Haubner's "Angel's Pharmacy," which served Vienna General Hospital and the area in which Freud lived, received a carton containing 15 g of hydrochloride of cocaine, and 5 g of cocaine freebase. That amount would be equivalent to approximately 150 lines of snorted cocaine, and 50 rocks of smokeable crack cocaine. Freud's initial purchase was only 1 g, which was all he could afford. One gram cost him one-tenth of his monthly salary.

The following week, Freud tried cocaine himself and was impressed. He decided to expand on the work done by Aschenbrandt, and by U.S. doctors who were publishing papers in a journal called the *Therapeutic Gazette*, edited by George Davis. The editor was, in fact, one of the owners of Parke, Davis & Company, a pharmaceutical company based in Detroit, Michigan. During the 1870s, Parke, Davis & Company manufactured a fluid extract of coca. During the 1880s, Parke, Davis & Company started to manufacture refined cocaine and ultimately challenged Merck for leadership of the cocaine market. In the early 1880s, Davis published an article by W.H. Bentley of Valley Oaks, Kentucky. Because the *Therapeutic Gazette* was written for advertising purposes, it is likely that Bentley was paid for his submission. Bentley claimed to have been successfully treating opium and alcohol addiction since 1872. The secret to Bentley's success was coca extract. Bentley singled out the extract of Parke, Davis & Company extract of mention in the article.

In addition to discussing his theory of addiction, Bentley offered opinions on some other diseases. Before condemning Freud too roundly for suggesting that cocaine could be used to treat morphine addiction, critics would be well advised to consider the state of medical thinking in the late 1870s. It is clearly reflected by Bentley's proposed etiology of tuberculosis:

> I think the brain and the nerves become enervated from various causes, and from whatever cause, digestion and assimilation become impaired; next the blood, by losing some of its healthy constituent becomes too thin and watery, and the circulation thereby languid and sluggish. Then, as it passes through the lungs, a spongy tissue, it parts with a portion of its fibrin, which, being semivitalized, organizes in the form of a tubercle.

The best that can be said is that Bentley's thinking about addiction was no more, and no less, magical than his thinking about infectious diseases. The worst that can be said is that Freud read this paper and actually took it seriously.

Another paper, also written for the *Therapeutic Gazette* and also quoted by Freud, was somewhat less theoretical. Dr. Edward Huse of Rockford, Illinois, described a 30-year-old Swedish man with a history of rheumatic fever. The man had been taking laudanum (a solution of opium taken orally) for over 2 years and had become addicted. According to Huse, the man's cravings disappeared over the course of 2 months of treatment. By the end of that time, the man had gained 17 pounds and claimed he had never felt so well in his life. His only treatment was "half an ounce of Parke, Davis & Co's fluid extract of coca, night and morning — no other medicine."

Freud also cited the papers of a Dr. Palmer from Louisville, Kentucky, the same Dr. Palmer who came to the aid of a lady "pedestrianist" in distress described in Chapter 3. Palmer claimed to have achieved near miraculous cures using coca elixir. Palmer managed to insert not just the name of Parke, Davis & Company in his paper, but also the advertisement on the back label of their fluid extract of coca. According to Parke, Davis & Company, this drug produces a gently excitant effect; is asserted to support the strength for a considerable time without food; in large doses produces a general excitation of the circulatory and nervous systems, imparting increased vigor to the muscles as well as to the intellect, with an indescribable feeling of satisfaction amounting altogether sometimes to a species of delirium, not followed by feelings of languor or depression.

All seven papers cited by Freud in his discussion of opium addiction were from the *Therapeutic Gazette*, published by Parke, Davis & Company, then America's largest cocaine manufacturer.

Freud found the reports fascinating, and he told von Fleischl-Marxow about them. He also told his fiancée. On June 2, 1884, while still working on the draft of *On Coca*, Freud wrote to Martha:

Woe to you my Princess, when I come. I will kiss you quite red and feed you till you are plump. And if you are forward, you shall see who is the stronger, a gentle little girl who doesn't eat enough or a big wild man who has cocaine in his body. In my last severe depression I took coca again, and a small dose lifted me to the heights in a wonderful fashion. I am just now busy collecting the literature for a song of praise to this magical substance.

One month later, at the end of May, the Physiology Institute where Freud had trained, and where von Fleischl-Marxow still worked, placed its first order for cocaine. The Institute purchased 10 g of cocaine at Haubner's "Angel's Pharmacy," the same place where Freud had made his purchases. However, because the Institute placed a larger order, for 10 g, it received a reduced price of five marks per gram. Von Fleischl-Marxow almost certainly was the one who placed the order for the Institute, and he soon became just as addicted to cocaine as he was to morphine. He began to order large quantities of cocaine from Merck, and the purchases immediately came to the attention of Merck administrators. From the time that Merck first started to make cocaine in 1862, until the time that Freud placed his first order in April of 1884, buyers for Merck cocaine had been notably absent. Officials at Merck wondered what on earth von Fleischl-Marxow and the Physiology Institute were doing with such a large amount of cocaine.

That summer, Merck officials wrote to von Fleischl-Marxow inquiring about his research. Von Fleischl-Marxow did not mention his own addiction. Instead, he wrote back to Merck and described Freud's experiments in some detail. He also discussed the possible use of cocaine in the treatment of morphine addiction. In October, Freud sent his own letter to Merck, outlining his research successes. Freud's correspondence with Merck was not entirely motivated by the desire to spread scientific knowledge. Freud sought, and later established, financial arrangements with both Merck and Parke, Davis & Company.

Emmanuel Merck recognized the possible promotional opportunities: if Freud's theories were accepted, Merck's cocaine sales could only increase. So, Merck summarized the letters sent by von Fleischl-Marxow and Freud and published several papers discussing advances in cocaine research. Because Emmanuel Merck was led to believe that von Fleischl-Marxow was Freud's collaborator, Merck's papers attributed the advances to both men.

Freud completed the final draft of *On Coca* in June 1884, and he managed to get it published the following month. The paper began with a summary of what had previously been written about the history and effects of coca and cocaine. He concluded it by recommending seven conditions for which cocaine treatment might prove useful, i.e., (1) as a mental stimulant, (2) as a possible treatment for digestive disorders, (3) as an appetite stimulant in cases of wasting diseases, (4) in the treatment of morphine and alcohol addiction, (5) as a treatment for asthma, (6) as an aphrodisiac, and (7) as a local anesthetic.

Freud's paper was widely read and, at least, initially, well received. Physicians, in very large numbers, began to prescribe cocaine for morphine addicts. Within a few months, clinics in Europe and the United States were packed with morphine addicts who were also addicted to cocaine. Less than 6 months after Freud's paper first appeared, Albert Erlenmeyer published a paper criticizing the practice. In his textbook on the treatment of morphine addiction, published in 1887, Erlenmeyer wrote:

> This therapeutic procedure (treatment of addiction with cocaine) has lately been publicly trumpeted and praised as a veritable salvation. But the greater the fuss made about this "absolutely precious" and "totally indispensable" route to health, the less efficacious it proved to be. These claims were made not only in medical journals but also in the popular press, a current practice that, at the risk of offending our profession, I must condemn. It was simply a question of propaganda expounded by individuals without any truly scientific experience, as objective analysis of the question easily demonstrated. But they persisted despite the warnings and ended up with the sorry and frightening result that use turned into abuse. The genies that they summoned up to help them turned into furies bearing misfortune and disaster.

Erlenmeyer was not the only one who had problems with the concept. As more bad results were reported, Freud was under pressure to defend his ideas in print. In 1887, he published another paper, making the feeble argument that addiction was a risk only in people who were already morphine addicts. But Freud also made the point, which was generally ignored or derided, that morphine addicts were getting into trouble because they were injecting themselves with cocaine, instead of taking cocaine orally, as Freud recommended. The distinction is, in fact, vitally important.

From the time that coca leaf was first introduced into Europe, sometime in the late 1600s, until the 1860s, cocaine was only taken orally. Practical hypodermic syringes were not yet commercially available, and no one realized that cocaine could be "snorted." Commercial production of hypodermic syringes only began circa 1855. Significant quantities of refined cocaine did not come on the market until 1885, nearly 30 years later. When cocaine finally became available in amounts large enough to abuse, it was mostly swallowed in solution.

Absorption of cocaine from the stomach is efficient, but when taken by mouth, much of the cocaine is metabolized and inactivated by the liver, long before it reaches the brain. Peak cocaine blood levels are reached more slowly when the drug is taken orally, and are much lower than if the same amount of cocaine is snorted or injected. The lower blood levels, and the longer the time required to enter the brain, the lower the addictive potential. Injected drug (no matter whether cocaine or morphine) reaches the brain very quickly, explaining the addictive potential of both drugs. Freud, of course, knew absolutely nothing about what happened to cocaine once it entered the body, but his observations were, nonetheless, valid.

Snorting cocaine produces results that are somewhere between swallowing and injecting. Based on the available medical evidence, it seems that no one thought about snorting cocaine until 1905 or 1906. Frequent bouts of cocaine snorting corrode the nasal septum, but the corrosion takes several years to develop. The first cases of perforated nasal septum in cocaine users were not described in journals until 1910, making it unlikely that this practice could have started much before then.

Freud's pronouncements on the use of cocaine as a local anesthetic were, and to some extent still are, the cause of contention. Freudians cite his recommendations in *On Coca* as evidence that Freud really thought of using cocaine as a local anesthetic before mentioning the idea to Koller. Detractors argue that Freud never pursued the idea and never conducted experiments, and claim that he was just quoting from von Anrep and Moreno y Maiz. Whatever the merits of these arguments, one thing is clear: Freud almost certainly had not read all of the research that he quoted in *On Coca*.

Freud wrote, "Cocaine and its salts have a marked anesthetizing effect when brought in contact with the skin and mucous membranes." However, that certainly is not the case, and the authors cited by Freud never claimed any such thing. Cocaine solutions produce an anesthetic effect when painted on mucous membranes, such as the lining of the nose or throat, but they have no effect on intact skin, because the solution cannot penetrate to the nerves that carry nerve impulses back to the brain. In order to anesthetize the skin with cocaine, cocaine-containing solutions must be directly injected into the skin so that the underlying nerve fibers come directly in contact with cocaine molecules. Both von Anrep and Moreno y Maiz realized that in order to be an effective anesthetic, cocaine would have to be injected.

Nowhere in *On Coca* does Freud mention that cocaine would have to be injected to produce an anesthetic effect. The omission raises the question of whether or not Freud actually read the papers by von Anrep and Moreno y Maiz. Physicians began injecting cocaine only after Koller's paper appeared. Freud was certainly not the first writer who did not bother to read the references he was citing. The practice still occurs today, and is especially common when authors not well acquainted with their subject write review papers. That seems to be an accurate description of Freud when he was writing *On Coca*.

Doctors in training at the Allgemeines Krankenhaus Wein (Vienna General Hospital) shared living space at the hospital. It was in the hospital's dormitory where Karl Koller first met Sigmund Freud. Letters discovered after Koller's death reveal that the two became close friends. Freud shared his aspirations with Koller, and he even shared his cocaine. During the summer of 1884, Koller helped Freud with some of his studies. They both took cocaine (orally) and then used various measuring devices to see if the drug could increase muscle strength.

Freud was so impressed with this experimental approach that, in January 1885, he published another cocaine paper, this one devoted to cocaine's effects on muscle strength. He used a "dynamometer" for the experiments. The device consisted of a spring-metal clip, which "upon being pressed together moves a pointer connected to it along a graduate scale." Freud would take cocaine, squeeze the clamp, and compare the results with measurements made without cocaine.

Freud was already convinced that cocaine was a wonder drug, so it is hardly surprising that he observed increases in his own strength. It is somewhat more surprising that he observed that the effects persisted for a number of hours at a time, when we now know that cocaine would have already been cleared from his bloodstream. These experiments were, of course, uncontrolled, unblinded, statistically insignificant, and totally unacceptable by today's standards. At the time, they passed as real science.

In September, Freud left town to visit Martha, no doubt with the intention of making her cheeks "quite red." Koller continued with the cocaine studies. During one of these experimental sessions, Koller gave some cocaine to another intern named Engel. Engel licked some cocaine from the tip of his penknife and remarked that the cocaine made his tongue numb. Koller wrote:

> ... in that moment it flashed upon me that I was carrying in my pocket the local anesthetic for which I had searched for some years earlier. I went straight to the laboratory, asked the assistant for a guinea pig for the experiment, made a solution of cocaine from the powder which I carried in my pocketbook, and instilled this into the eye of the animal.

When Koller put the cocaine drops into the guinea pig's eyes, they became insensible to pain. Koller and his laboratory assistant, Dr. Gaertner, then put cocaine into each other's eyes and found that they could feel nothing. Freud's official biographer, Ernest Jones, recounts the story somewhat differently, but Koller's account was confirmed by Gaertner, who went on to become a successful physician and the editor of a medical newspaper. On the 35th anniversary of Koller's discovery, Gaertner published an editorial recalling the events. The contents of the editorial match exactly the description given in Koller's diaries.

Koller and his family were hardly on speaking terms. When Koller first made his discovery, just a few weeks before the Heidelberg Ophthalmological Society was due to hold its annual meeting, he did not have enough money to get to Heidelberg. He convinced a friend, Joseph Brettauer of Trieste, to go to the meeting and present a paper in Koller's name. Brettauer presented Koller's paper on September 19, 1884. Brettauer also conducted a demonstration on a patient from the eye clinic.

In attendance at the Heidelberg conference was an American, Dr. Henry Noyes from New York City. Noyes mailed an account of the discovery to the editors of the New York Medical Record. It was published on October 11, 1884, not quite 1 month after the meeting, and 1 week before Koller was able to present the same material on October 17, at the meeting of the Viennese Medical Society.

The Noyes report electrified doctors and energized drug makers. Within 6 weeks of the publication of Noyes' report, Squibb's drug company received 300 orders for cocaine. In fact, the day after Noyes' letter was published, there was a rush to buy cocaine. Only one druggist in New York City had any cocaine in stock, and he had less than 1 gram. As demand for cocaine increased, so did the price. During the first week or so after Noyes' report was published, a 2% cocaine solution sold for $0.04/g. The price of cocaine in New York City rose from $1/g to $2.50/g to $7.50/g. In 2004 dollars, the price was more than four times as high as current wholesale prices on the black market. By the end of 1884, less than 2 months after the Heidelberg Congress, and less than 5 months after the publication of *On Coca*, cocaine production at Merck increased from three quarters of a pound in 1883 to 3179 pounds in 1884, and to 158,352 pounds in 1886.

One of the first Americans to experiment with cocaine was Dr. William Stewart Halsted (1852–1922), a young surgeon, then chief of Roosevelt Hospital's Outpatient Department and a visiting surgeon at Bellevue Hospital in New York City (Figure 6.2). Within 1 week of hearing about Koller's discovery, Halsted and his associates, Richard Hall and Frank Hartley, not only experimented on themselves but on their surgical colleagues, and students, not to mention the occasional patient. It became apparent to Halsted, and to his group, that cocaine could do much more than just make the eye insensible to pain.

Halsted observed that if cocaine was injected directly into a nerve, the perception of pain in that area would be blocked. The first paper published by Halsted and his group described nerve blocks performed by Halsted and Hall. It was published 6 weeks after they read Noyes' account of the Heidelberg Congress. One of the cases described by Hall was his own; Halsted

Figure 6.2 William Halsted was one of America's greatest surgeons. Unfortunately, he and most of his close staff members became cocaine addicts. (Courtesy of the Clendening History of Medicine Library.)

injected Hall's inferior dental nerve. Anyone who has ever had a cavity filled in a lower tooth is familiar with the procedure first devised by Hall and Halsted.

In the 1800s, doctors thought nothing of experimenting on themselves. Herman Knapp, editor of the *Archives of Ophthalmology,* also read Noyes' report, and set to work testing Koller's claims. He experimented on himself, his patients, and his 15-year-old son. Knapp described the results in an article he wrote for the October 25, 1884, issue of *Medical Record.* He stated that he placed cocaine drops in his own eyes, ears, nose, mouth, throat, urethra, and rectum. He then applied silver nitrate to his eye and to the end of his penis. Silver nitrate is used to cauterize bleeding from small blood vessels, and its application is normally very painful. Knapp found that when cocaine was applied to his eye and his urethra, the silver nitrate produced no pain whatsoever. Perhaps his enthusiasm had waned by the time he got around to checking his rectum, because he applied no silver nitrate there, believing it sufficient to observe that he experienced a feeling of numbness.

Within 1 year, William Halsted's group had used nerve blocks on more than 1000 patients, allowing the physicians to carry out surgical procedures that were never previously thought practical. In 1885, Halsted traveled to Europe, visited Vienna General Hospital, and taught Christian Billroth's assistant, Adolph Wölfer, how to produce anesthesia by injecting cocaine directly into nerves. Wölfer had already experimented with cocaine anesthetics, but without much success. Wölfer declared that the whole business was a waste of time. After Halsted showed Wölfer the proper techniques, Wölfer became a convert and began publishing his own papers on cocaine anesthesia.

Another Viennese surgeon, Carl Ludwig Schleich, took Wölfer's work one step further, finding ways to avoid cocaine's side effects by using highly diluted cocaine solutions ("infiltration anesthesia"). One of Halsted's students, Leonard Corning, is credited with the discovery of spinal anesthesia, again using cocaine. As was the case with Freud and Koller, a dispute arose over whether it was Halsted or Corning who first discovered spinal anesthesia. Like the dispute between Freud and Koller, the question is now one of only academic interest.

Not surprisingly, Halsted, Hall, and several of Halsted's assistants became addicted. Hall retired from academics and moved to California, where he founded the Santa Barbara County Medical Society. He became the first surgeon at Santa Barbara Cottage Hospital. Unfortunately, it appears that Hall remained addicted, as Halsted certainly did. Halsted's friend, William Welch, a pathologist at Bellevue Hospital, tried to break Halsted's cocaine habit by chartering a schooner with a crew of three and sailing Halsted around the Caribbean.

When that did not work, Halsted checked into Butler Hospital in Providence, Rhode Island. The staff at Butler cured him of his cocaine addiction, but only by addicting him to morphine. After a second admission to Butler in 1887, Halsted was pronounced "cured" of his newly acquired morphine problem, and he went on to become the first professor of Surgery at Johns Hopkins School of Medicine, where he spent the rest of his career. After Halsted's death, his friend William Osler, the first professor of medicine at Johns Hopkins, confirmed that Halsted had never been cured of his addiction, and that Halsted was still using morphine at the time of his death.

History has not been particularly kind to these researchers. Had all of these men been archaeologists, working in Egyptian tombs, the question of a mummy's curse would surely have arisen. Von Anrep was imprisoned by Russian revolutionaries and died an exile in Paris. Niemann died prematurely, but the cause remains unknown. Moreno y Maiz disappeared from public life almost as soon as his paper was published, and no one knows what happened to him. Freud lived into his 80s, but died a lingering and painful death from cancer of the mouth. Halsted spent the rest of his life addicted to cocaine and morphine. Several of Halsted's colleagues were said to have died of drug abuse. Schleich was nearly laughed out of the meeting hall at the German Surgical Society Congress in Berlin in 1892, when he suggested that local anesthesia might be much safer than general anesthesia. No one in Germany ever took Schleich seriously afterward (even though he was correct).

Koller was challenged to a duel by an anti-Semitic junior surgeon working for Christian Billroth. Even though Freud maintained that Koller had only one dueling lesson, Koller was actually a reserve army officer and an experienced fencer. Koller won the duel but realized that his possibilities for advancement, as a Jew in Vienna, were, to say the least, limited. He immigrated to New York where he died in 1944. He was never eligible for the Nobel Prize, because it was not created until after his discovery. The only physician to profit from cocaine during this epoch was Arthur Conan Doyle. Doyle was never successful as an ophthalmologist, but he attended lectures at Vienna General Hospital, and he learned all about cocaine. Doyle's knowledge of cocaine and its side effects may explain why Sherlock Holmes made such a convincing addict.

By today's standards, cocaine is only a moderately good local anesthetic, but in 1884, it was the only local anesthetic, and the medical community became fascinated with its possibilities. During the 2 years immediately following Koller's discovery, hundreds of clinical reports, mostly singing the praises of cocaine, were published. A few of the reports mentioned toxicity and untoward reactions, but the reports were played down. Drug companies could not keep up with the demand for cocaine, and their eyes then turned to South America, while some visionaries looked toward Southeast Asia.

Death by Misadventure

7

In the rush of euphoria that followed Karl Koller's discovery that cocaine could be used as an anesthetic, medical professionals, the press, and readers of the daily papers believed what they wanted and discounted most of the bad news. Sigmund Freud, in his eager and uncritical enthusiasm for cocaine, had shown, to say the least, a rather selective reading of earlier accounts of coca's effects. He seized on Johan von Tschudi's story of Hataum Humang's extraordinary feats as confirmation of coca's miraculous powers. But von Tschudi had hardly written a blanket endorsement of coca. In fact, anyone who read all of von Tschudi's book would have known that he was also very concerned about coca's undesirable side effects, and that he even expressed concerns that Europeans might be more at risk for toxicity than the natives who had grown up chewing coca. It was not just that the habit disgusted him ("all who masticate coca have a very bad breath, pale lips and gums, greenish and stumpy teeth and an ugly black mark at the angles of the mouth"), he was also concerned that their habit was making them sick. As evidence, he cited their "sunken eyes, yellow skin" and "general apathy," which all bore "evidence of the baneful effects of coca juice when taken in excess."

Freud also read the accounts by another Amazon explorer, Edward Poeppig. When William Hooker published his drawings of the coca plant in Kew's *Companion to the Botanical Magazine*, he also translated part of Poeppig's account of his 5 years in the Amazon, *Travels in Chile, through Peru and Down the Amazon*, and published it in the same issue.

Like von Martius, Poeppig, and most of the other early Amazon explorers, believed that coca users had increased endurance, but they also believed that, in many respects, coca users resembled opium eaters, and all of them warned against the immoderate use of coca. A British-born, French-naturalized explorer, Hughes-Algernon Weddel, held more moderate views. Weddel was the designated botanist on a French expedition to Bolivia in 1843. His book, *Voyage dans le nord de la Bolivie*, was later translated into English and extracts were published in U.S. medical journals. Weddel disagreed with most of what Poeppig had to say, but he never did believe that there was not a downside, stating that coca chewing "does sometimes produce evil consequences among Europeans who have not accustomed themselves to it." He also reported that chewing too much coca could result in a "peculiar aberration of the intellectual facilities indicated by hallucination."

Freud dismissed most of these warnings as unrepresentative and inaccurate, but he was nearly the only scientist to do so. To be fair, Freud also quoted parts of von Tschudi's book that described both the attractions and the dangers of the drug:

> He who indulges for a time in the use of coca finds it difficult, indeed almost impossible to relinquish it... They give themselves up for days together, to the passionate enjoyment of the leaves. Then their excited imaginations conjure up the most wonderful visions.... I have never yet been able to ascertain correctly the conditions the Coquero (coca-chewer) passes through on returning to his ordinary state; it, however, appears that it is not so much want of sleep, or the absence of food, as the want of Coca that puts an end to the debauch.

Von Tschudi and Weddell were both exploring the same parts of Peru at the same time, but somehow never met. Von Tschudi's completed book was first published in French in 1847 and was translated into English in 1854. Von Tschudi was not the only person to write about "wonderful visions." They were experienced firsthand by Paolo Mantegazza, an Italian physician and anthropologist working in northern Argentina during the 1850s. Like Freud, Mantegazza was happy to experiment on himself, and he used prodigious quantities of coca extract. He praised "the very strong digestive power of this leaf," which "eliminates the most uncomfortable complications of alcoholic overindulgence," but he also wrote vivid descriptions about his coca-related hallucinations. A description of one of his hallucinatory experiences is still widely quoted, probably because the prose was so overheated:

> I sneered at the poor mortals condemned to live in this valley of tears while I, carried on the wings of two leaves of coca, went flying through the spaces of 77,438 words, each more splendid than the one before.... An hour later I was sufficiently calm to write these words in a steady hand: God is unjust because he made man incapable of sustaining the effect of coca all life long. I would rather

have a life span of ten years with coca than one of 10000000...(and here I had inserted a line of zeros) centuries without coca.

Mantegazza's account, and von Tschudi's observation that "want of coca," was the only factor limiting use, illustrates a fascinating and frightening feature of cocaine — it is extremely addictive. Laboratory animals connected to a source of heroin will give themselves injections on a regular basis, but not to the exclusion of all other activities. Animals instrumented to self-inject cocaine will continue doing so until they die. No other drug, with the possible exception of methamphetamine, exerts that effect.

Despite all the negative reports, Freud concluded that "other observers affirm that the use of coca in moderation is more likely to promote health than to impair it." In this, he was telling the truth, at least as far as he knew it. Freud's big mistake was confusing coca with cocaine. Coca leaf contains only very small amounts of cocaine, usually much less than 1%. Vascular disease and sudden death, now so common among heavy cocaine users, was, and still is, unheard of among coca-leaf chewers. Freud found out the hard way that use of purified cocaine is an entirely different matter. Even when swallowed, purified cocaine is more toxic than the chewed leaf, simply because more cocaine gets into the body more quickly. Both the amount of cocaine used and the way it is taken determine toxicity and addiction. In other words, the severity of cocaine toxicity is, to a great degree, determined by technology. First, there have to be ample supplies of purified cocaine, and then there have to be more efficient ways to get the cocaine to the brain.

The addiction potential for any drug depends mainly on how much drug actually reaches the brain and how quickly it gets there. When pure cocaine is taken orally (many laboratory studies are done this way), it exerts a more potent effect than does cocaine derived from chewing leaves. Even so, it is unlikely to be very toxic, and it will not produce much of a "high," at least when compared to cocaine injected under the skin or into a vein. The reason for this has to do with the considerable time lag between the moment when cocaine gets out of the stomach and into the bloodstream, the time it takes for the cocaine to arrive in the brain, and the amount of cocaine that finally arrives there.

Cocaine in the stomach enters the bloodstream much more slowly than cocaine injected into a muscle or vein, and the increase in levels in the blood is much slower. The result is a less intense high and less likelihood of toxicity. When cocaine is injected, however, the time lag between ingestion, and the time when its euphoric effects can be felt, is much shorter, and the levels in the blood are much higher. Not only does injecting produce a more intense high, it also increases the risks of addiction and toxicity. Smoking crack cocaine produces levels in blood similar to those in intravenous users, but smoked cocaine ("freebase" or "crack") produces the most intense stimulation, the greatest risk of addiction, and the greatest risk of toxicity.

These facts explain the apparent absence of vascular toxicity in coca-chewing natives of the Andes — at any one time, the amount of cocaine in their blood is quite small, and it never rises to high enough levels to put coca chewers at risk. Comparing coca leaves and cocaine is like comparing fire hoses and flamethrowers. While there are occasional reports describing sores in the mouths of coca chewers, similar to those seen in people who chew tobacco, reports of vascular disease remained rare, or at least they were until recently, when some of the indigenous young people of the Andes began smoking partly refined cocaine.

It would take an enormous amount of coca leaf, and a great deal of chewing, to extract enough cocaine from coca to produce a toxic reaction. And, as Freud quickly found out, using purified cocaine causes very different effects than just chewing coca leaves. Both the amount of cocaine used and the way it is used are codeterminants of toxicity. In a real sense, the history of cocaine toxicity is determined by technology.

Until Freud and Koller published their observations, hardly anyone in Europe or the United States ever heard of cocaine, and physicians had no experience with the problems of cocaine toxicity. There was just none to be had. On September 2, 1885, the *New York Times* wrote:

> Recent publications on the subject of cocaine and the various therapeutic use to which it can be put have caused a widespread demand for the valuable drug. The increased demand for cocaine is a source of marked satisfaction among all the druggists because, like everything else which is new and valuable, it commands a large price and issues a handsome profit.

True, large amounts of coca were being produced in the Andes, but the leaf that left South America was used to make wine, not purified cocaine.

The medical community only learned gradually about the dangers of cocaine, for there was little cocaine to be had. It would take more than 20 years for the full picture of the dangers of cocaine use to emerge. During the 1870s, virtually all of the cocaine consumed in Europe was in the form of coca wine. No one had yet thought to inject cocaine, and, even if they had, syringes were not yet being mass produced. Freud took his cocaine by mouth, and so did his friends, at least until Fleischl-Marxow started to give himself subcutaneous injections, and until surgeons started injecting cocaine anesthetics into their patients.

"Sniffing" or "snifting" cocaine (as "snorting" was referred to at that time) only became common after the turn of the century. While not nearly as efficient a way to get cocaine into the bloodstream as injecting cocaine, sniffing it allows it to enter the bloodstream more quickly than swallowing it. With the enhanced absorption, a user is much more likely to become addicted, or poisoned.

Chronic cocaine snorting produces a characteristic pattern of changes in the tissues lining the nose. Cocaine causes all blood vessels to contract (the process is called vasoconstriction). Sometimes the vessels contract so intensely that no blood can pass through them. When cocaine is snorted, the blood vessels in the cartilage in the middle of the nose (the septum) are temporarily deprived of their normal blood supply. Blood flow only returns to normal as the cocaine effects wear off. As a consequence, two things occur: (1) the tissue swells when the blood supply is restored, which explains why cocaine users tend to have stuffy, runny noses, and (2) the tissue repeatedly deprived of its blood flow is weakened, eventually destroyed, and a hole develops in the nasal septum (the piece of cartilage that divides the nose). The first cases of perforated nasal septum were not reported until 1910, which suggests that the practice of snorting cocaine could not have begun much before 1905.

Freud's friend, von Fleischl-Marxow was one of the first to start injecting himself with cocaine — not into a vein, but under the skin (subcutaneous is the proper word, but on the street it is called "skin popping"). And once people started injecting cocaine, the results were predictable. As dosages escalated, so did the medical problems. News about Koller's discovery of cocaine anesthesia spread like wildfire. Doctors in Europe and the United States began to use cocaine to treat a host of unrelated conditions. Enthusiasm often got the better of common sense, and, frequently, cocaine was prescribed for conditions that today are not even recognized as diseases. Cocaine was said to be a cure for almost every conceivable disorder, from prostate enlargement to nymphomania, asthma, seasickness, hemorrhoids, and hay fever.

Some of these treatments made more sense than others. Cocaine raises blood epinephrine (adrenaline) levels, and epinephrine-like drugs are a recognized treatment for asthma. Using cocaine to treat nymphomania, on the other hand, was probably not wise. Cocaine can be a potent sexual stimulant, simultaneously increasing libido and decreasing inhibition. Many addiction specialists believe that cocaine-related compulsive sexuality contributes to failure of their treatments leading to a chronic relapse into drug use. Even 100 years ago, the phenomenon of sex-for-drugs may have contributed to the spread of syphilis.

Cocaine is a local anesthetic vastly more effective than anything ever used before. Koller showed that cocaine drops applied to the membranes of the eye made the eye insensible to pain. The next logical step was to apply cocaine solutions to other surfaces of the body, such as the urethra, bladder, rectum, and vagina. Applications of cocaine worked well in those locations, too, but cocaine injected into body tissues worked even better.

When cocaine solutions are applied to body membranes, they are rapidly absorbed. When only a few drops of dilute cocaine solution are placed in the eye, detectable concentrations of cocaine appear in the bloodstream a few seconds later. Most of the early eye surgeons used relatively small amounts of cocaine, so complications were uncommon. When larger doses of cocaine were used, or when the cocaine was injected directly into the lining of the eye, complications began to occur.

Less than a year after Koller's discovery, an eye surgeon in Danzig, Poland, Dr. Anton Ziem, published a paper describing 17 instances where cocaine anesthesia caused serious side effects. As ophthalmologists soon found out, large doses of all local anesthetics (not just cocaine) can cause seizures. If the seizures are prolonged, coma and death follow. In addition, many other eye surgeons noticed that patients treated with cocaine solutions developed eye infections at a much higher rate than those who were not. The observation greatly dampened the initial enthusiasm.

Fortunately for the eye surgeons and their patients, humans have small eyes (at least relative to the total size of their bodies). Instilling large volumes of cocaine-containing solutions is difficult, though not impossible. This fortunate circumstance was coupled with another fortunate circumstance, namely, that cocaine is not a potent local anesthetic (the more potent, the greater the toxic side effects). Still, with so many physicians prescribing cocaine for so many people, complications were inevitable.

Deaths from cocaine anesthesia were not rare, although they were certainly not everyday occurrences. The first recorded surgical death due to cocaine occurred in 1886. It was the result of cocaine administered during rectal surgery. Gonorrhea and syphilis were rampant in the late 19th century. Those suffering from these venereal diseases, and some patients suffering from tuberculosis, were prone to inflammation, scarring, and, occasionally, ulceration of the rectum, urethra, and bladder. Filling the urethra and bladder with cocaine-containing solutions allowed for the painless insertion of instruments and also rendered the bladder wall insensible to pain. However, the bladder wall provides a tremendous surface area for absorbing cocaine, especially if the wall is already inflamed. The same danger existed during surgery to the rectum and vagina.

The death toll slowly continued to mount. In 1887, Professor Sergei Petrovich Kolomnin from St. Petersburg treated a young woman with an open sore inside her rectum, a presumed complication of tuberculosis. Kolomnin decided to scrape and cauterize the lesion, using cocaine as an anesthetic. He had never used cocaine in this procedure before, but he read reports from other physicians who claimed great success. One particular report from France described using cocaine in an operation exactly like the one that Kolomnin was planning. To be on the safe side, Kolomnin injected the patient with only 1380 mg of cocaine, half as much as the French surgeon had recommended, but still a very large amount — the equivalent of approximately 20 to 30 lines of cocaine.

The surgery was uneventful. Kolomnin scraped the ulcer, packed it with gauze to prevent bleeding, and sent the woman back to her room. Half an hour later, he was called to her bedside. Her pulse was weak, her face was blue, and she was barely breathing. Kolomnin tried everything he could think of, including, "Faradization [electric shocks], artificial respiration, hypodermatic injection of ether, administration of ammonia, tracheotomy for the inhalation of oxygen, [and] stimulating and nutrient enemata," but the woman could not be revived.

Analysis of the ulcer scrapings taken at surgery revealed that the woman was not, after all, suffering from tuberculosis, and that the surgery was almost certainly not necessary. Shortly afterwards, Kolomnin committed suicide, telling friends that, "I cannot help feeling at times that I killed her."

Cocaine is no longer used for rectal or vaginal surgery, though application of cocaine to those areas as an exercise in eroticism is still widely practiced, and deaths associated with genital cocaine application are still fairly common, at least in countries where cocaine is readily available. Death is especially likely to occur during sex play, when levels of stress hormones (adrenaline, also called epinephrine, and norepinephrine) are elevated. Pathologists generally believe that because cocaine also elevates levels of these same hormones, application of cocaine to the vagina or rectum, where the drug is readily absorbed, may precipitate fatal cardiac rhythm disturbances.

The first cocaine anesthetic death to occur in London took place 2 years later in 1889. A man named Charles Sidney Fletcher was admitted to the University College Hospital where he was scheduled to have surgery on his tuberculosis-scarred bladder. A concentrated cocaine solution, containing 1200 mg of cocaine, was to have been injected into Fletcher's bladder. Instead, it was mistakenly given to him to drink. The uncontrolled convulsions that followed were fatal. Although it was not recognized at the time, Fletcher's autopsy revealed the typical findings seen in cocaine-associated deaths: a swollen brain and fluid-filled lungs.

It took still another 2½ years before the first anesthetic-related deaths occurred in New York City. In 1892, a 42-year-old tailor, Benjamin M. Noe, went to Bellevue Hospital for hand surgery. Noe's hand was injected with a 4% cocaine solution. He developed uncontrollable convulsions and was dead within 5 minutes. The autopsy disclosed "congestion" of the major organs, but the inquest panel was unsure how to interpret those findings. As in the London case, the autopsy disclosed fluid in the lungs and "congestion" of the abdominal organs. The findings of the inquest read as follows:

> It is supposed that this intense congestion was caused by the cocaine, but as there has been no other death after the administration of cocaine in this city, the medical profession is not familiar with the effects of the drug.

Even though the inquest panel ruled that death was caused by the cocaine injection, it was decided that the surgeon had exercised proper judgment. The panel felt that death was in some way due to "a peculiar, unknown existing idiosyncrasy."

Dentistry was another problem area. Dental hygiene during the "Gay Nineties" was not good, and before the advent of cocaine injections, dental procedures were extremely painful. Injecting cocaine directly into the gums surrounding a tooth produced a reasonably good level of anesthesia and required a good deal less skill than finding and injecting the nerve to the lower jaw, as was done by William Stewart Halsted. Unfortunately, most of the cocaine injected into the gums goes directly into the bloodstream, producing dangerously high levels in the blood. Seizures — occasionally fatal — regularly occurred in dental surgeries.

Many of the complications ascribed to cocaine would have occurred even if the unfortunate patients had been given excessive amounts of today's local anesthetics, such as lidocaine or marcaine. However, cocaine is more than a local anesthetic, and cocaine does things that other local anesthetics do not. At the turn of the century, autopsies were rarely performed in cocaine-related deaths, so there is no good way to determine how many of these deaths were due to heart disease and how many were due to cocaine. But it seems likely that many were due to unrecognized, underlying, heart disease. Rheumatic heart disease was rampant in the late 1800s. Many of those sitting in the dentist chair already had damaged hearts, and they would have been particularly vulnerable to the effects of cocaine.

For those with heart disease, a visit to the dentist could be deadly. The demise of Jane Favish was typical. She died on January 25, 1908, in a dental surgery, in London's Soho district. The dentist, an unqualified illegal immigrant, injected the woman's gums with 30 mg of cocaine before extracting numerous teeth. Favish died before the dentist finished. An autopsy disclosed that she had a badly scarred mitral valve, a consequence of childhood rheumatic fever. The dentist was charged with manslaughter.

Dr. J.B. Mattison from Brooklyn, New York, was the first person to carry out a large-scale "pharmacovigilance" study of cocaine. Mattison reported his findings in 1887. He managed to collect reports on four deaths, and on 46 other cases where serious adverse complications had occurred in conjunction with cocaine anesthesia. Six months later, Mattison found three more cocaine-related deaths and 73 more cases with severe complications. Four months later, there were another six deaths and 53 additional cases where patients experienced life-threatening side effects.

Mattison was not the only physician worried about the cocaine problem. In January 1886, Dr. George Catelet wrote to the *Medical Gazette* describing the case of Ester C., a 39-year-old mother of four children. Ester had been admitted to the State Lunatic Asylum in St. Joseph, Missouri. One year prior to admission, her behavior started to change, and she would make periodic threats of killing herself and her baby. Six months of intensive treatment improved things, and her husband thought it safe to remove her from the hospital. She was readmitted 3 months later, worse than ever. Because she had become so depressed, her doctors decided to treat her with cocaine. She was given a 60 mg injection of cocaine every morning, with another dose, of equal size, late in the afternoon. The treatment continued for 2 weeks.

Catelet's patient seemed to be getting stronger, and she was eating more, but she remained depressed. The cocaine injections made her feel better while they lasted, but she felt worse than ever when they wore off, and she was constantly asking for more. She woke one morning complaining of swollen eyes, headache, and feeling weak. She died 30 hours later. A review of her chart showed that after each injection her heart rate had increased by 25 beats a minute, and that her blood pressure "rose considerably."

Ester C. had all the symptoms of what would now be described as a cavernous sinus thrombosis, a type of stroke. It is a somewhat uncommon disorder, usually seen in women with clotting disorders, either pregnant women or women taking birth control pills. But the evidence suggests that cocaine can also promote this sort of clotting disorder.

For several decades, medical journals regularly ran articles describing the dangers of cocaine use. More than a few of these reports described doctors who became totally incapacitated by cocaine use, and who sometimes managed to kill themselves. One such doctor was Daniel McIntyre, a 27-year-old surgeon at Edinburgh University, who tried to cure his toothache by applying cocaine crystals directly to the tooth. The coroner's jury returned a verdict of "Death by misadventure."

A New Disease Emerges

8

By the turn of the 20th century, there was a glut of cocaine on the market. Cocaine could be purchased from the local chemist, usually without a prescription. Cocaine was also sold openly in the streets. Even in cities where pharmacy sales were regulated, enforcement was lax, and there was no shortage of doctors and pharmacists willing to make money by selling drugs. There were also many patent remedies on the market that contained large amounts of cocaine. As the number of cocaine users grew, so did the number of cocaine-related deaths. In fact, the cocaine problem, when expressed as a proportion of the U.S. population, was probably worse then, than it is today.

According to a U.S. government report, the total number of deaths from heroin and cocaine in the United States constitutes a smaller percentage of the total population now than it did in 1912, when the number exceeded 5000. Today, the number of cocaine-related deaths is nearly three times that high, but the U.S. population is four times what it was then. The exact numbers are impossible to determine, because the U.S. agency charged with tracking the totals changed its format and no longer publishes national totals.

A partial resolution of the anesthesia problem was found at the dawn of the 20th century. During the 1890s, toxic reactions usually occurred because doctors had given their patients too much cocaine at one time. After the turn of the century, the pattern gradually changed, as physicians learned more about cocaine. They began to use it more sparingly and with much more caution. In 1924, an investigation commissioned by the American Medical Association recommended using less cocaine and avoiding injections of it altogether. Thereafter, the number of reported deaths from cocaine rapidly declined.

Cocaine-associated medical disorders decreased in the 1920s, but they did not disappear. They just changed in character. When problems occurred, they were more likely to be the result of using large amounts of cocaine for too long a time than from taking one enormous dose. The most striking disorders associated with chronic cocaine use, apart from sudden cardiac death, are some very strange psychiatric syndromes. They result from long-term alterations of brain chemistry. Freud's addicted friend, Ernst von Fleischl -Marxow, was probably the first to suffer from one of these syndromes. One night in June 1885, Freud and his friends spent the evening trying to calm von Fleischl-Marxow. He had become quite psychotic — convinced that white snakes were crawling over his skin.

This belief that small animals are crawling out of, or through, a cocaine user's skin has come to be known as Magnon's syndrome, named after the French neurologist Valentine Magnon, who first recognized this unique complication of cocaine abuse. In 1898, at a meeting of the French Biological Society, Magnon reported on three patients who had symptoms almost identical to those of Freud's friend. One patient claimed to be covered with lice, that his clothes and all the objects around him were full of "microbes." In his attempts to remove them, he scratched himself raw and was covered with sores and abscesses. Another claimed he could feel cocaine crystals under his skin. He kept scraping his tongue and scratching his hands to rid himself of them. Another, a 39-year-old physician, claimed he could feel liquid crystals of cocaine under his skin. He was almost continuously scraping his tongue and scratching his skin in an attempt to remove the crystals.

Medical accounts of this disorder even began to appear in the lay press. The *Scientific American* (March 20, 1897) published another account — by a reformed cocaine abuser:

> Other dreadful hallucinations I had in thousands, all of a perse-cuting character, and frightening the life out of me so long as the effects of the drug lasted. You see small animals running about your body, and feel their bite.

At least victims of Magnon's syndrome were only a danger to themselves, unlike those suffering from "excited" or "agitated delirium," the other important behavioral disturbance associated with cocaine abuse. Victims of this disorder become grossly psychotic and physically agitated, often perform amazing feats of strength. They have also elevated body temperatures. After a few minutes or hours, victims grow quiet and die.

This syndrome, first recognized more than 100 years ago, qualifies as a true medical emergency. Most cases occur as the result of prolonged stimulant abuse, though the syndrome may also be seen as a complication of some purely medical disorders, such as hyperthyroidism, and even schizophrenia. When pure cocaine first became available, most of the cocaine abusers were members of the medical profession who were experimenting with cocaine on themselves. Toward the turn of the century, cocaine use reached epidemic proportions in the United States, not so much among the middle classes, but mainly among the poor people, especially in the Southern United States. The demographic shift was partly prompted by the tendency of some farm owners to pay sharecroppers in cocaine, or at least make it cheaply available.

The first newspaper accounts of agitated delirium appeared in the *New York Times Sunday Magazine* section for February 8, 1914. The actual cover, containing the headline "Negro Cocaine Fiends are a new southern menace," can be seen in Figure 8.1 Edward Williams was reporting on a series of murders and violent crimes allegedly committed by black people under the influence of cocaine. According to Williams, cocaine made the perpetrators crazed and resistant to bullets because they had a "temporary immunity to shock." He even described a man who had been shot through the heart but who was able to continue fighting with police officers. Williams also claimed that cocaine had the ability to enhance the user's ability to shoot straight, making them all the more dangerous.

Figure 8.1   Dr. Edward Williams. Writing in the February 8, 1914, issue of the *New York Times*, Williams breathlessly described how "cocaine crazed negroes" threatened the "New South." Much of the violence he described was probably a consequence of chronic stimulant abuse — in this case, cocaine. From the *New York Times* with permission.

The account offered by Williams is so bizarre and so mixed with racist hysteria that it is difficult to take anything he says seriously. To be fair, Williams was reporting only what other people were saying. Twelve years earlier, a *New York Times* correspondent wrote:

> Physicians say that if the habit (cocaine use) among the negroes is not suppressed and radical steps to this end taken very quickly, it will mean the utter ruin and extermination of the race in the South… the press of the State is taking up the subject favoring the adoption of some radical method to save the negro from self-destruction. (November 2, 1902)

The charges continued to escalate. The *New York Times* of December 6, 1907, carried a report from a correspondent in Augusta, Arkansas, who described the death of Wash Mussay, " a negro who shot seven white persons, two were women." According to the account in the newspaper, "The negro was finally surrounded in the railroad yard and shot to death by a posse, fighting until he fell literally riddled with bullets." In 1809, another *New York Times* correspondent, this one reporting from Monroe, Louisiana, described how "Half-crazed, either by whisky or cocaine, Bill Way, a negro from Pine Bluff, Arkansas, dashed down the main street of Monroe to-day with a double-barreled shotgun, firing in every direction. Citizens returned the fire and the negro finally fell dead after receiving a score or more wounds. Twenty-one persons were injured in the fight." Mr. Way's body was "placed on a pile of rubbish and about ten gallons of coal oil poured over it."

Just a few months before Williams' article appeared, the *New York Times* correspondent in Harrison, Mississippi, reported (September 28, 1913) that a "reign of murder, started early this morning by two negro boys who were crazed by cocaine developed into a race riot which ended only after three white men, four negro men, and a negro woman had been killed, a score of persons wounded, and two boys lynched." Williams was not the only medical practitioner to mix racism and drug abuse. In 1908, Dr. Leonard Corning (the inventor of spinal anesthesia) wrote:

> The use of "coke" is probably much more widely spread among negroes than among whites. "Heaven dust" they call it. There is little doubt that every Jew peddler in the South carries the stuff, although many States have lately made it a felony.

A partial explanation for what was occurring is supplied by the subtitle of Williams' article, "Murder and Insanity Increasing among Lower Class Because They Have Taken to 'Sniffing' Since Being Deprived of Whisky by

Prohibition." Much of the most outrageous language was generated by the fight over prohibition. Williams argued that the emergence of this new "menace" was attributed to the restriction of alcohol sales: as more cities closed bars and limited alcohol sales, a switch to other drugs was inevitable. During prohibition, this line of argument was frequently used by the "wets," those individuals opposed to limiting the sale of alcohol. The Williams article, according to some writers, had the effect of giving police in the South an excuse for upgrading their .32 caliber guns for the heavier .38 handguns still used today. It is interesting, and perhaps not so surprising, is that the same sort of reasoning is being used to sell other, less lethal, means of restraint today.

Racist though Williams may have been, when his observations are compared to descriptions from modern medical literature, there are some striking parallels. The cocaine-related deaths described below occurred in Miami, Florida, in 1985. The descriptions were contained in a report that appeared in the *Journal of Forensic Science*. Pathologists in Miami noticed that, as more cocaine appeared on the streets, more people were dying of excited delirium:

> A 37-year-old white male drank some beer with a friend. A short time later he was observed in a van, racing the engine and blowing the horn. He then rammed the vehicle into the front of a residence, jumped out, and began running about the neighborhood jumping over fences and pounding on doors. He was yelling and screaming that people were after him. When the police arrived, they found him hiding in some bushes. They coaxed him out and began a "pat down," whereupon the subject began to violently fight the police. Four officers finally restrained and subdued the victim and he was handcuffed. When placed in the police vehicle he began to kick out the windows.

> Then there was the case of the 26-year-old man who took off his clothes, began yelling and screaming, and ran about the apartment smashing a variety of objects. Medical rescue units were called when he punched through a window and lacerated his arm.

The authors then explain that both men died shortly after they reached the hospital.

At the beginning of the 21st century, new case reports of agitated delirium are increasingly common, both in the United States and Europe. If any further proof was needed that Europe was developing a cocaine problem, it is to be found in the increasing number of agitated delirium cases being encountered by British and European police and pathologists. The strange behavior of people afflicted with this disorder invariably attracts police attention, which means that when victims die, they die in police custody. Allegations of police brutality inevitably result. Virtually no one recalls that the disorder was common a hundred years ago, and it is difficult to persuade the public that drugs, and not the police, are usually the cause of death.

Modern research indicates that the likelihood of developing agitated delirium may be genetically determined. Fortunately, only a very small percentage of the population has this genetic propensity. One consequence is that the incidence of this disorder can be used as a marker for cocaine use. If cases of agitated delirium occur with any frequency, it can only mean that very large numbers of people are using cocaine. No new cases of cocaine-related agitated delirium were reported in the United States between 1914 and 1981. During those years, cocaine supplies were scarce, and cocaine was very expensive. In the early 1980s, as soon as the cocaine supply increased, so did the number of agitated delirium deaths. Until the mid-1990s, cases were unheard of in the United Kingdom, but as the cocaine supply has increased in the United Kingdom, so has the number of cases of agitated delirium. There may be a "war on drugs," but more cocaine is available on the street today than ever before, and there are more reported cases of agitated delirium than ever before. It is not hard to see the connection. The number of newly reported cases is once again on the increase. Whether this reflects wider use of cocaine or the increased availability of methamphetamine, which can also cause psychosis, is hard to say.

Coca Java

9

...while its price is higher than that of any other known substance used in medicine, yet so beneficial are the results obtained from a very small amount of it that it is comparatively cheap.

The Pharmaceutical Record, 1884

Merck began producing small amounts of cocaine in 1862 but found few customers. In 1883, the year before cocaine's anesthetic properties became widely known, Merck's total output of cocaine amounted to less than half a pound. Doctors were unable to determine what, if anything, cocaine did to the body. The general opinion was that, if it had any effects at all, cocaine was probably not much different than caffeine. And, caffeine was abundant and cheap.

Perceptions changed drastically in 1884, when Sigmund Freud published *On Coca* in April, and Karl Koller announced his discovery of cocaine anesthesia the following October. Freud's publication generated considerable interest, but it was after Koller's discovery that cocaine sales went through the roof. Before Koller, eye surgery was almost impossible, and surgery on other parts of the body was limited to procedures that could be performed in seconds. Demand for cocaine became insatiable.

There was, however, very little cocaine to be had, and what little there was sold out almost overnight. Prices for cocaine rose dramatically. In December 1884, Messrs. J.W. Drysdale & Sons, an old-line British pharmaceutical manufacturer, sold 6 ounces of cocaine to European buyers for the astronomical sum of £250 (approximately U.S. $1212.50). No one complained. Attention turned to alternate sources of supply. The most important alternate source proved not to be South America. For several decades, Indonesia was the world's chief producer of coca leaf. Strangely, the same scientists and administrators

85

responsible for bringing quinine to Europe were also involved in the transfer of cocaine to Asia.

Cocaine does not grow naturally in Southeast Asia — it is a New World plant. But once it was established on plantations throughout Java and Sumatra, it grew very well. With a little help from Japan, coca plantations were soon to be found in Taiwan and Iwo Jima. Coca, with the valuable cocaine it contained, was not the first valuable medicine to be imported from South America. In fact, it was the second, and it is only a matter of the purest luck that either plant was successfully cultivated.

Quinine came first. It was extremely valuable, because it was the only effective treatment for malaria, and malaria was rampant throughout the British Empire. The only source for quinine was the Pacific Coast region of South America, generally in the area of Peru. British and Dutch colonial governments (Indonesia was then a Dutch colony) simultaneously launched efforts to obtain seeds for quinine cultivation, hoping that the precious bark could be grown in their Old World colonies.

Botanists from the Royal Botanical Gardens at Kew, just outside of London, established cinchona plantations in Ceylon and India. Dutch agriculturalists did the same in western Java, but with vastly more success than their English counterparts. The first cinchona trees were planted in Java in 1852, though much to the chagrin of the administrators, the initial plantings were a failure.

Initial Dutch and British attempts at producing quinine were not successful, mainly because the British and Dutch explorers both gathered seeds from the wrong type of cinchona tree. There were no field tests for quinine. Explorers were forced to make their choices by the look of the tree. Bark from these trees selected by the leader of the British expedition, Clements Markham, contained quinine, but not very much, certainly not enough to merit efforts at cultivation. Unfortunately, that deficiency was not discovered until more than a million trees were successfully planted in India and Ceylon. They all had to be ripped out. The correct seeds were finally obtained in 1864, but only by chance. A British trader named Charles Ledger, living in Puno, Peru, managed to acquire 14 pounds of seeds from high-yield tress. He sent the seeds back to his brother living in London, hoping his brother could sell them to the botanists at Kew. The botanists were not interested, but Dutch planters were. Within a few years, new, government-sponsored cinchona estates (using high-yielding hybrids now named *Cinchona ledgeriana*) were established in the Pengalengan highlands of southwestern Java.

Officials at Kew, still thinking they were successful with their quinine project, envisioned a similar scenario for coca leaf. Unlike quinine seedlings, seedlings of the coca plant are hardy. They were often sent via the regular mails, packed in a little moist soil. Kew officials sent coca seeds from the plant they were growing in Kew to the Botanical Gardens at Calcutta, to the Peradeniya Gardens in Ceylon, to the Agricultural Society of India, and to agricultural stations at Assam and Darjeeling. Seeds planted at the Botanical Gardens outside of Lagos, Nigeria, and in Sierra Leone, did very well, as opposed to those sent to Jamaica, which, for some reason, failed to flourish. For a time, the Blue Mountain area of Jamaica was planted with coca, but Blue Mountain coca did not grow as successfully as Blue Mountain coffee, and attempts at coca growing were abandoned after several years. Coca growers in India met with more success, particularly in the Tea Estates of Assam, where coca remained a minor cash crop for at least 20 years.

A botanist named Justus Karl Hasskarl spent several years in South America as head of the Dutch mission to look for the high-yielding cinchona trees. Like Markham, he brought back the wrong ones. By coincidence, however, he became well acquainted with the habit of coca chewing and the fundamentals of coca cultivation. He was impressed with what he saw (the areas where the two plants grew were not that far apart). On his return to Indonesia, Hasskarl wrote a letter to the Dutch Colonial office suggesting that coca offered economic opportunities nearly as good as those of cinchona. Hasskarl described how coca chewing imparted energy and feelings of well-being, and he outlined in some detail his reasons for believing that coca plants were well adapted for growth in Java. However, his suggestions were rejected by the chief of the Public Health Service and the head of the Department of Agriculture.

Both of the supervising Dutch colonial officials were convinced that once the Javanese found out how good coca could make them feel, they would not be "morally strong enough to refrain from excessive use." They also argued that there was really no need to start growing another dangerous stimulant. After all, coffee already grew in Java. Why risk the "moral health" of the country just to make more money? Despite the early decision not to pursue commercial coca development, just to be on the safe side, Melchior Treub (1851–1919) (Figure 9.1), then the director of the government's botanical research station in Buitenzorg, decided to start a trial garden, with the intent of raising enough coca for "chemical and physiological" studies (Figures 9.2 through 9.5).

Buitenzorg is 2600 feet above sea level, and it was consciously modeled along the lines of Kew when it was founded in 1815. Creation of the garden received the active support of Sir Joseph Banks (the real father of Kew and, of course, the founder of the Royal Society), and Sir Stamford Raffels (who governed Singapore and, for a time, Java). Even though the gardens belonged to competing Empires, there were always strong connections between Kew and Buitenzorg. British botanists James Hooper and William Kent worked at both gardens, and the samples of rare specimens were often exchanged between the two gardens.

Figure 9.1 Melchior Treub (1851–1819), scientific director at Buitenzorg, started the first experimental coca plots at Buitenzorg in the mid-1860s. (From *Science and Scientists in the Netherlands Indies*, published by the Board for the Netherlands Indies, Surinam and Curaco, New York, 1945.)

In 1868, the Dutch appointed a new director, R.C. Sheffer (circa 1850–1920). Sheffer changed the focus of Buitenzorg from pure scientific research to applied agriculture. He wanted to grow plants that made money. It would have been Sheffer who placed an order for coca plants with the firm of Herman Linden, a Belgian seed exporter located in Ghent. Initial experiments with the new coca plants were encouraging, so much so that seed was provided to growers throughout Java. Cultivation efforts at other plantations in Java and Sumatra were not nearly as successful as those at the botanical garden. Much of Java is too wet to permit coca cultivation. But seeds planted at higher elevations, and shrubs planted between existing trees, did very well. By 1883, the year before the cocaine market took fire, modest quantities of

Figure 9.2 Henry H. Rusby, a physician and Amazon explorer in the employ of Parke, Davis & Company. He devised the formula for making crack cocaine. From *A History of Cocaine, The Mystery of Coca Java*, Royal Society of Medicine Press, with permission.

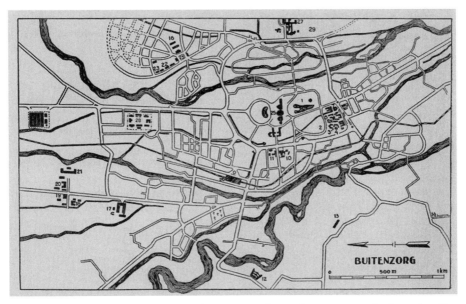

Figure 9.3 Map of Buitenzorg, the Botanical Garden at Bogor, Indonesia. The first experimental plots for growing coca were planted therein. Samples of coca originally found by Kew scientist, Richard Spruce, were first planted in the late 1850s. This is a schematic drawing of the garden circa 1895. Origin unknown.

coca leaf, mostly for use in the production of coca-based wines, were being exported from Madera and Sumatra for auction in Amsterdam.

Figure 9.4 Coca plants growing at the Botanical Gardens at Buitenzorg. In 1817, the Dutch established a research station, modeled after Kew Gardens, just southeast of Jakarta. Dutch administrators were concerned that the Javanese might not be "morally strong enough to refrain from excessive use," so they vetoed an initial proposal for commercial coca production. To be on the safe side, seedlings were planted with the intent of raising enough coca for "chemical and physiological" studies. (Courtesy of the Royal Tropical Institute, Amsterdam [633.888.16, N 14]. The photograph was taken by Professor L. Ph de Bussy. The date is unknown.)

By 1885, coca seed was in such demand that the agriculturists at Buitenzorg could not keep up with all of the requests. Many of the Dutch tea growers wanted to switch to coca and give up growing tea entirely. They were advised not to. A colonial office agriculturist, Nikolas Van Gorkum (1835–1910), wrote a newspaper article advising the tea growers to plant coca only between rows of tea bushes, as a supplemental crop. Van Gorkum warned that if the growers planted too much coca, prices would go down, and coca cultivation would eventually not be worth the effort. Six years later, in 1889, leaf from Java finally began to appear at London's Mincing Lane auctions, just off

Figure 9.5 Bringing the coca leaves to the factory of the estate at Tegallega. Photograph taken by Professor de Bussy. It shows leaves being gathered after drying in the sun. The plantation was located on Java's northern coast, roughly midway between Jakarta and Surakarta. (Courtesy of the Royal Tropical Institute, Amsterdam [633.888.16, N 16].)

Fenchurch Street, where most trade with British Colonies was carried out (also where the tea brokers Ferguson and Muirhead, clients of Sherlock Holmes, were located).

Buyers for the Great European drug houses had almost no interest in product that was grown in South America. They were skeptical about the kind of coca being grown in Java, almost as skeptical as they were of the state of industrial chemistry at the time. And the shipping problem proved to be a nightmare. If the leaves are improperly packed, they become too damp and will ferment in transit. Leaves that were overly dry lost their cocaine content. For nearly a decade, the Indonesians used tin-lined chests that they soldered closed, but even these did not solve the problem of leaf deterioration, and they too were eventually abandoned.

Figure 9.6 Initial phase of the cocaine extraction process. The hollowed logs shown here have now been replaced by plastic-lined shallow pits, but otherwise, little has changed in the last 100 years. In order to extract the cocaine from the leaves, the leaves must first be soaked in a dilute solution containing water and a strong alkali, such as lime. (Courtesy of the Royal Tropical Institute, Amsterdam [633.888.16, N 18]).

The South American growers solved the problem of shipping and deterioration, but only because the leaves they were working with were easier to purify, and because of the work of an American botanist named Henry H. Rusby, who found a way to eliminate the shipping problems almost entirely.

Almost as soon as Parke, Davis & Company (the same company that printed the fake journals that influenced Freud so greatly) was incorporated in 1871, George Davis began sending out teams of explorers in the hope of discovering new and exotic medications. The initial results of the expeditions were not exactly earth shaking. Explorers from Parke, Davis & Company brought back guarana (the main source of caffeine in commercially prepared food), bearsfoot root, and eucalyptus, the latter being "especially recommended in malarial diseases and for its influence on the mucous membrane in croup, diphtheria, catarrh, etc." In the early 1880s, several years before the discoveries of Freud and Koller, Parke, Davis & Company began to market a line of products made from coca leaf extract. After 1884, Parke, Davis & Company began supplying purified cocaine for use as an anesthetic and expanded its product line to include a range of cocaine-containing preparations.

Like all of the other large drug houses, Parke, Davis & Company feared it would be unable to keep up with the explosive demand resulting from

Figure 9.7 The Nederlandsche Cocaine Fabriek. The Dutch Colonial Development Board and coca growers in Java formed a joint venture and built a cocaine refinery to better compete with Merck and other German cocaine manufacturers. The NCF opened in Amsterdam on March 12, 1900. The plant was so successful that a second story was added in 1902. By 1910, NCF claimed to be the largest cocaine manufacturer in the world, producing more than 1500 kg of refined cocaine per year. This photograph, of the interior of the factory, is from a trade publication, *Het Pharmaceutisch Weekblad*. It is the only known surviving photograph of the factory. (Courtesy of Marcel de Kort, Netherlands Ministry of Health.)

Koller's discovery. Almost as soon as Davis heard of Koller's discovery, he approached a young chemist working in the laboratories of Parke, Davis & Company and asked him how soon he could leave for Bolivia. The chemist was Henry H. Rusby, a recent medical school graduate, with an additional degree in botany (Figure 9.6). On January 10, 1885, the Pacific Mailship S.S. Acapulco sailed from the foot of Canal Street in New York with Rusby aboard. Rusby had doubts about the trip almost as soon as the ship sailed out of the harbor. One of the passengers was Frederick Carl Lehman, another botanist. Lehman had spent the last 10 years exploring Colombia, Ecuador, and northern Peru. When Rusby told him that he planned to cross the continent, Lehman laughed, and suggested that by the first night camping out, Rusby would probably die from insect bites.

Despite the warnings, Rusby persevered. After sailing through violent storms, which washed one of the passengers overboard and then back onto the ship, Rusby finally made land. He hiked across the Isthmus of Panama, and then made his way south along the coastal roads of Colombia, Ecuador, and Peru to La Paz, Bolivia. In Bolivia, he organized an expedition that included two Texans who were fleeing the law, and an Indian guide whose participation was not quite voluntary. Rusby then crossed the Andes and traveled down the Amazon River, collecting specimens and recording his observations.

By any standard, Rusby's expedition was a success. As instructed by his employers, he identified potential new sources of coca leaves. But Rusby did something more important than identify new sources; he solved the shipping problem. Almost as soon as he arrived in Lima, he organized a large shipment of coca leaves to return to the United States. The leaves, however, never reached their destination. A civil war in Columbia placed an effective halt to all shipping. And, while Rusby's leaves were rotting in a Colombian warehouse, the price of cocaine fell precipitously. A competitor of Parke, Davis & Company had arranged huge shipments around Cape Horn, bypassing the war zone, and undercutting Parke, Davis & Company's price. Rusby concluded that shipping coca leaf was a risky proposition, and he determined to find a better way. Rusby set out to devise a method for making semirefined cocaine. He knew the general principals for extracting alkaloids, like cocaine and quinine, and thought he might be able to develop a simplified approach, one that could be accomplished outside of the laboratory. He used his hotel room for a laboratory.

Rusby's hotel room in La Paz had no running water. This was not surprising, because at that time, the only water in La Paz was carried in by laborers every morning. Some people might question the thinking of a trained chemist who set up an alcohol still in a room with no water, but that was exactly what Rusby did. The still was a crudely made affair of heavy tin with a copper bottom. Rusby was in the process of distilling off alcohol from a 5-gallon batch of coca leaf extract, and had placed the still directly over a charcoal fire, when a seam in the still came apart, leaking alcohol into the open fire, and causing an explosion and a giant plume of flame. Rusby remained calm enough to throw the still out onto the hotel veranda, where, instead of burning down much of La Paz, the alcohol quietly burned itself out.

Despite getting some blisters, Rusby carried on with his experiments. Even though he is generally given credit for discovering the process, a Peruvian chemist, named Alfredo Bignon, devised a similar process years before Rusby ever set foot in South America. Rusby never made mention of Bignon in any of his writings, and it may be that he was unaware of Bignon's process because it was proprietary.

Andes historian Jo Ann Kawell, an expert on the early years of the South American coca industry, believes there is evidence suggesting a link between Bignon and French cocaine manufacturers. It may well be that Bignon's process was kept secret in order to give the French drug makers a competitive advantage.

Clandestine chemists in South America still use the same basic process pioneered by Rusby, except on a vastly larger scale. The initial steps in the process are the same. Leaves are soaked for 3 or 4 days in a dilute solution of water and alkali, usually lime. Rusby added alcohol to the mixture, but today's illegal producers use gasoline or kerosene, taking up the dissolved cocaine. The leaves are discarded, and dilute sulfuric is added. Lime or ammonia is used to neutralize the acid, causing the dissolved cocaine to come out of the solution and collect on the bottom of the container. The liquid is discarded, and the crude cocaine is allowed to dry in room air. The final product is very much like crack cocaine. Called *buzco*, it can be smoked, and it is widely smoked in South America today.

Rusby's extract was not as pure as the refined product sold by drug houses, but it had two important advantages over coca leaf: the semirefined material did not lose its potency when stored, and it could be transported in a fraction of the space required to ship coca leaf. In one stroke, Rusby succeeded in converting coca from a perishable commodity to a stable commodity, like copper or silver. The problem for the Indonesian coca producers was that their coca was not nearly as simple to refine, and the only people who could do it reliably were in Europe, and that meant shipping. For a time, ambitious Dutch growers considered the possibility of developing their own refinery, but the plans were never realized.

The leaves grown in Java contained a great deal more cocaine than the leaves grown in South America, but it was much harder to extract, and most chemists just were not up to it. All cultivated coca comes from two closely related New World species: *Erythroxylum coca Lamarck*, and *Erythroxylum novogranatense* from New Granada, the former name of Columbia. Each of the two species has two distinct varieties. The seeds that botanists at Kew Gardens sent British experimental gardens around the world were, almost certainly, *E. coca novogranatense* var. truxillense. But the variety most commonly grown in the Amazon basin was *Erythroxylum coca Lamarck*. The first seeds of *E. coca novogranatense* did not even arrive at Kew until 1870. They were collected from the vicinity of Huánuco by the Bishop of Huánuco. Once enough of the Bishop's plants were germinated, Kew botanists distributed seeds to agricultural stations in most British colonies. Unfortunately, Kew botanists repeated the same mistake they made with quinine — they obtainedthe wrong seed stock. The seeds that the Kew botanists chose to distribute were not those that produced the most extractable cocaine.

During the late 1800s, chemists trying to extract cocaine from coca leaves divided the extracts into two categories: "crystallized" and "uncrystallized" alkaloid. "Crystallizable" alkaloid is another word for cocaine. Uncrystallized alkaloid is another way of referring to other molecules, closely related to cocaine, that are also contained in the coca leaf. At the turn of the century, no one had any idea of what to do with the uncrystallized alkaloid. Cocaine was what everyone wanted, so leaves containing the most crystallized, and the least uncrystallized alkaloid, were the leaves most highly valued. That was not the only problem with coca grown in Indonesia. It, like the South American types, just did not travel well. To get around this, the South American producers packed their leaves in tin containers that had been soldered closed.

The total alkaloid content of *Erythroxylum coca Lamarck*, at least at the turn of the century, was usually in the range of 0.5%, nearly all of it crystallizable. The alkaloid content of *Novogranatense* varieties was between 1% and 2%, but only one-third was crystallizable. That explains why the experts at the time felt that leaf coming from Southeast Asia had no value, except to make wine and other beverages. The experts were partially correct, but just before the turn of the century, German chemists figured out how to convert uncrystallizable alkaloid to crystallizable cocaine.

In 1898, Farbwerke, a German chemical manufacturer, devised a patented process to convert all of the alkaloid in Java coca leaf into usable cocaine, providing a yield much higher than could be obtained from leaves grown in South America. The high alkaloid content of Java coca leaf, combined with the fact that the weather allowed for four crops to be harvested each year, made Java coca leaf a desirable product, but only to chemists at Farbwerke, who knew how to refine it.

Farbwerke's factory was located in Germany. Bulk coca leaf still had to be shipped to Germany for processing and remained, therefore, a perishable commodity. Unfortunately for Farbwerke, there were no patent agreements between the Netherlands and Germany. The Dutch Colonial Development Board and coca growers in Java formed a joint venture and built their own refinery, the Nederlandsche Cocaine Fabriek (NCF), which opened on March 12, 1900, in Amsterdam. It is shown in Figure 9.7.

Even though Java leaf still had to be shipped halfway across the world, the presence of a second factory in Amsterdam broke Farbwerke's stranglehold on the Indonesian market. The Amsterdam plant was so successful that a second floor was added to the factory in 1902. By 1910, NCF claimed to be the largest cocaine manufacturer in the world, producing more than 1500 kg per year of refined cocaine. NCF moved to new, even larger, premises that same year.

In 1903, when Farbwerke's patent expired, other German chemical makers began using the same process. Privately owned Dutch plants opened and went into competition with NCF. A disgruntled NCF employee established the first of these in nearby Bossum. Another plant, called Brocades and Steehman, opened in Meppel. From that point forward, coca exports from Java began to increase at a steady pace. Leaf exports rose from 45 tons in 1904 to 83 tons in 1906 and to 1300 tons in 1913. Exports peaked at 1650 tons in the 1920s, but were still substantial with more than 740 tons exported in 1927. Representatives of German and Japanese drug houses purchased all Java leaf that was not shipped to Amsterdam. Merck and other drugmakers, including the Japanese, eventually bought their own plantations in Java, avoiding the brokers, and shipping coca leaf directly to their factories.

Once the Netherlands ratified the 1925 Geneva Convention, which required import and export certificates, growers in Java and operators of the NCF in Amsterdam could no longer continue to produce cocaine on a massive scale and to expect to find legitimate buyers for their product. With the medical use of cocaine already declining, there was simply no way to hide, or justify, the enormous amount of cocaine being produced. The magnitude of the surplus production can be gauged from the fact that during the months leading up to the implementation of import certificate regulations, more than 220 tons of stored coca leaf was shipped from warehouses in the Netherlands. The other event that crippled the Dutch cocaine industry had to do with Japanese politics and industry.

When pharmaceutical companies in Japan first began producing cocaine, it was from Indonesian coca leaf purchased through Japanese brokers. In Tokyo, there were two major companies selling Java leaf: the Sumatra Industrial Company and the Trading Corporation of Japan (Koeki Eidan). A third firm, Nonomiya and Company, located in Lima, Peru, supplied coca leaf from South America. Many of the Japanese companies emulated the German cocaine producers and acquired their own plantations in Java. During World War II, the Japanese government, through its Medicine Controlling Company, became the sole importer of coca leaf and took over distribution of refined cocaine.

As Japanese cocaine production increased, Japan's drugmakers moved to ensure their raw supply and reduce their costs. In 1918, Hoshi Pharmaceuticals, with approval from both the Japanese Home Ministry and Ministry of Welfare and Social Affairs in Peru, purchased a 500-acre coca plantation outside of Lima, and began shipping coca leaf directly to its Tokyo factory. At the same time, Hoshi Pharmaceuticals began growing coca in the Kagi district of Formosa. Takeda Pharmaceutical Industries of Osaka, through one of its subsidiaries, purchased 102 acres of land on Okinawa and began growing its own supply of coca.

Koto Pharmaceuticals, another of the major Japanese drug houses, started its own plantations on Iwo Jima and Okinawa. Shionogi Pharmaceutical Company purchased crude cocaine from the Taiwan Shoyaku Company Limited, located in Formosa, and from Nonomiya and Company in Lima. In interviews taken in preparation for the Tokyo war crimes trials, Saburo Hagiwara, manager of Shionogi's Tokyo branch, said they had to stop buying coca leaves from their Lima exporter because of pressure from the Japanese government "to patronize their home markets in an effort to build up their trade balance." From 1938 forward, all of Shionogi's crude cocaine came from Taiwan.

At an even earlier date, Japan's central government intervened to limit the amount of coca leaf being imported from Indonesia. Beginning in 1929, they simply stopped granting import permits for Java coca, unless, of course, the leaves came from plantations owned by Japanese companies operating in Java. The Dutch Coca Producers Association was, understandably, upset by this move, and filed a series of complaints with the Colonial Minister's office in Amsterdam. Japan ignored the complaints. The simultaneous shrinking of legitimate markets, coupled with Japan's refusal to use coca leaf not grown on Japanese soil, spelled the death knell for Indonesia coca growers. By 1937, Java's exports of leaf fell to 41 tons. Professor Van Gorkum was correct. Coca was an unreliable cash crop.

The business of Japanese cocaine producers, however, continued to grow, although deceptively. In 1934, in response to a request from the U.S. Secretary of State, the American Consul queried the government in Taiwan and was told that a total of 694 acres was devoted to coca cultivation (Taiwan Shoyaku 448 acres, Hoshi Pharmaceuticals 246 acres); that in 1930, a total of 179,939 kg of coca leaf was grown for a yield of 506 kg per acre, and that 785 kg of cocaine was produced from those leaves. The numbers make no sense, and the figures supplied to the U.S. Consul were surely fabricated.

Refiners in Tokyo and Taiwan were accustomed to working with coca leaves from Indonesia with its high alkaloid content. It can be presumed that the estates in Taiwan, Iwo Jima, and Okinawa planted a similar, if not identical, strain to the Indonesian variety, a strain with a yield of substantially more than 1% cocaine.

Dutch agronomists at Buitenzorg went to the trouble of planting sample plots and precisely measuring output. They found that in Java, 1 acre of coca plants produced 285 pound of dry leaf, containing 1.5% alkaloid, per acre. That amount of alkaloid, using the Farbwerke process, would have yielded 3.4 kg of purified cocaine. And in Java, four crops could be harvested each year. Thus, if only 500 acres were under cultivation in Taiwan, the expected yield should have been closer to 6800 kg (500 acres × 3.4 kg per acre × 4 crops per year = 6800 kg, or 3.4 metric tons). The number was equal to approximately three times the reported total cocaine production for the entire world during the mid-1930s. But at least the Japanese trade representatives filled out the required form neatly, and in triplicate.

Production in Taiwan was understated by almost 70%, and perhaps by as much as 90%. In fact, so much surplus cocaine was accumulating in Taiwan that a special meeting was held at the Foreign Office in Tokyo to decide what to do with the surplus of 2500 kg that was sitting in storage. But, at the same time, Japan's reports to the League of Nation's Opium Committee put total cocaine exports at less than 10 kg per year. With so much cocaine to sell, and so little legitimate demand, sale on the black market was inevitable. Moving so much product eventually required the active participation of Japan's Army, Navy, and Foreign Office.

A Beautiful White Powder

10

...a whole new field has been opened up by the availability of Parke's cocaine, a reliable, effective, and purer cocaine. This is beautiful white powder (available at a low price).

Herman Guttmacher, Editor, *Vienna Medical Press,* **August 9, 1885**

Sigmund Freud and Karl Koller were successful in their research, while others failed, because Freud and Koller had easy access to purified cocaine. Yes, coca wines and tonics were popular in Europe long before either Freud or Koller even enrolled in medical school, but the coca extracts prescribed by physicians were notoriously unreliable; the cocaine content was unpredictable and, therefore, so was its effect. Before Freud and Koller published their observations, there was no demand for purified cocaine. The miniscule amounts produced by reputable chemists, such as Merck, were so expensive that few could afford them. After Freud and Koller published their findings, demand for cocaine was insatiable, but supplies were, at first, limited.

South American coca leaf was scarce, the coca plantations of Southeast Asia were yet to be planted, and few drug houses had mastered the chemistry of large-scale alkaloid extraction. Almost overnight, two players came to dominate the cocaine market: E. Merck and Sons of Darmstadt, Germany, and Parke, Davis & Company, of Detroit, Michigan. Both companies had financial arrangements with Sigmund Freud.

Freud bought his first cocaine from Merck. E. Merck & Son was founded more than two centuries earlier by an apothecary named Jacob Freidrich Merck. In 1654, Merck purchased the Angel Pharmacy, located near Schiller Platz in Darmstadt, Germany. When Merck died in 1678, George Fredrick Merck, a distant relative, assumed management of the pharmacy. George Fredrick died in 1715 and left the pharmacy to his twice-married son, Johan Franz Merck (1687–1741). Johan's son from his first marriage, Johan Justus Merck, took over the pharmacy in 1754. He died at the early age of 30, when his son, Johann Anton Merck was only 2 years old. Johann Anton, however, managed to retain ownership, and the pharmacy apparently prospered during the years the young man was away at school. Few noticeable changes occurred at the pharmacy during the century that elapsed between the time that Jacob Fredrich Merck purchased the Angel Pharmacy, and the time that Johann Anton Merck took title to it in 1769.

The clinical practice of medicine had changed very little since the Middle Ages, but during the second century of Merck ownership, apothecaries working at Angel Pharmacy watched the practice of medicine undergo a series of profound changes. The Merck family's contribution to those changes was substantial. Johann Anton's son, Heinrich Emanuel, along with another famous Darmstadt resident, Justus von Liebig, were important participants in that revolution. Heinrich Emanuel Merck (1794–1855), who was born in the same year that the cotton gin was invented and just 2 years before Edward Jenner popularized vaccinations for smallpox, took over management of the pharmacy in 1816. The death of Angel Pharmacy's acting manager forced Heinrich Emmanuel to give up his studies in Vienna and return home to manage the business. Heinrich Emmanuel was 22 years old at the time.

Heinrich Emmanuel and von Liebig were contemporaries and friends. Von Liebig (1803–1873), more than any other person, laid the foundations for the modern science of organic chemistry. As we have already learned, von Liebig was unique for being the first respected scientist to exploit his reputation in order to make money. (Mariani does not count — he was a showman, not a scientist.) There is, however, no doubt that von Liebig had a profound influence on his friend, Heinrich Emmanuel Merck.

Heinrich Emmanuel Merck first became interested in alkaloid chemistry when he was a student. At the time, techniques for isolating and purifying medically useful chemicals from plants were less than 10 years old. Of course, plant extracts were used as medicines for thousands of years, but systematic attempts at isolating the active agents in the plants were not made until the beginning of the 19th century. Friedrich Wilhelm Sertürner isolated morphine from opium in 1805; quinine was successfully isolated from cinchona bark the following year; and a succession of other alkaloids followed. Because Heinrich Emmanuel Merck was a gifted alkaloid chemist, and because he was also well acquainted with the principles of industrial chemistry espoused by von Liebig, it was only natural that he would be the first to build a factory designed for the mass production of pharmaceuticals.

After Freud and Koller's discoveries became known, the complexion of the cocaine business changed almost overnight: cocaine selling turned into a very big business, and a very profitable one at that. Shortages of raw materials were quickly remedied, resulting in excess production, then market manipulation, and, eventually, to the dumping of excess product on the black market. At first, South American coca leaf was scarce, and only a few drug houses had mastered the chemistry of large-scale alkaloid extraction, a process that was crucial to producing cocaine at a profit. Almost immediately, two players came to dominate the cocaine market: the German company of E. Merck and Sons of Darmstadt, and the American company of Parke, Davis & Company of Detroit.

The original Angel Pharmacy, located across from the castle in old Darmstadt, was not large enough to house a factory. So Merck bought a small house outside of town and converted it to a factory where he began drug production in 1827. The first product made at Merck's new factory was morphine. Other alkaloids were added to the product line in rapid succession. Codeine production began in 1832, followed by quinine production in 1833. There was such demand for Merck products that larger production facilities were built around the original house, and steam power was introduced at the factory in 1843. By 1848, the process of running both the pharmacy in town, and the factory outside of town, became too much for Heinrich Emanuel. He assigned his son, George Franz, to run the pharmacy in town.

Wilhelm Ernst studied cocaine breakdown products, especially one called benzoylecgonine. He discovered that much of the cocaine produced by coca leaves disappears after the leaves are picked, because the cocaine is converted into benzoylecgonine. Wilhelm Ernst's great discovery was finding a way to convert the benzoylecgonine back into cocaine, making it possible to extract considerably more cocaine from the leaves. For a time, Merck had a great advantage over other cocaine producers.

In 1862, just 2 years after cocaine had been isolated and purified by Albert Niemann, Wilhelm Ernst began manufacturing cocaine, even though there was virtually no market for it. It appears he undertook the project as a matter of principle: as the leading maker of alkaloid drugs, the firm simply wanted to offer the most comprehensive range of alkaloid plant products. For the next 20 years, cocaine sales amounted to less than 1pound a year. In 1884, Merck's cocaine sales began to perk up. Merck directors were, at first, puzzled when they started receiving cocaine orders, albeit small, from Vienna. The orders were coming from Freud, and from his addicted friend Ernst von Fleischl-Marxow, both unknowns at the time. However, von Fleischl-Marxow was a pathologist working at the well-known, highly respected, Vienna Physiological Institute, and he was ordering cocaine through the Institute.

Records show that sales of cocaine remained stagnant for the next 20 years. Many of Merck's records were destroyed during World War II, but the records of Carl Scriba (1854–1929), who was the production manager at

Merck from 1908 through 1926, survived. Scriba's records contain summaries of production figures dating back to the beginning of cocaine production at Merck. According to Scriba, the annual production of cocaine, for the first decade, at least, amounted to less than 1 pound per year.

With such unimpressive sales, Merck was forced to look at some of the other compounds contained in the coca leaf, hoping that one might prove to have some commercial value. He observed that another compound found in coca leaves, named ecgonine, shared some chemical properties with cocaine. Merck contacted Freud and Fleischl-Marxow and inquired if they would be willing, for a fee, to study the effects of ecgonine. They were. On October 21, 1884, the factory in Darmstadt sent Freud a 100-g sample of ecgonine. He tested it on both animals and humans, and apparently on himself. Unfortunately for Merck and Freud, ecgonine is essentially devoid of stimulant, or any other clinically useful properties. In reality, ecgonine is formed when the breakdown product, benzoylecgonine, itself breaks down.

Between the end of 1884 and the end of 1885, Merck imported 1.9 tons of coca leaves, from which 30 kg of purified cocaine was produced. Demand continued to grow, with production more than doubling to reach 70 kg in 1886, all because of Koller's discovery and Freud's paper. In 1887, Merck, and most of the other German manufacturers, stopped importing coca leaf and began importing raw, semirefined cocaine, manufactured in Peru. As demand grew, Merck and most of the other German manufacturers developed their own suppliers in South America and stopped importing coca leaf on the open market. Instead, they began importing raw, semirefined cocaine, manufactured in Peru, usually by German companies that had opened up refineries there. Merck bought most of its raw cocaine from Kilz & Co., a German refinery located in Lima. Boehringer in Waldhof, and Knoll in Ludwigshafen, were Merck's two largest competitors. Merck ultimately produced about half of all the cocaine made in Germany. All told, from 1887 until 1913, and the beginning of World War I, Merck imported 88 tons of semirefined cocaine and used it to manufacture 76 tons of pure cocaine, an average of nearly 3 tons of pure cocaine each year.

Merck's cocaine production figures were inconsequential by today's standards — South American production of refined cocaine today is well in excess of 500 tons, and the real number may be closer to 800 tons. It all depends on which official agency you care to believe. Such quantities of refined cocaine were never available before. The amounts being produced were wildly in excess of the world's legitimate medical needs, and had only one place to go — onto the world's black market. During the period just before World War II, a select committee of experts working for the League of Nations estimated that medical and scientific requirements for cocaine, worldwide, amounted to less than 1 ton. Still, the market continued to grow.

In 1906, Merck began to import coca leaves from plantations it had established in Java. Between 1906 and 1918, Merck managed to extract and sell almost a ton of Javanese cocaine each year, bringing its total cocaine output to almost 4 tons a year. With so much cocaine coming to market, prices inevitably dropped. Merck had been charging 6 marks per gram prior to the Heidelberg Congress, but over the course of a few weeks, Merck raised its price to 15 marks. As other competitors entered the market, including competitors from the United States, supplies increased, and prices dropped almost as rapidly as they had risen. By 1887, the cost of cocaine had decreased by almost 90%, from 15 marks to 85 pfennigs per gram. The drop in price was largely the result of price competition from Merck's U.S. competitor, Parke, Davis & Company.

Parke, Davis & Company, the other major player, also started as a drugstore, but it was hardly a family operation. A physician named Samuel P. Duffield founded the drugstore in 1862, in Detroit, Michigan. Duffield studied chemistry in Berlin and was conversant with the modern approaches to chemistry taught by von Liebig, and so successfully utilized by Merck. Duffield hoped to emulate Merck's success in America. Duffield's Pharmacy also contained a small manufacturing facility. His initial product offerings included "Ether, Sweet Spirit of Nitre, Oil of Wine, Hoffman's Anodyne, and Blue Pill Mass, a mercury-containing remedy not unlike calomel, a very popular medication at the time." For whatever reason—the names really were not that outrageous for the times—Duffield had trouble selling his products, but he persisted. By 1866, he was ready to expand. Duffield sought outside investors. Two were recruited, but within the first year, both investors dropped out. The last one to quit the enterprise, Francis Conant, sold his interest to C. Parke. Duffield was able to increase production and sales, particularly on the Atlantic coast. This, unfortunately, prompted a price war with other larger and better-funded drugmakers located in New York and Philadelphia. When the eastern firms launched an aggressive marketing campaign, Duffield and Parke decided to recruit their own marketing expert. The man they chose was George Davis.

Like Parke, George Davis was a wealthy man. He knew nothing about chemistry, but he was a charismatic salesman who believed in advertising. Duffield apparently felt uncomfortable with the way the business was evolving and decided to return to medical practice, leaving Parke and Davis to run the company. For advertising and branding purposes, they chose to emphasize the purity and reliability of their products. Even in the 1880s, quality control was unheard of, and manufactured drugs were notoriously unreliable products. Parke and Davis were convinced they could gain a competitive edge by selling products that reliably produced the same effect each time they were used. They also decided to emulate Merck and concentrate on alkaloids, drugs derived from plants.

In 1871, hoping to discover new products, Parke and Davis started to finance expeditions to remote areas of the globe. In 1874, the expeditions bore fruit, of a sort. Parke and Davis introduced three new products: extracts of guarana, bearsfoot, and eucalyptus. All three products were well received, although they are of no known medicinal value. It is difficult today to imagine just what benefit doctors thought they were conferring when they prescribed the new Parke, Davis & Company products.

Parke and Davis had their first big success in 1875 when they introduced an extract made from coca leaves. The following year, their drug company finally turned a profit. The next decade was marked by nearly continuous expansion. New production facilities were built, and Davis assembled an impressive sales organization. Not only did he personally train all of the salesmen, but he also published a series of booklets, pamphlets, and magazines targeting physicians and pharmacists. Today, these journals would be called "throwaways," an acknowledgment of the fact that individuals reading them know that they are really advertisements published by drug companies, and the information contained in them was not "peer reviewed." In fact, the concept of "peer review" did not come into existence until the early 20th century. In the late 1880s, the line between serious medical journals and advertising tracts was not always clear.

The flagship in Davis' line of publications was a monthly medical newspaper called the *Therapeutic Gazette*. It contained no disclaimers and made no mention of its relationship to Parke, Davis & Company. But not surprisingly, it often carried articles detailing therapeutic successes attributable to Parke, Davis & Company products. Davis' biggest success may have been a series of articles he ran in the *Gazette* that described morphine addicts who were successfully cured after treatment with a Parke, Davis & Company coca elixir. Freud read the papers on morphine addiction that appeared in Davis' publication, and he quoted from them in *On Coca*. The papers quoted by Freud not only mentioned giving cocaine to morphine addicts, but they specifically recommended the Parke, Davis & Company formulation.

There is nothing to suggest that at the time he wrote *On Coca*, Freud knew that he was quoting from paid advertisements. Rather, he treated the papers as if they were legitimate contributions to the medical literature. Had Freud realized he was quoting from a cocaine manufacturer's throwaway, one wonders whether he would have recommended cocaine as a treatment for morphine addiction. In any event, Freud's endorsement of cocaine therapy, and Koller's discovery of cocaine's local anesthetic properties, did wonders for the cocaine business. Advertising helped as well. Beginning in 1885, Parke, Davis & Company promotional materials cited Freud's writing as proof that cocaine was an effective treatment for morphine addiction. They never mentioned the fact that Freud first got the idea from reading Parke, Davis & Company promotional materials.

With supplies of cocaine increasing, and wholesale prices declining, Parke, Davis & Company, like other manufacturers, tried to increase sales by expanding its line of cocaine-based products. Their products included a coca wine, a coca soft drink designed to compete with Coca-Cola, coca-containing cigarettes, a cocaine formulation designed for inhalation, an assortment of different cocaine salts, and a kit for injecting cocaine (Figure 10.1). The kit contained 300 mg of powdered cocaine divided into five capsules. It also included a solution for dissolving the cocaine, a camel brush, and a syringe for injecting the drug. The kits retailed between $2 and $3. Parke, Davis & Company also expanded its service area. It sent sales representatives to Europe and began competing head to head with Merck for cocaine sales.

Breaking into the European market proved more difficult than Davis imagined. Merck had the advantage of brand name recognition in general, and for cocaine-containing products, in particular. Freud and Koller both used Merck cocaine. In fact, Freud mentioned Merck's cocaine by name in *On Coca*, mainly, it appears, so he could complain about how expensive it was:

> I used the hydrochloric preparation of cocaine as described by Merk [sic] in Darmstadt. This preparation may be bought in Vienna in Haubner's Engelapotheke am Hof at a price which is not much higher than Merk's [sic], but which must, nevertheless, be regarded as very high. The management of the pharmacy in question is trying, as they have been kind enough to inform me, to lower the price of the drug by establishing new sources of supply.

Inspired, no doubt, both by the successes of Angelo Mariani's wine, and by von Liebig's even greater success at exploiting his meat extract, Davis knew how potent a tool the endorsement of a celebrity scientist could be. And because Freud was clearly upset by what he perceived as price gouging on the part of Merck, Davis saw an opening he could exploit. Davis offered Freud money (60 guilders, roughly $24) if he would endorse Parke, Davis & Company cocaine. Sometime in April 1885, Freud accepted the offer. The endorsement took the form of an article, written under another person's name, and published in the August 9, 1885, issue of the *Viennese Medical Press*. Supposedly, the journal's editor, Herman Guttmacher, wrote the article, and he may actually have done that. But within the body of the article, Freud is quoted directly:

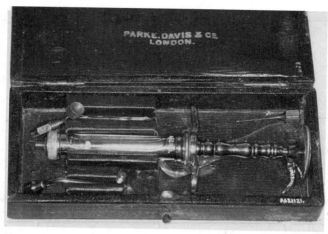

Figure 10.1 Among other product offerings from Parke, Davis & Company was a kit containing everything needed to inject yourself (or your friends) with their pharmaceutical grade cocaine.

> I have examined cocaine muriaticum produced by Parke, Davis…and can state that it is fully equal in effect to the Merck preparation of the same name…. The only difference I can detect between the two preparations is that in their taste. The satisfactory results found with Parke cocaine are probably the result of the greater availability of coca leaves in America, and since the price is lower than European products because of lowered transportation expense, this preparation should have a great future.

Just in case Freud's endorsement proved to be too subtle for the general readership, Guttmacher added his own opinion that "a whole new field has been opened up by the availability of Parke's cocaine, a reliable, effective, and purer cocaine. This is beautiful white powder, available at a low price."

Needless to say, Heinrich Emanuel Merck was not happy with the article. On October 1, 1885, he wrote a letter to the Viennese Medical Press and complained, "Under the pretense of scientific research, this material was written merely to further the interests of an American firm." Merck pointed out that Parke, Davis & Company prices were just slightly less than his own, and he argued that his company was entitled to charge more, because purchasers of Merck cocaine are guaranteed "obtaining a totally usable cocaine…. For the physician, a fact not to be overlooked!" Merck's note concluded with the statement, "…it remains a mystery why the author of said article directs the attention to America and forecast the 'greatest future' for American cocaine." Whether it was really a mystery, or whether Merck knew that Freud was paid to write the article, is impossible to say.

What no one appreciated at the time was that Freud was already acting as a shill for Parke, Davis & Company, only he never knew it (unless, of course, he made the discovery in later years). This was the doing of Davis. Beginning in 1885, promotional materials for cocaine produced by Parke, Davis & Company always cited Freud's writings as proof that cocaine was an effective treatment for morphine addiction. No one ever mentioned that Freud first got the idea from reading Parke, Davis & Company promotional materials.

In 1917, the U.S. division of Merck became a war prize of World War I and was seized by the U.S. Government. Parke, Davis & Company survived somewhat longer, but finally lost its corporate identity when it was taken over by Warner Lambert. However, Merck and Parke, Davis & Company were far from the only players in the cocaine business. In 1906, Merck formed a joint venture with Knoll and Boehringer and produced cocaine under the MBK label. It took only a few years before other drugmakers, in other countries, entered the market. Several of the other cocaine-producing firms were located in Germany, including Boehringer and Sons, near Mannheim, and Knoll Pharmaceuticals, located in Ludwigshafen. With supplies of cocaine increasing, and wholesale prices declining, Parke, Davis & Company, and other manufacturers, tried to develop new markets by expanding its line of cocaine-based products.

The First Cocaine Cartels

11

The first cocaine cartels were formed in Europe, probably around 1910. A group of eight European drug manufacturers met and agreed, if not to fix prices for cocaine, then at least not to start any price wars. The group was actually referred to as the Cocaine Manufacturers Syndicate, not cartel, and its existence was kept a secret. To counter the pressures exerted by the Cocaine Manufacturers Syndicate, Dutch growers in Java formed their own syndicate.

In 1929, Englishwoman Dame Rachel Crowdy (1884–1964), Chief of the League of Nations Opium Traffic and Social Issues Section, wrote a letter to W.G. Van Wettum, then the Dutch Colonial Administrator and also the Netherlands' representative at the League of Nations Opium Committee. Crowdy was planning a conference on cocaine and opium production limitation, and she just heard rumors about the existence of a cocaine producer's syndicate. She complained that "practically no information has so far been available to the Committee regarding the organization and working of this convention." Only after a month did Van Wettum reply:

> …all correspondence regarding the Convention being confidential, the opinion of the manager of the cocaine factory at Amsterdam is that he cannot give the information off-hand and he is therefore consulting his fellow members in the question.

Another month passed before Van Wettum informed Dame Crowdy that the Convention, or Syndicate, consisted of eight members:

C.F. Boehringer & Soehne, G.m.b.H., Mannheim, Waldhof
C.H. Boehringer Sohn, A.G., Hamburg
F. Hoffman-La Roche & Co., A.G., Berlin

F. Hoffman-La Roche, & Co., A.G., Basel
Knoll, A.G., Ludwigshafen a/Rh.
E. Merck, Chem Fabriek, Darmstadt
Nederlandsche Cocainefabriek, N.V., Amsterdam
Etablissements Rocques, S.A., Paris

Crowdy was told that all the European manufacturers were members of the syndicate, except for Buchler, Brunswick, and Sico of Paris, and the British firm of May and Baker. Some factories in Russia wanted to become members, but because they were refining coca paste only, not extracting it from leaves, they were ineligible.

Not only were the American producers excluded from this cartel, but they also competed against themselves. Parke, Davis & Company faced stiff competition from Squibb Pharmaceutical (now incorporated into Bristol Meyers Squibb) and Dohme Pharmaceuticals (which was ultimately absorbed by the American Branch of Merck, as a component of Merck Sharpe & Dohme).

Members of the cocaine manufacturers syndicate were under no obligation to limit output and could sell their product wherever it was legal. They also agreed not to dump products. Any member could sell in any country as long as the company met the import and export regulations of the countries involved. Rather than stabilizing prices, the Syndicate's real purpose was to maximize profits. Not only did the producers not compete, they also conspired to force down the price of raw materials. Growers and crude cocaine refiners in South America were not as well organized as the Syndicate. At one point, when greater quantities of leaf from Java, Borneo, and Sumatra became available, the Syndicate stopped buying crude cocaine from South American exporters. Semirefined cocaine accumulated in South American ports, and prices fell substantially. Representatives of the Syndicate were there to buy it at reduced prices.

Allowing for market disruptions brought about by World War I, and for the occasional, unpredictable disruption in supply due to local conditions, the amount of cocaine produced by legitimate manufacturers increased steadily from 1885 until the end of World War I. The increase was surprising only if one presumes that the increased production was intended for legitimate medical use. By the end of the First World War, the world's medical community had largely lost interest in the drug — it simply had too many life-threatening side effects. Toxicity problems or not, the large drug manufacturers continued to produce and sell prodigious amounts of cocaine, all the time knowing that the cocaine was being diverted to the black market.

Things went well for the cocaine cartel, at least until the early 1930s, when a new player entered the market: Japan. Japan's production eclipsed that of producers in the United States and Germany. In the 1930s, manufacturers in the United States produced 21.3% of the world's refined cocaine, Germany 15%, the United Kingdom 9.9%, and France 8.3%. Japanese pharmaceutical houses accounted for 23.3% of total production.

Japan produced much more cocaine than it reported to the League of Nations, and all of the surplus was sold on the black market — facts that came to light only after World War II. In fact, Japanese drug dealers were able to sell much more of the drug than they could produce and were forced to import cocaine in order to meet the demand. In this, they had no difficulty. German and Swiss members of the syndicate were happy to supply the Japanese with as much refined cocaine as they required. The League of Nations was well aware of that fact.

On March 20, 1930, Dame Crowdy wrote to Dr. H. Carrière, the Director of the Swiss Federal Health Service, and complained about the enormous quantities of cocaine and heroin, much of it bearing the Hoffman La Roche label, finding its way into Occupied China. Two months later, Carrière wrote back to Crowdy saying that he checked with Hoffman La Roche and could find no evidence that the sales she was referring to had ever taken place. Carrière hedged his bets by pointing out that even if such sales had occurred, they would have been legal under Swiss law. Carrière was being as diplomatic as he was disingenuous. European drug manufacturers had been exporting huge quantities of narcotics to the Far East since just after the turn of the century, and Hoffman La Roche was one of the largest exporters.

As producers of both cocaine and heroin, Hoffman La Roche did everything possible to accommodate its Far Eastern clients. Buyers in Tokyo and Shanghai were provided with secret codes, allowing them to check on-spot drug prices and available inventories of heroin and cocaine. A cable to Hoffman La Roche's offices in Bern was all that was required. League of Nations' reports frequently singled out Hoffman La Roche for attention. In the early 1920s, their drug transactions were legal. But, after the adoption of the Hague Treaty in 1925, and the Geneva Treaty of 1931, such transactions violated international law. European manufacturers were then forced to resort to subterfuge.

Mislabeling shipments was the preferred method for shipping larger quantities of drugs. Smaller shipments were often sent through the post, or simply smuggled on board outbound freighters. Some drugmakers used all three methods. On March 15, 1928, customs officers in Rotterdam carried out a routine inspection of the *Gemma*, a Dutch steamer bound for Osaka. They found 60 kg of heroin in a crate that was supposed to contain medicines and perfumes. Markings on the container indicated that the crate originated at the Naarden Chemical Factory at Bossum, just outside Rotterdam.

The local police were contacted, and a search warrant was obtained. By the time the search party reached the factory at Bossum, most of the records and correspondence had been destroyed. But the remaining records were revealing enough. Over the preceding 2 years, officials at Naarden had shipped 664 kilograms of morphine, 2112 kilograms of heroin, and 56 kilograms of cocaine to Far Eastern buyers. More than half the shipments were sent to Japan and Japanese possessions in the Far East, even though the owners of Naarden never bothered to obtain export certificates. These transactions were actually legal. It seems there was a problem with the import–export regulations, and the drugmakers were quicker to spot the problem than was the government.

By the late 1920s, the League of Nations established an elaborate system of import and export controls. And, because all of the major governments had a good idea of what Japan was doing with its imported narcotics, it became increasingly difficult to get the import certificates needed for shipments to Japan. The terms of the Limitation Act of 1925 required that each country file an annual report estimating legitimate medical needs within that country, and then limit imports to conform to that number. Because the estimated yearly morphine requirement for Japan was well less than 600 kg, the Japanese government could not justify issuing certificates for multiple 1000 kg purchases. Similar considerations applied to cocaine. Enterprising drug exporters found a way to get around that problem too.

The Naarden Chemical Factory was able to circumvent the law, because treaty requirements for imports and all signatories to the treaty did not uniformly implement export certificates. Not every country required both types of certificates, at least not at first. Until late in 1929, the Netherlands issued import certificates only when the exporting country requested them. Germany was one of the countries that did not ask for them at all. German narcotic manufacturers, particularly C.H. Boehringer Sohn of Hamburg, and C.F. Boehringer & Soehne of Mannheim (Figure 11.1), availed themselves of this happy circumstance and shipped their products to legitimate narcotic factories in Holland. There, the drugs were stored in bonded warehouses. A technicality in Dutch law permitted the firms owning the warehouses to withdraw drugs, repackage them, and then ship them overseas. As far as the Dutch government was concerned, the drugs were never there. They were simply in transit, and never appeared, either as imports or exports, in the Dutch statistics reported to the League of Nations.

Sandoz Pharmaceuticals and Hoffman La Roche, both in Basel, were two of Naarden's best customers. There can be no question that the executives of the Swiss pharmaceutical houses knew that the drugs shipped through Naarden were being sent to fictitious shell companies in Shanghai, Tientsin, Darien, and Osaka. Nor can there be much doubt that they knew the Asian shell companies were owned by notorious drug smugglers who made little effort to hide the fact. Several of the companies that regularly placed large orders for drugs from Germany and Switzerland even shared the same mailbox.

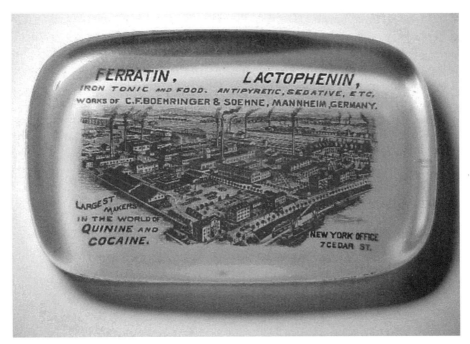

Figure 11.1 Paperweight advertisement for C.F. Boehringer & Soehne (Mannheim, Germany), "largest makers in the world of quinine and cocaine." This chemical manufacturer was a member of the original cocaine makers' cartel, founded in Switzerland. The paperweights were given away as part of an advertising promotion, probably sometime around 1905. Reliable figures are not now available, but Boehringer's claim of being the biggest cocaine manufacturer probably were not true. (Courtesy of the Addiction Research Unit at University of Buffalo.)

"Larger" drug dealers had adjacent mailboxes. Naarden had many customers in Shanghai, all in the same post office. Holland Company had Naarden ship drugs to P.O. Box 1604, Boonhua & Co., to P.O. Box 1607, Ting Long & Co., to P.O. Box 1608. The Paul Yip Opium Syndicate, and its front operation, the Own Trading Company, owned all the postboxes.

U.S. producers were never able to participate in the booming Japanese market for abused drugs. By the 1920s, U.S. drug and import regulations made large-scale cocaine production and diversion all but impossible. There would have been no way to import sufficient raw material to produce finished drugs. There was, however, a U.S. connection to the Far East drug industry. The largest Japanese cocaine manufacturer, Sankyo Pharmaceutical, had close ties with Parke, Davis & Company. In fact, the chairman of Sankyo's board, Jokichi Takamine, had, earlier in his career, worked for George Davis as a consultant.

At one time, Parke, Davis & Company successfully sold a digestive designed by Takamine, called "Taka-Diastase." They also manufactured another Takamine discovery: adrenaline, which they manufactured. Takamine was even placed in charge of setting up production. In his position as a supervising industrial chemist at Parke, Davis & Company, Takamine would certainly have been well acquainted with their latest techniques for making cocaine. That knowledge almost certainly was of some use to Takamine when he returned to Japan and went to work for Sankyo, one of Japan's major cocaine producers. Under Takamine's guidance, Sankyo was able to produce more cocaine than either Heinrich Emanuel Merck or George Parke would ever have imagined possible. Of course, none of the cocaine was destined for use by doctors.

Risky Business 12

> We are a drug-habit Nation and alcohol is only one of the many kinds that are being used to excess. The medical profession is doing everything it can to save the Nation, but it is not doing enough. Personally, I shall be glad to see this country have universal prohibition, not only of drugs but of liquor of all forms.
>
> **Dr. Harvey Wiley, head of the Bureau of Chemistry in the U.S. Department of Agriculture**
>
> *Addressing the New York City Republican Club, February 18, 1911*

At the turn of the last century, encounters with the average country doctor were a risky business. More often than not, patients came off worse for the experience. Patent medicines were popular, because they were cheaper than doctor visits, and they were likely to produce about as much good. At a minimum, most patent medicines contained a generous dose of alcohol, often supplemented with cocaine or morphine. No wonder then that these products made patients feel better, even if only for a short time, and even if the price of the cure meant being exposed to an addictive or toxic drug. Alcohol supplementation eventually caused a range of problems for patent medicine makers, especially in the States, because the prohibitionists were opposed to alcohol in any form, medicinal or not.

At the end of the 19th century, chemists were much more sophisticated than the doctors they served and that reality helped to explain some of the more bizarre aspects of U.S. drug law. It was much easier to make and detect chemicals than it was to work out what those same chemicals did once they were inside the human body.

This disparity between medical and chemical knowledge also helps explain the strange legal action filed against the Coca-Cola Company in 1911. Company officials found themselves in federal court charged with, among other things, poisoning the youth of America with caffeine. They were also charged with the crime of failing to put any cocaine into Coca-Cola®.

Coca-Cola's problems were a direct consequence of Mariani's successes. While some of the claims for Mariani's wine may have been overblown, there was never a doubt that the product contained only wine and coca. Mariani made his product from coca leaf, the only source of cocaine available. It would be another 20 years before purified cocaine would become available in commercial quantities.

Using coca leaf meant there was a limit on how much cocaine Mariani could get into the wine. Add too much leaf and the final product would taste so strongly of tannin that it would be undrinkable (imagine trying to drink a 6-month-old Bordeaux, even a very expensive one). By the mid-1890s, however, there was a glut of cocaine on the market, and patent drugmakers were able to dump large amounts of pure cocaine into their products. This made the products popular and encouraged the proliferation of coca-based remedies. The number of dangerous cocaine-containing products on the market exploded. There were coca cheroots, enemas, and eye drops, not to mention Kumfort's Coke Extract, Rococola, Pillsbury's Coke Extract, and Inca Cola.

Surprisingly, as far as anyone knows, no one became ill, let alone addicted, to Vin Mariani, or any other coca-based wine. That was because Vin Mariani contained only a very small amount of cocaine, probably less than 6 mg/oz, not enough to produce any toxic effects. When combined with alcohol, however, a 6- to 8-ounce serving would have been more than enough to create feelings of well-being. Mixing cocaine with alcohol exaggerated the effects of both.

The original Coca-Cola contained even less cocaine than Vin Mariani. According to a formula held by the great-grandson of Frank Robinson, one of Coca-Cola's founders, 10 pounds of coca leaf was used to make 36 gallons of syrup. Coca leaf from South America contains very little cocaine, probably less than 0.5%, and not all of that can be extracted. So, Coca-Cola, in its original form, would have contained about 22.5 mg of cocaine per gallon (10 lbs = 4.5 kg; 0.5% × 4.5 kg = 22.5 mg), far less than the amount of cocaine in Vin Mariani.

Such minute quantities would certainly not have been enough to produce a detectable physiological response, and it is absurd to suggest that Coca-Cola ever had addictive properties, or that its cocaine content was responsible for its success. Coca-Cola was successful for the same reason that Vin Mariani was successful: it was brilliantly promoted, and people liked drinking it.

John Styth Pemberton (1831–1888), born in Knoxville, Georgia, was the man who invented Coca-Cola. He originally trained as a physician at a medical school founded by an herbalist named Samuel Thompson. Thompson's approach to medicine relied on treatments that used various combinations of exotic herbs. While not qualifying as either rational or scientific, Thompson's theories were at least less dangerous than other approaches fashionable at the time (such as bleeding patients in order to remove imagined toxins circulating in their systems). Pemberton also trained for a year as a pharmacist, and he ultimately chose pharmacy over the practice of medicine. He opened his first pharmacy in Columbus, Georgia, in 1852. In 1869, Pemberton moved to Atlanta, which was then going through a post-Civil War building and financial boom.

In 1876, Pemberton read, and was fascinated by, Sir Robert Christison's paper describing the magical properties of the coca leaf. And, of course, Angelo Mariani's advertisements for his coca-based wines were seen everywhere. Taking his inspiration from Mariani, Pemberton began to make and sell Pemberton's French Wine Coca. According to advertisements for Pemberton's concoction, it contained not only Peruvian Coca, but also an extract of African cola nuts (which are said to contain more caffeine than very strong coffee), and "true Damiana" (*Turnera diffusa*, a plant that grows wild in the western United States, where its use was believed to be a surefire way of promoting libido).

Pemberton's claims for his drink were primarily medical; advertisements said it was "the greatest blessing to the human family," in that it would cure "nervous trouble, dyspepsia, mental and physical exhaustion, all chronic and wasting diseases, gastric irritability, constipation, sick headache and neuralgia." In clear homage to Mariani, Pemberton also claimed that his product was an "intellectual beverage," one that could be used to good end by "scientists, scholars, poets, divines, lawyers, physicians and others devoted to extreme mental exertion." Most important, it was "a most wonderful invigorator of the sexual organs."

Pemberton's wine sold fairly well, but not enough to make him rich. His fortunes should have changed in 1884, after the publicity surrounding Freud and Koller piqued the public's interest in cocaine. But disaster struck: the temperance movement took hold in the South, and, late in 1885, Atlanta voted to outlaw alcohol. Pemberton immediately set to work reformulating his product. The formula he finally settled upon included fluid extract of coca, lime juice, sugar, vanilla, and the oils of lemon, orange, neroli oil, cinnamon, coriander, and nutmeg. Attention always focused on the coca in Coca-Cola, but Pemberton's inclusion of neroli oil (which contains *citrus aurantium*) deserves mention. The active ingredients in the oil are similar to those in the recently banned (and then unbanned) ephedra plant. Many of today's herbal supplement makers have reformulated their products with neroli instead of ephedra. Their hope is that the mild stimulant properties of neroli can cause as much weight loss as ephedra.

Pemberton needed more capital to launch the new product, and in 1886, he was forced to take in new partners. One was Frank Robinson, who not only thought up a new name for the alcohol-free product, Coca-Cola, but also designed the logo that is now recognized around the world. Carbonated water, commercial refrigeration, and the soda fountain were all invented during the mid-1870s and were especially popular in the southern United States. Coca-Cola was, like Vin Mariani, sold as a patent medicine, but Robinson hit on the brilliant idea of selling it as a soda fountain beverage. The approach vastly increased the potential number of purchasers and gave Coca-Cola many more sales outlets than Vin Mariani ever could have hoped to have. The combined advantages probably explain why Coca-Cola ended up with the giant share of the coca drink market.

Pemberton filed a patent on Coca-Cola on June 6, 1887. In 1889, Pemberton, who was now a morphine addict, sold ownership of Coca-Cola to another chemist, Asa Candler. Candler's zealous approach to marketing and advertising ensured that Coca-Cola would remain in the public eye. By the turn of the century, Coca-Cola had dropped its medicinal claims, possibly a result of a special tax passed by the U.S. Congress in 1898 to help pay for the Spanish-American War. Under this new tax, medicines were taxed but soft drinks were not. Candler refocused his marketing strategy to include middle-class urban whites who frequented the soda fountains, and he began to sell Coca-Cola in individual bottles, which meant that now anyone could buy it, without going to a soda fountain.

Candler's only problem with his product was that cocaine was fast developing a bad name. Cocaine use was being linked, by the popular press at least, with the underclass, and most especially with violence in the underclass. In 1901, it was claimed in the *Atlanta Constitution* that, "use of the drug among negroes is growing to an alarming extent." In the public mind, using cocaine was a practice associated with the underprivileged, uneducated, and, by extension, sexually menacing. In 1903, Candler struck a deal with the Schafer Alkaloid Company, of Maywood, New Jersey (later known as the Maywood Chemical Company), to remove the cocaine from coca leaves and provide Coca-Cola with only the essential oils contained in the leaf (still referred to today as "Merchandise No. 5").

Recently, exporters in South America have begun to rethink the idea of coca-based soft drinks. In April 2004, the *Associated Press* reported that two new coca-based soft drinks were being sold in Peru (Kdrink™ and Vortex Energy Drink™). Introduction of the products was prompted by the increasing popularity of coca-based teas. These cocaine-containing drinks are sold to tourists with the intent of warding off altitude sickness. Like Coca-Cola, these products are made with decocanized leaves, and each bottle is said to contain 0.6 mg of cocaine. Makers of the product would like to go international but have run afoul of U.S. and United Nations' regulations.

Coca-Cola's supplier of decocanized leaf, the Stepan Company, successor to Maywood Chemical, has annual sales of $400 million and is traded on the American Stock Exchange. Still located in Maywood, Stephan is said to import 175,000 kg (nearly 200 tons) of coca leaves into the United States each year. It appears that the leaves come from some of the same farms that supply the Columbian drug cartels, although the cocaine is removed from the leaves before it is sold to the Coca-Cola Company. The truly noteworthy aspect of this news is the amount of coca leaf that is being used. Most government estimates put total Andean production at less than 600 tons. If these figures are correct, and they appear to be, then one-third of the world's coca production is going toward the manufacture of soft drinks.

While Candler was reformulating Coca-Cola, Congress moved to regulate the food and drug industry. The public had been calling for some type of regulation for nearly a quarter of a century. In 1880, Edward Robinson Squibb, the same Squibb who, unable to procure adequate supplies of coca leaf, had declared that there was no future for the cocaine business, managed to get the New York State legislature to pass a bill that served as the model for the one finally passed by Congress, in 1906: the Pure Food and Drug Act. This new act superseded an assortment of ineffective state laws. It gave federal regulators some authority over the production, distribution, and marketing of food and drugs, and it also established the U.S. Pharmacopoeia as the legal standard of official preparations. Patent remedies containing compounds not listed in the Pharmacopoeia were required to list those ingredients on the label.

The law was badly needed. By any rational standard, the contents of many turn-of-the-century remedies could only be described as criminal. Combinations of alcohol and cocaine were popular, but not in so much demand as combinations of morphine, opium, and alcohol. Coca-Bola, a cocaine chewing gum invented by a certain Dr. Mitchell from Philadelphia, was supposed to be chewed at "occasional intervals throughout the day." It contained 710 mg of cocaine per ounce of gum. Each piece of gum would have contained the equivalent of nearly 10 lines of cocaine. Dr. Tucker's Asthma Specific, formulated and sold by Nathan Tucker of Gilead, Ohio, was even more dangerous, because it was sprayed into the lungs. When cocaine comes into direct contact with the lung's surface, much more gets absorbed into the body than when it is swallowed. Analysis by government chemists revealed a cocaine content of 420 mg/oz, but that did not make Dr. Tucker's product illegal. Tucker correctly stated the cocaine content on his product label, so under the terms of the new act, sales remained legal.

Figure 12.1 Harvey Wiley was the first director of the Division of Chemistry in the Department of Agriculture. From www.cfsan.fda.gov/m/rdstamp.html.

If our drug policies appear convoluted today, think how they must have looked to the owners of the Coca-Cola Company just after the turn of the century. In 1911, company officials found themselves in federal court, charged with, among other things, not putting cocaine in Coca-Cola. Popular histories of this period usually lump Coca-Cola with the other quack nostrums, often suggesting that the problem of cocaine abuse in the United States was, in some way, connected to the successes of the Coca-Cola Company. Except for the titillation factor, the idea has little else to recommend it. Even when Coca-Cola contained cocaine, the quantities were trivial; too small to produce measurable physiologic or behavioral changes. Coca-Cola was not

Figure 12.2   Dr. Wiley (third from right) with his staff. From www.cfsan.fda.gov /m/rdstamp.html.

responsible for the U.S. cocaine problem, but government harassment of the Atlanta soft drink maker marks an important turning point in the development of U.S. drug policy and is worth examining in some detail.

Government moves against Coca-Cola were a consequence not so much of the Pure Food and Drug Act, but rather of Dr. Harvey Wiley (1844–1930), the person in charge of implementing it (Figure 12.1, Figure 12.2). Wiley was the first head of the Bureau of Chemistry within the Department of Agriculture, the agency given overall responsibility for enforcing the act. He was one in a series of government officials, such as Hamilton Wright and J. Henry Anslinger, who made their living by campaigning against the evils of drug abuse. These antidrug crusaders had more in common than just the desire to rid society of its drug problem: all were willing to use very bad, sometimes fraudulent, science to advance their arguments. The dual problems of "drug careerism," and the tendency to use political considerations as a means of determining scientific truth have not entirely gone away. Witness the administration claims that global warming is not occurring. The issues were, however, more clearly framed in the early 1900s.

A few years before taking on Coca-Cola, Wiley set out to prove that adding benzoic acid (now known to be an exceptionally safe food additive) was a dangerous practice.

Discoveries made by innovative chemists, such as W.E. Merck and Justus von Liebig, were not immediately integrated into the medical practice. Turn-of-the-century chemists were much more sophisticated than turn-of-the-century physicians and they were also more effective, which partially explains some of the convoluted dynamics involved in the writing of American drug laws. It was much easier to make and detect chemicals than it was to figure out what those same chemicals did once they were incorporated into the human body.

Wiley studied a group of 12 men, all U.S. Department of Agriculture employees. They came to be known as "Doctor Wiley's poison squad" (Figure 12.3). They were housed together and fed an assortment of adulterated foods, while continuing their normal work. Half were given a particular item of food obtained from one source. Their reactions were compared to the reactions of the other six subjects, who were fed a similar food item from still another source containing benzoic acid. However, this was far from being a double-blind experiment. Everyone, doctors and participants alike, knew from which source the food came. Study subjects were closely monitored, but regardless of whether or not they were given benzoic acid, they were all given plenty of fruit. As fresh fruit contains benzoic acid, all the participants were receiving supplementary amounts of benzoic acid, totally invalidating the study. Another defect of the study was that it was "unblinded." Studying the behavioral effects of a drug can only be reliable if neither the test subject nor the experimenter knows whether drug or placebo is given.

Figure 12.3 Wiley with "the poison squad." From www.cfsan.fda.gov/m/rds-tamp.html.

Freud committed the same type of error when he measured his own muscle strength before and after taking cocaine. The force of muscle contraction is, in large part, voluntary. As Freud knew he was taking cocaine, and because he freely admitted that he wanted to prove that cocaine was a valuable drug, it should have come as no surprise when he found that cocaine increased muscle strength. Wiley did much the same thing. He gave his subjects chemicals that he was sure were harmful, and then he looked for harmful effects. It would have been surprising if he had not found any. Wiley was able to conclude, just as he expected, that "preservatives used in foods are harmful to health."

Scientific American magazine waged a solitary battle against Wiley and his Bureau of Chemistry, pointing out the flawed nature of Wiley's methodology, which should have been clear to anyone who gave the subject a second thought. But in the end, the persuasiveness of Wiley's personality, and his bully pulpit as chief government chemist, proved to be more important than the credibility of his science. Later, long after Wiley was dead, the government classified benzoic acid as a "generally...safe" compound.

Bogus though Wiley's experiments may have been, they struck a responsive chord, and he became both famous and powerful, just the man to enforce the new laws enacted in 1906. The law provided that substances could be added to food only if they were safe for human consumption and that addition of the substances to the food served some useful purpose. Actually, the law came as something of a relief to patent drugmakers. In 1905, at a secret meeting, the trade organization of proprietary drug manufacturers passed a resolution calling on its members to tone down their more outrageous advertising claims. In particular, members were advised to reduce the alcohol and narcotic contents of their products. Even the Coca-Cola Company supported reform legislation, believing it had nothing to fear. It was, after all, truthfully labeled and made from pure products.

The 1906 Pure Food and Drug Act should have led to important changes in the drug industry, but they were very slow to occur. George McCabe, head legal counsel of the Department of Agriculture, repeatedly criticized Wiley's plodding approach and berated him, sometimes in public, for not going after more patent drugmakers. Wiley's response was that there were over 25,000 such products on the market, and he did not have the staff or the facilities to analyze even a small fraction of them.

Even if Wiley had the manpower, there are several reasons why he could not have done the job. Most importantly, neither he nor his staff had any command of the technology needed to measure the subtle drug effects of all the possible adulterants; existing technology was only good enough to detect the presence of adulterants in food, but the actual effects of these adulterants could not be accurately measured once they were in the body. The other problem was his legal authority. The act applied only when substances like heroin and cocaine were added surreptitiously to a product. If the drugs were listed on the label, there was nothing illegal about their presence or the sale of the product.

In reality, the situation was even worse than it sounded. Rusby called the act a complete failure. The law was easy to circumvent, because it was so narrowly drafted. It was common practice for quack drugmakers to ship the individual ingredients that comprised their products across state lines, where they could then be legally blended by local manufacturers. For reasons that remain unfathomable, Wiley next became convinced that caffeine was even more dangerous than benzoic acid, even though caffeine was not on the list of dangerous drugs specifically regulated by the Pure Food and Drug Act, and even though Coca-Cola contained less caffeine than tea and coffee, Wiley took it upon himself to stamp out caffeine use.

Executives of the Coca-Cola Company had supported the Pure Food and Drug Act. John Candler, Asa's brother, even went to Washington, D.C. to testify at congressional hearings in favor of the bill; Coca-Cola's management assumed that passage of the bill would likely lead to increased sales. When the act was finally passed, Cola-Cola was even able to boast in its advertisements that it was "Guaranteed under the Pure Food and Drug Act."

Coca-Cola's support for the act infuriated Wiley. Given what is known about Wiley's personality, it may be reasonable to suppose that he thought Coca-Cola was actually mocking him when it publicly endorsed the Act. For whatever reason, Wiley began an organized campaign of government harassment against Coca-Cola. He convinced the Acting Secretary of Agriculture to threaten legal action unless Coca-Cola stopped claiming it was pure. Wiley then formed an alliance with Martha Allen, head of the Woman's Christian Temperance Union, and persuaded the U.S. Army to ban Coca-Cola from its bases.

Earlier, in a Congressional tax hearing held in 1901, evidence was introduced showing that Coca-Cola contained alcohol. Trace amounts were, in fact, required to dissolve the flavoring essences used to make the product. Wiley and Allen recycled the testimony from the former hearings and wrote to the Army's Surgeon General, claiming that Coca-Cola contained as much alcohol as beer and, in addition, an "indefinite amount of cocaine." And so, for a few months in 1907, at least until the absurdity of the claims became clear, the U.S. Army banned Coca-Cola from its bases. Wiley was never reprimanded for making what he clearly knew were false claims. Instead, he launched another federal investigation into Coca-Cola's bottling practices.

By then, Candler had opened more factories and was beginning to establish networks of distributorships that would transform the small Atlanta firm

Figure 12.4 Dr. Harvey Wiley as Uncle Sam, protecting the masses from the evils of soft drink makers and purveyors of caffeine. A cartoon appearing in an issue of *Good Housekeeping* magazine.

into a global giant. So, it came as something of a shock when, in 1909, Wiley, acting with the full approval of the U.S. Department of Agriculture and the Solicitor General, seized a shipment comprised of 40 barrels and 20 kegs of Coca-Cola syrup. The government claimed that the syrup contained a poisonous ingredient that might be hazardous to health. Coca-Cola was also charged with false labeling: it contained no coca and hardly any cola. The case was tried in a federal court in Chattanooga in March 1911.

At trial, Wiley directed much of the cross-examination. One of the expert witnesses for the prosecution was none other than Henry H. Rusby, the former Parke, Davis & Company employee who secured new coca supplies for his employers, and who had, in the process, revolutionized the cocaine industry by devising a way to produce crude, semirefined, cocaine on site (Remember, Rusby basically invented "crack"). At the time of the trial, Rusby had been appointed professor of Materia Medica (pharmacology) at Columbia University, and also one of the three editors of the *National Standard Dispensary*, a semiofficial book on pharmacology. The other two editors of this book also testified for Wiley.

Although it was never mentioned at trial, Rusby was also a full-time government employee, which later proved to be a problem for Wiley. Rusby's presence at trial was probably not even necessary. Even before he appeared, the jury heard a Harvard Medical School professor describe the terrible effects observed when frogs were injected with Coca-Cola syrup. Another government "scientist" described the painful deaths experienced by rabbits when Coca-Cola syrup was poured into their lungs. Still another prosecution witness assured the jurors that drinking Coca-Cola encouraged boys to masturbate.

While the assault on Coca-Cola continued in Tennessee, Wiley was hatching even grander plans. On March 20, long before the trial came to a close, a representative of the Bureau of Chemistry called a press conference in New York City. Dr. W.L. Baldwin, who was acting chief when Wiley was out of town, announced plans for a "strenuous warfare on all cooling concoctions that are alleged to contain harmful ingredients." Just what was considered harmful by the Bureau of Chemistry's standards was anyone's guess. But Baldwin announced that a list of "alleged harmful soft drinks" was already prepared, and that "every soda fountain and soft drink store in Washington will be visited several times each week by government inspectors, with a view to learning if they contain cocaine, coca leaf, or caffeine." Judge Edward Terry Sanford was not impressed with Wiley's case against Coca-Cola, and he ordered a verdict in favor of Coca-Cola. "Coca-Cola," he said, "without caffeine would not be Coca-Cola."

The fallout from the trial took years to sort out. The government appealed, and in 1912, the Pure Food and Drug Act was amended, and caffeine was added to the list of dangerous drugs. The government lost its initial appeal but eventually won in the Supreme Court. In 1917, Coca-Cola reached an out-of-court settlement and agreed to reduce the amount of caffeine in its finished product. Under mounting pressure and accusations of incompetence, Wiley left his government post shortly after the trial. Among other things, he was accused of paying Rusby too much for his expert testimony. Wiley went on to write a column for *Good Housekeeping* magazine. In one column, he touted the virtues of coffee, claiming it had become "America's beverage" (Figure 12.5).

The final outcome of the Coca-Cola Company case could not have been gratifying to Wiley. He had to drop his planned offensive against the soda fountains of America, and, for all his effort, his only real accomplishment was to have run up a large legal bill for Coca-Cola. It was estimated that the cost of the first trial alone was more than $200,000, an enormous sum for 1911. It is not clear whether publicity from the trial helped or hurt Coca-Cola's sales.

Much more important than the outcome of the trial, however, was the precedent it set: the U.S. government learned how to use pseudoscience to meet its own ends in court. The Coca-Cola trials were just a reprise of Wiley's benzoic acid research, where he had basically manufactured evidence to "prove" what he already "knew." Wiley was so firmly convinced of the evils of Coca-Cola, that he was not at all bothered by the accuracy or legitimacy of the data he presented in court.

Granted, turn-of-the-century medical experiments lacked sophistication, but because Wiley later expounded on the virtues of coffee drinking, it is hard to suppose he could have had much faith in the evidence he or his where simple but nutritious lunch could be bought for a penny by some of those who were unable to bring proper food from home. Where this experiment has been tried it has been the universal consensus of opinion that the scholarship and deportment of those who received these simple benefactions have been improved. To show the hold that mercenary interests have on the country I may say that, when these attempts were made in Washington to supply wholesome and nutritious luncheons to the poor children, protests were made by dealers in candies, etc., in the vicinity of the school, against the practice, on the ground that serving the luncheon in the school room prevented the children from coming into their stores and buying their goods. Happily this commercial objection did not succeed in breaking down the plan adopted by the school authorities in Washington.

A still more important problem is that condition of school children which, for lack of a better term, is called nervousness. What is it that has ruined the children's nerves? In my opinion it does not as a rule come from over-study, though occasionally that might have been the case. The trouble with the children of this country is that after the manner of their parents they are subjected to exhilaration by stimulants of various kinds, which have no food value and can work only injury. I refer especially to coffee and tea at home, the acquisition by the young boys of the tobacco habit, and the indulgence by the boys and girls in the so-called soft drinks which contain cocain or caffein. Fortunately the effectiveness of the campaign against cocain has driven most of the beverages containing it from the soda fountains, but this is not true of those containing caffein.

690

Coffee is too powerful a stimulant for children

CAFFEIN

And Coca Cola and other caffeinated drinks are open to the same objection

The Drug Division of the Department of Agriculture secured the names of over one hundred so-called soft drinks sold at soda fountains which contained either caffein or cocain or both. As a rule no soda fountain sells over two or three of these soft drinks, but they are offered in the large numbers which I have mentioned in the various parts of the country. Inasmuch as every authority has agreed that cocain is a substance to be kept out of foods, I shall confine my remarks solely to those products containing caffein.

The health officers of Washington issued a letter of caution to parents in which it was urged that they should not allow their children to use tea or coffee at home. Nothing was said in this circular, however, about patronizing soda fountains where beverages containing caffein were sold. In point of fact, it is commonly admitted by experts that caffein-bearing beverages taken upon an empty stomach are more injurious than the same amount of caffein would be, consumed with meals. Now the consumption of tea and coffee at home with meals is less harmful than the drinking of caffeinated beverages at the soda fountains. The name of one of these beverages most frequently found is Coca Cola. Indeed, it is somewhat rare at the present time to find a soda fountain that does not sell this beverage. A glass of Coca Cola contains about the same amount of caffein as a cup of tea or coffee, and children in drinking this are doing the very thing their parents would not have them do if they knew it. The authorities should be as careful to caution against the use of Coca Cola as against coffee and tea. It is bad enough for grown people to drink these beverages without offering them to children.

But there is another reason why the children suffer with that indescribable condition called nervousness. While we may not

Figure 12.5   Wiley an excerpt from *Good Housekeeping*. Note the child in the Cola glass being tormented by the devil caffeine.

experts presented at trial. The willingness to resort to pseudoscience, along with his refusal to accept the obvious fact that the amount of drug used has something to do with the effects that a drug produces, makes Wiley the father of what is now the central element of American and International drug policy, the concept of "zero tolerance."

The "Legitimate Business of Poisoning Hindoos"

13

...they (the German representatives at Geneva) don't understand action based on humanitarian motives and...would understand it still less when called on to enact legislation to restrict German traders in "the legitimate business of poisoning Hindoos and Chinese."

From a British representative at the Hague Conference to the Foreign Office in London, 1909

Drug control policy was never considered a fit subject for diplomacy until the government of the United States decided to formulate policy. In 1906, the United States launched a series of initiatives aimed at curtailing the illicit drug trade. These efforts were not made in response to any serious drug problems within U.S. borders, or anywhere else in Europe, for that matter. Rather, they were exercises in international relations, designed to serve U.S. political needs. The United States was not an opium producer, and there were relatively few addicts within its borders. But in 1898, at the end of the Spanish-American War, the United States had taken possession of the Philippine Islands, and it found itself in much the same position as Japan in 1905, when it acquired Taiwan — ward to a large population of addicted opium smokers.

The situation in the Philippine Islands was not nearly as bad as it was in Taiwan, when Japanese administrators found that a sizable portion of the population was addicted. When the United States took possession of the Philippines, there were fewer than 50,000 opium addicts, almost all Chinese, and opium imports amounted to only 100 tons per year. At first, opium traffic in the Philippines was unregulated, and the U.S. occupation government helped balance its budget by taxing opium imports. But then, the U.S. Congress appointed a commission to study the problem. Episcopal Bishop Charles H. Brent (1862–1929) was appointed its leader. The committee was supposed to investigate opium use in the Philippines and make recommendations to Congress.

The commission reached essentially the same conclusions that the Japanese had come to a few years earlier: form a government monopoly, prohibit nonmedical use of opiates, license opium smokers, and try to educate the public about the dangers of opium smoking. The commission made its report to Congress in 1905. Congress rejected the findings and recommendations and, instead, voted for an absolute prohibition. The prohibition went into effect in March 1908.

Overnight, smuggling in the Philippines became a major problem. There are hundreds of islands in the Philippines and thousands of landing sites for smugglers transporting opium from Borneo and Singapore. Policing the borders began to consume a major portion of the local constabulary's budget. Echoing a theme still heard today, the Chief of Philippine Customs wrote to Bishop Brent and complained that his department was receiving only "about one tenth of the amount necessary to enable this bureau to fully prosecute this prohibited evil!"

Not long after the U.S. Congress outlawed opium in the Philippines, the government of China passed an edict prohibiting opium cultivation in that country. That same year, Bishop Brent, frustrated by the flood of opium smuggled into the Philippines, wrote to President Theodore Roosevelt and suggested international action. Brent realized, even if Congress did not, that the United States and the Philippines could not simply make drug policy in a vacuum. Congress could pass all the absolute prohibitions it wanted. Enforcing them, without cooperation from the producing countries, was another matter.

Brent's suggestion was eventually implemented. The United States invited 14 countries, all with major financial interests in the Far East, to participate in a drug conference. Each of the invited countries generated revenues by growing, refining, or selling opium. Thirteen of the countries agreed to send representatives to a meeting. Turkey was the only major opium producer that refused.

The delegation from the United States was led by Bishop Brent, but most of the proposals offered by the U.S. delegation were written by Dr. Hamilton Wright (1845–1916), an American physician who was appointed to the U.S. negotiating team. Wright certainly was not chosen for his diplomatic skills. In fact, he had no diplomatic training and managed to alienate nearly every European diplomat he dealt with. But no one in the Congress cared about that minor defect. Wright was chosen because he knew the region and was, presumably, well acquainted with the problems of opium addiction.

It may seem surprising that Great Britain agreed to attend the conference. The colonial government in India was, after all, partially financed by taxes on opium sales. But Bishop Brent was not the only one concerned about the opium problem. In England, pressure was mounting in Parliament to outlaw the opium trade altogether. The pressure came partly from the general public, but mostly from missionary groups, frustrated with their lack of success in converting the Chinese to Christianity. Past attempts at legislative reform were unsuccessful, but in the Parliamentary election of 1906, reform candidates handily beat the Tories and finally forced the government into action.

After much debate, Great Britain eventually agreed to curtail Indian exports of opium to China, provided that, at the same time, China reduced domestic production and imports from other countries as well. The latter condition was a recurring European theme in all drug control negotiations. England, like Germany and France, was home to an advanced pharmaceutical industry, and India, her possession, was a major opium producer. England did not plan to stop selling drugs to China only to see some other producer take its place.

After prolonged negotiations over the agenda, the commission finally met in Shanghai in 1909, from February 1 to 29. The American representatives submitted eight resolutions. Hamilton Wright drafted all but one of the resolutions, and they were not exactly the proposals that the other countries wanted to hear. Wright wanted the commission to agree that opium should be used only for medical purposes, and that bans on opium smoking should immediately be put into effect. Only China and Canada found the terms acceptable.

The proposals were far too draconian and far too radical for the other countries to accept. Not that they could have done much to implement such proposals, even if they had agreed to them. As the head of the British delegation, Clementi Smith (1840–1916), pointed out, such a ban would be impossible to carry out; there were not enough soldiers in all of Britain to police an area as vast as India. Instead of an outright ban on opium smoking, Wright was only able to negotiate a resolution favoring gradual reductions in opium production coupled with agreements that opium smoking should be gradually regulated and suppressed. Another of Wright's suggestions, to impose export controls on producing countries, was accepted in such a watered-down version, so universal and so general, that it actually made narcotic smuggling easier. What began as a proposal for strict international regulation of drug sales became, in its final form, an agreement that drug control was a local, not an international, problem. The resolutions finally adopted by the commission were nonbinding.

The conference was an abject failure, but there was a general consensus that something had to be done about the drugs. As one British delegate put it, the "opium question required firmer handling." Dr. Wright wrote a report that described what transpired at the Shanghai meeting, but it did not exactly agree with the recollection of the other diplomats in attendance. It did, however, portray the actions of Dr. Wright and the American delegation in a very good light. Even though nearly the entire set of U.S. proposals was rejected out of hand, when the conference proceedings were reported to Congress, Wright indicated they were "waived for the sake of harmony." In internal memos, British diplomats confirmed that absolutely no agreement regarding the necessity of international drug regulation was reached, or even considered. But when Wright wrote his report to Congress, he insisted, "it was recognized that such action (international regulation) was necessary." The foreign diplomatic corps, particularly the British, were not happy with Wright, or with his claims, or with the United States in general.

Wright spent the next 2 years organizing a second conference to be held in The Hague. There was considerable foot dragging, both by the U.S. State Department and by the Foreign Office in England. While the foot dragging was going on, Wright had time to craft 14 new proposals. These were forwarded by the State Department to the Foreign Office in London. As before, at the top of Wright's wish list were laws to control opium production and gradually limit opium smoking. There were also many other proposals designed to make it more difficult for drug producers to move drugs across international borders. Wright suggested that an international commission be appointed and charged with supervising drug production. None of the 14 new proposals submitted by Wright mentioned that cocaine, unlike opium, was a problem within U.S. borders.

In correspondence with the various governments prior to the meeting in The Hague, U.S. State Department representatives claimed that their main concern was the eradication of opium smoking in China, and in the Far Eastern possessions owned by the various participating European countries. They insisted that problems associated with the use of other drugs were not to be discussed. British diplomats did not much like that approach. Britain derived too much revenue from Indian opium sales, and, in addition, many colonial administrators felt that the habit was not all that pernicious. When the British Foreign Secretary, Sir Edward Grey (1862–1933), finally accepted the U.S. invitation to attend another conference in September 1910, he pointed out that his acceptance was only provisional. Britain had no intention of attending, unless all:

> ... the other participating Powers are willing that the conference should thoroughly and completely deal with the question of restricting the manufacture, sale, and distribution of morphia...and also with the allied question of cocaine. In India, in China, and

in other Eastern countries the importation of morphia and cocaine from occidental countries, and the spread of morphia and the cocaine habit, is becoming an evil more serious and more deadly than opium smoking, and this evil is certain to increase.

British diplomats were, in fact, seriously grappling with the entire issue of drug production and drug misuse, and they understood the relationship between growing opium and coca, manufacturing cocaine and heroin, and distributing these drugs, far better than did their U.S. counterparts. The British diplomats' reasons may not have been entirely altruistic, but their vision was far more reaching, and their assessment of the situation, and the potential for disaster, was far more accurate.

As was clear from Grey's letter that British leaders were not enthusiastic about holding another conference. They were even less enthusiastic when they noticed that none of Wright's proposals mentioned cocaine. Regulating one drug, but not another, seemed to make little sense. British diplomats were more concerned with regulating the manufacturing process than with cultivation. In retrospect, the British approach was somewhat surprising. At the time, Great Britain was second only to Germany in the drug refining business. However, the British government was increasingly embarrassed by its role of English producers in the illegal drug trade. Although not of the epic proportions attained prior to World War II, Japanese sales of heroin and morphine in occupied China were substantial. British and European drug-makers were supplying most of the drugs sold by the Japanese. Britain refused to attend the second conference unless the problem of other drugs was also placed on the agenda. Eventually, the British got their way.

Even with the benefit of hindsight, it is impossible to understand how Wright, or anyone else for that matter, could entertain the idea of solving the opium problem without, at the same time, addressing the problems of morphine and cocaine production. British emphasis on the control of drug manufacture as the key to limiting the spread of drug use, was in stark contrast to that of representatives in the United States, who were chiefly concerned with the production of raw materials. Both approaches, however, proved to be equally shortsighted.

When the convention was finally convened in The Hague in 1912, most of the U.S. proposals were promptly abandoned. The first two chapters, regarding opium, were generally uncontroversial and passed easily. The third chapter (each of the conclusions is referred to as a "chapter") of the convention had to do with manufactured drugs, and was hotly debated. This section was written by the British delegation and would have had the effect of severely limiting sales of all refined narcotics. Germany, the home of Merck and Bayer, then the world's largest cocaine and heroin manufacturers, vigorously opposed the provisions. The financial underpinnings of the negotiations were a source of outrage to many. Max Mueller (1823–1918), one of the British negotiators, a former chargé d'affaires in Peking with firsthand knowledge of the opium problem, wrote to his superiors that the representatives of the German delegation "don't understand action based on humanitarian motives and…would understand it still less when called on to enact legislation to restrict German traders in the legitimate business of poisoning Hindoos and Chinese."

Financial considerations almost guaranteed that no serious agreement would come out of the Hague conference. Except for the United States and Canada, where there were no pharmaceutical giants, drug manufacturing was a major industry in all of the participating countries. In the unlikely event that humanitarian consideration might convince one country to get out of the drug business entirely, other manufacturers would have been more than happy to supply any shortfall. Implementation of the agreement became a real problem. Short of all countries signing on the same date, producing countries that signed earlier would lose revenues, while those that signed later would reap windfall profits. Two additional conferences were convened, in 1913 and 1914, solely to find a way to actually implement the agreements reached in 1912. The meetings were unsuccessful, and negotiations were continuing at the outbreak of World War I.

Ratification of The Hague treaty finally became possible at the end of World War I. Turkey and Germany lost the war. Both were major drug-producing countries, and they were not enthusiastic about The Hague treaty. American President Woodrow Wilson linked the founding of the League of Nations, the predecessor of today's United Nations, to the peace treaty. Few of the Allies shared his passion: France strongly objected, England offered half-hearted support, and the U.S. Congress was not as enthusiastic as England. Wilson finally had to threaten to sign a separate peace treaty with Germany if the rest of the Allies did not support him on the League's formation. Once the League of Nations was accepted, it was only logical that the terms of the unratified Opium Convention be included in the League of Nations' charter. Germany, the world's largest narcotics producer, and Turkey, one of the world's largest opium growers, had no choice but to become signatories, and to limit their drug sales. According to Article 23 of the League of Nations Covenant, members "entrust the League with the general supervision over agreements with regard to…the traffic in opium and other dangerous drugs."

At the first meeting of the League in 1921, the Assembly voted to create the Advisory Committee on Traffic in Opium and Other Dangerous Drugs. The committee was charged with finding ways to implement the provisions of the 1912 Hague Convention. Many approaches to the problem were discussed, but only two were seriously considered: production controls and sales controls. Drug manufacturing countries were heavily represented on the committee, and they effectively stonewalled any proposal to limit production. The approach ultimately chosen relied on the regulation and control of drug sales.

A system of import and export certificates was devised. Narcotic exports were only permitted if buyers could produce certificates attesting to legitimate medical need. There were, of course, certain problems with this approach. For instance, there was no agreement as to what constituted legitimate medical need. Per capita cocaine and opiate consumption varied widely from country to country, partly because of differences in medical practices, partly because of sloppy bookkeeping, and, in the case of countries such as Japan and Switzerland, because the government condoned fraud and deception. During the 1920s, League of Nations experts estimated that the legitimate medical requirement for cocaine in countries with developed medical systems was not more than 7 mg per person. Japanese production, alone, amounted to far more than that amount.

Enforcement was another problem. It clearly was not working. According to a joint resolution approved by the U.S. Congress on March 2, 1923, the Opium Committee's approach had "utterly failed to suppress such illicit traffic." And the reason for the failure, according to the U.S. Congress, was that the League had wrongly emphasized the regulation of transport and sale. According to Congress, the failure to "provide adequate restrictions upon production has resulted in extensive and flagrant violation of the laws."

Another convention was held in Geneva in 1925. U.S. suggestions were, again, largely ignored, and the Americans walked out of the meeting. Europeans continued to focus on manufacturing. The Americans felt that that approach was totally wrongheaded. In a memorandum to the president of the conference, one of the American delegates wrote:

> There is, however, no likelihood of obtaining a complete control of all opium and coca leaf derivatives. Irrespective of the measure of control provided for manufactured drugs, it is believed that, by reason of the very small bulk, the ease of transportation with minimum risk of detection, and the large financial gains to be obtained from their illicit handling, such drugs and their derivatives can only be effectively controlled if the production of the raw opium and coca leaves from which they are obtained is strictly limited to medical and scientific purposes.

The committee did not agree, and its focus remained on drug sales and distribution. It is not clear from the records why the Europeans were so opposed to the U.S. emphasis on limiting raw materials, but they were certainly correct in this opposition; they understood that any of the dangerous drugs could be produced anywhere. The number of acres devoted to opium and coca in the 1920s amounted to only a tiny fraction of the acres under cultivation today, even though a host of laws and treaties prohibit cultivation of both coca and the poppy.

In none of these deliberations is there any evidence to even remotely suggest that any U.S. delegation member considered the possibility of clandestine production, now the main source of heroin and cocaine. For reasons that are impossible to fathom today, not one participant at the League of Nations, except Japan, realized that large-scale narcotic production could occur totally outside of government production controls. The Japanese understood that extracting cocaine from coca was a relatively simple procedure, but not even the Japanese recognized the possibility of small, underground laboratories. Japan's government saw this opportunity for what it was, and began to finance its territorial expansion with drug sales.

Two further conventions were held before the outbreak of World War II. The Geneva Convention of 1931 prohibited members from producing or importing more drugs than they actually needed. The Geneva Convention of 1936 called for the enactment of measures to prevent drug smuggling, and measures to facilitate extradition for drug offenses. The treaties were a blessing for Japan's war chest, allowing them to dump millions of dollars worth of drugs onto the black market. But signing the treaties proved to be a mixed blessing, and eventually became a liability for Japan. Violation of the various drug treaties was cited as one justification for holding the Tokyo War Crime Trials at the end of World War I.

Harpies in the West End
14

In England, at the beginning of the 20th century, laws regulating drug sales were very lax, and there were hardly any limitations on sales of cocaine and heroin. There were some laws about selling and dispensing, and provisions of the 1908 Pharmacy Act made it difficult, though not impossible, for addicts and recreational users to buy drugs. Pharmacists merely had to keep records and properly label their products. In this way, British law resembled provisions of the U.S. Pure Food and Drug Act of 1906; almost any amount of any drug could be added to a patent remedy, provided the content was listed on the label. Policing was left to the pharmaceutical society, acting for the Privy Council. Cocaine could still be purchased with a prescription, but under the new laws, it was no longer possible to obtain an unlimited number of prescription refills. People who really wanted to buy drugs could, but not many did, and there was no need for extensive regulation.

The number of drug deaths reported by coroners was miniscule. The small number proves, as well as it ever can be proven, that there was a lack of demand. Except for alcohol, England was relatively drug free. Until the outbreak of World War I, the only real drug problem faced by the Home and Foreign Offices, and various Colonial Offices, was the existence of a massive trade in illegal narcotics manufactured in the United Kingdom and sold in the Far East, mainly in China, through the agency of Japanese black marketers.

The advent of World War I had a profound effect on pattern and extent of drug use in England and the United States, not so much for soldiers in combat, but for civilians on the home front. A black market for opium and cocaine quickly sprang into existence, selling mostly drugs that were smuggled into England by Chinese immigrants living in Liverpool and in the Limehouse area of London. At the same time, the U.S. West Coast steamer ports proved an increasingly easy portal of entry for smuggled narcotics that had been manufactured in Japan. Steamship owners found themselves acting as unwilling participants in the drug trade. The ship owners had more than simple moral objections to selling drugs; their ships were being impounded, and the owners were being fined. It was costing them money.

Complaints from the ship owners, especially in the United Kingdom, became so vocal that the Colonial Office convened an interdepartmental meeting to deal with the problem. It was held on June 19, 1916. The explicit purpose of the meeting was to find ways of limiting the narcotics trade (and thereby protecting the shipping industry). Britain signed The Hague convention in 1914. Having signed, England was obliged to pass internal legislation that would control the use of narcotics and dangerous drugs within its borders. For the same reason, not because of any massive drug problem within its borders, the United States had already passed the Harrison Narcotic Act.

Serious attempts at implementation of these new laws were hampered by the outbreak of the war. The owners of the English shipping line could not wait for new laws to be drafted, and they pressured the Colonial Office to act. Decisions made at the June meeting eventually led to the introduction of stricter regulations, but not exactly of the sort that one might expect. The Colonial Office reasoned that the best way to limit exports and eliminate the black market for cocaine and heroin was to limit production. The conclusion was not unreasonable. Except for the Japanese producers, virtually all the heroin and cocaine in the world was produced by legitimate pharmaceutical companies — the clandestine underground drug lab was yet to be invented. And, the Colonial Office assumption proved to be correct. Morphine exports (comparable figures for cocaine are not available) plummeted from 204,742 oz in 1915 to near zero in 1918.

Even so, a war was in progress, and there was concern about drug use by enlisted men. Most of the problems had to do with cocaine. During World War I, cocaine use was more prevalent in France than in either the United States or the United Kingdom. Returning soldiers often brought home not just memories, but also souvenirs, including a taste for cocaine. In 1916, the British Army Council made it a crime to supply cocaine, or any other narcotic drug, to members of the armed forces.

Whether or not the number of addicted was very great is hard to say, but the government was being pressured. Just a few weeks before the council reached a decision, the press gave extensive coverage to the arrest of a prostitute named Rose Edwards, and her pimp, Horace Kingsley, who were sentenced to jail for having sold cocaine to Canadian troops stationed outside London. Newspaper circulation got another boost in February 1916, when both the famed Harrods Department Store and the Savory & Moore Department Store (which no longer exists) were fined for violating the Pharmacy Act. The previous Christmas, both stores advertised candies made from cocaine and morphine, promoting them as ideal gifts "for friends at the front." At trial, the Crown made the case that provision of these drugs posed a danger to troop morale and effectiveness.

As the war progressed, reports became more numerous, and articles about the abuse of drugged soldiers became a regular feature in most of the daily papers. One editorial writer opined that returning soldiers remembered "the transitory bliss of the drugged sleep and forget(s) the aftermath.... Nurses in hospitals have little difficulty in procuring quantities of anything from cocaine to heroin" (December 21, 1918). Country boys from Canada and the United States were said to be especially easy prey. According to the *News of the World*, vendors of cocaine-laced cigarettes were regularly seen selling their wares, and their bodies, to soldiers visiting Piccadilly and Leicester Square (December 22, 1918).

The tendency for writers to link drug usage and sex was almost irresistible. The linkage would, no doubt, have been made even without a war going on. But, intended or not, because of the war, women were entering the workforce in record numbers. Production lines needed staffing, and all the available men were already fighting in Europe. For many, the presence of all the liberated women in the workplace was threatening. These same liberated women frequented the West End of London, spent their nights out in clubs, and even had sex with off-duty soldiers. Such behavior would have been irresistible to tabloid writers.

On December 15, 1918, the ever reliable *News of the World*, informed its readers:

> ... there are harpies in the West End and the East End who batten and grow fat by pandering to the cravings of victims of the drug habit, who make enormous sums by selling drugs to them, receiving pounds for shillings-worth; and these modern vampires supply the drugs taken at doping parties which are now a feature of West End life. These orgies are of the most disgusting character.

Public fascination with "disgusting" orgies can always be counted on to sell newspapers, and it probably accounts for the intense media coverage accorded the death of Florence Leonora Stewart, otherwise known as Billie Carleton (Figure 14.1). It also explains why so much attention was devoted to these orgies at the subsequent coroner's inquest. At the time of her death, Carleton was a 22-year-old musical comedy performer, said to have been a rising young star, with, according to newspaper accounts, "thousands" of admirers. Her photograph shows her as a fashionably plump, squared-jawed, young woman of her time, hardly the image of a long-term addict, as was later alleged at the inquest.

Figure 14.1 Billie Carleton (nee Florence Leonora Stewart) (1896–1918), a dancer and singer. André Charlot and Charles B. Cochran, the leading impresarios of musical plays and revues during World War I, both gave her leading roles, Cochran in *Watch Your Step* (1915) and Charlot in *Some* (1916). Carleton died, allegedly of a cocaine overdose, after an all-night party following a Victory Ball at the Royal Albert Hall in November 1918. Her death caused a flurry of press coverage, and the trial of her accused drug supplier caused even more. In many ways, her death drew attention to the problem of cocaine abuse in much the same way as did the death of basketball player Len Bias more than 75 years later. (From the National Portrait Gallery, London. With permission.)

According to the account given at her inquest, on the evening of November 27, 1918, Carleton attended a Victory Ball at the Royal Albert Hall, then returned home and had breakfast with some friends. Her maid found her dead in bed the next day. A coroner's inquest was held, and it was determined that her death was the result of using cocaine. Reggie de Veulle (a friend of indeterminate sex status) was said to have given her the cocaine, and was later charged with manslaughter for having provided it.

A *News of the World* reporter who attended the inquiry recounted testimony that:

> Young women and men have frankly confessed to being drug-takers — the drugs indulged in being cocaine and heroin. So far as it has gone, the inquiry into the death of Billie Carleton has shown that in the West End of London, in the quiet seclusion of luxurious flats, the "most disgusting orgies" take place.

The staid *London Times* (December 21, 1918) was more explicit, and even described one of Carleton's drug-taking episodes. "There were about five or six of them. Miss Carleton arrived later at the flat from the theater, and she, after disrobing, took her place in this circle of degenerates." One witness subpoenaed to appear at the trial of Carleton's supplier was a man named Don Kimfull, who was also thought to be one of Carleton's drug suppliers. Kimfull reemerged some years later as the owner of a bar in Tangier called Dean's Bar. Dean's was a favorite watering hole for actors Errol Flynn, Ava Gardner, and even Ian Fleming, and is said to have been the model for Rick's in *Casablanca*.

Public reaction to Carleton's death mirrors, in many ways, American response to the cocaine-induced death of basketball player Len Bias. Both events made the public finally accept that drug use was occurring on a much broader scale then anyone in society wanted to admit. What differentiates the two events is that the Carleton trial sparked a whole literary genre, and the death of Bias sparked changes in U.S. law.

The most famous of the English writers to capitalize on the drug trade was Arthur Henry Ward, better known as Sax Rohmer (1883–1959), creator of the Fu Manchu mystery series. One of the central elements of the Fu Manchu stories was the existence of a narcotics ring based in Limehouse. (Limehouse is located on the northern bank of the River Thames, opposite Cuckold's Point. The area was notorious for crime and opium dens in the late 19th century, a notion often repeated in pulp fiction works by Sax Rohmer and others.) Rohmer's novel, *Dope: A Story of Chinatown and the Drug Traffic* (1919), basically retold the Billie Carleton story. The cover of the original edition states that it was "based upon actual conditions as they existed in London." Novels by Thomas Burke (1886–1945) took up the same theme. Aleister Crowley (1875–1946), novelist and, some would also say, a sex-crazed deranged magician, wrote a novel in 1922 called *Diary of a Drug Fiend*. The hero, Peter Pendragon, is introduced to heroin and cocaine by his true love, Lou. The story was played out within Mayfair's café society, and, again, some of the settings and incidents almost sounded like testimony at the Carleton inquest.

The British government's response to the perceived drug menace (the less charitable interpretation would be to say the government's response to the barrage of press coverage) was to modify something called the Defense of the Realm Act (DORA). The act was passed just after the beginning of World War I, in 1914. More than anything else, with DORA, the government gained central control over the economy. The government also gained almost unlimited powers to do what was necessary to win the war. Land could be seized from individuals, newspapers could be censored, and people could be arrested without cause. When the act was first promulgated, there was no mention of heroin or cocaine, although DORA required beer manufacturers to water down their products in order to reduce drunkenness and make workers more productive. The original version of DORA did not address the problem of cocaine abuse, mostly because abuse of cocaine was simply not seen as a problem. Two years later, using special powers granted to the government to help fight the war, additional laws (Regulation 40B) were enacted. Unlike earlier laws passed by the British, this regulation mirrored those on the books in the United States, making not just the sale, but also the possession, of drugs illegal.

Nearly a century later, the United States had its own version of the Billie Carleton saga. It centered on a man named Len Bias, a gifted college basketball player. Bias died of a cocaine overdose in 1986, 2 days after being drafted by the Boston Celtics. Here was another young, talented person whose life had been cut short by drug use. Ensuing media reports highlighted the health risks of cocaine, and drugs become a hot political issue. If the Billie Carleton saga inflamed public passions, the Bias story poured kerosene on them. A government response was required, if for no other reason than to appease the press and the ever more worried voters.

The U.S. Congress passed a series of draconian drug laws, and specially earmarked funds were made available to help control the problem. A series of "Len Bias laws" was enacted in the same year. Selling drugs to someone who died of drug use now carries special criminal penalties, and possession of even very small amounts of cocaine leads to long prison sentences.

Under most circumstances, federal law today provides a maximum punishment of 20 years in prison without parole, plus a fine up to $1 million, for persons convicted of simple distribution of cocaine. In addition, the federal Anti-Drug Abuse Act of 1986, passed by the U.S. Congress in response to the Bias death, provides a minimum mandatory sentence of 20 years in prison without parole, and a possible maximum sentence of life without parole, for persons convicted of distributing controlled substances that result in death. Under the terms of this law, which are inflexible, if two teenagers pool their allowances to buy some Ecstasy (or cocaine, or fill in the blank), and one should die, the other would be accountable for his or her friend's death. Such cases are being tried with increasing frequency.

One direct consequence of this approach is that now, with the exceptions of Russia and Rwanda, the United States incarcerates a greater proportion of its population than does any other country. Approximately 2 million Americans now reside in prisons across the United States, and 450,000 of them are there for drug offenses. The number of Americans now incarcerated for drug offenses is greater than the number incarcerated in the European Union (an entity with roughly a third of the population of the United States) for all crimes combined.

Japan's Adventures in the Cocaine Trade

15

How the import of raw material is to be limited without keeping an exact record of these imports transcends one's comprehension, though possibly to the statisticians in Japan it may not be so difficult.

Letter from the British Consul in Formosa to the British Ambassador in Tokyo (1911)

The original Mitsukoshi Department Store in Tokyo was modeled after Selfridge's Department Store in London, except that it was constructed of white bricks, instead of granite. Two bronze lions, similar to those at the base of Admiral Horatio Nelson's pillar in London, guarded its main entrance. The floors were covered with straw matting, and Japanese shoppers were required to remove their shoes before they could enter. Western tourists were issued cloth covers to put over their shoes. The building boasted all the modern conveniences, including central heating, a sprinkler system, and elevators. A roof garden was open from June through September, and a band played daily.

Tourists entering the store probably would not have known that the store was founded by the Mitsui Company, or that Mitsui was, at that time, the largest company in Japan, and quite possibly the world. The average tourist would have been even less likely to know that until the end of World War II, Mitsui generated some of its profits by operating coca plantations and refineries in Taiwan. They certainly would never have guessed that Mitsui subsidiaries were major suppliers of cocaine and opium. They would have been incredulous if they were told that Mitsui held a government-sanctioned franchise for opium sales in occupied China, and that the Japanese government had a financial stake in Mitsui's drug sales.

Nor would the visitor have realized that other Japanese conglomerates, of nearly equal size, were engaged in exactly the same business of selling illegal drugs. Mitsubishi, the second-largest company in Japan, along with Mitsui, shared the lucrative franchise for opium and heroin sales in occupied China. Sumitomo Bank, the third-largest commercial entity in Japan, participated in a war bond offering that was guaranteed by heroin and opium sales. How did these household names get into the drug business? And how did the Japanese government come to be their partner? There is no simple answer.

Nearly every aspect of Japanese government and industry was involved, including the armed forces. The description written by a bemused British embassy officer in 1928 summed up the situation: "That corruption should exist in connection with the drug traffic is not surprising when it is remembered that the standards of right and wrong in this country are frequently very different to what we are taught. Scandals…in connection with drug cases…are associated with all classes, from Prime Ministers downwards."

If drug dealing is viewed simply as a business, then there should be nothing surprising about the fact that, in Japan legitimate business enterprises dominated the narcotic trade. It is somewhat more surprising to learn about the participation of the government and the military. But by the 1920s, the Japanese Army controlled the civilian government, and both needed cash.

At the close of World War II, the Allies, under General Douglas MacArthur, occupied Japan. MacArthur had a large staff of intelligence and counterintelligence officers. But when the decision was finally made to hold War Crimes Trials and to specifically charge Japan with crimes against humanity for its drug sales, there was not enough manpower to do all the investigating. One of MacArthur's aides contacted the head of the U.S. Bureau of Narcotics and asked for help. Only after resolving disputes over pay grades, did Harry Anslinger, then the director, dispatch several of his field agents. The narcotics agents were given temporary army appointments to MacArthur's staff. The magnitude of the drug business unearthed by investigators came as a stunning surprise.

The boundaries between Japanese industry, the Japanese Army, and the Japanese government were often blurred, mainly as a result of events that occurred after Japan opened its doors to the West. Very special relationships came to exist between the Japanese government and the great Japanese trading houses, referred to as the *zaibatsu* ("financial clique"). Japanese commerce, and, to a large extent, Japanese society, were dominated by a handful of giant trading companies. In a very real sense, the *zaibatsu* families dominated Japanese society.

Mitsui has, of course, been out of the illegal drug business since the end of World War II, but it still is the most important of the *zaibatsu* companies, and probably still the largest single business enterprise in the world, with reported gross revenues in 1994 that were in excess of $171 billion. It operates 742 different companies around the world. Slightly more than half of its companies are located within Japan. In modern-day terms, it is difficult to conceive, but at the time of World War II Mitsui actually controlled nearly 25% of all Japanese foreign trade.

Mitsubishi was the second-largest company in Japan. It also made money by selling drugs. Compared to Mitsui, however, the family-held Mitsubishi Company was an upstart company, less than 70 years old when World War II began. Its founder, Yataro Iwasaki, and his successor, Baron Yanosuké Iwasaki, became rich in the steamship business. In 1916, the Mitsubishi Company was divided into ten separate divisions that included trade and banking, as well as mining and shipbuilding. The trading and shipping divisions were both involved in the drug trade.

Mitsubishi's relationship with the government is illustrative, and typical of the way that Japan did business. Mitsubishi owned Japan's largest and most important steamship line, Nippon Yusen Kaisha (NYK). NYK received large Imperial subsidies and used them to operate fast mail and passenger services around the world. During the 1920s, a sizable, though not controlling, number of NYK shares were held by the Imperial family. Members of the NYK Board of Directors served in the government, and government officers served on the NYK Board — a relationship such as is not to be found today. Of course, cronyism still occurs today, but never quite this floridly. Regardless of the criticism raised when reconstruction contracts for the rebuilding of Iraq were awarded to Vice President Dick Cheney's former employer (Halliburton), neither President George W. Bush nor Vice President Cheney would ever be allowed to sit on the Board of the Halliburton company, at least not while still holding office.

As a result of the overlapping directorships, the government always knew what NYK was doing, because, in a real sense, NYK and the government were one and the same. What NYK was doing, besides delivering the mail, was delivering drugs. The relationship between NYK, the state, and the Imperial family was not at all unusual.

Japan entered the drug trade by chance when a unique set of circumstances made it easy to flout international law. International efforts at controlling the illicit drug trade first began in the early 1900s. Beginning in 1912, four separate international treaties on drug abuse had become law, and Japan had signed three of the four (The Hague International Opium Convention of 1912, The Geneva International Opium Convention of 1925, and the Convention for Limiting the Manufacture and Regulating the

Distribution of Narcotic Drugs of 1931). The net effect of the three agreements was to restrict, and in some cases prohibit, the production, distribution, import, and export of commonly abused drugs.

The Convention of 1925 established a Permanent Central Board, responsible for monitoring the production and consumption of illicit drugs. The actual day-to-day monitoring process was carried out by the Opium Committee of the League of Nations. Members from each of the producing countries were appointed to the committee that met once a year in Geneva. The committee's policy formulations were based solely on data submitted to the committee by participating countries. The Opium Committee did not have its own investigative branch. It learned of violations only when they were uncovered by the intelligence services of other committee members. Even when the Opium Committee was advised of a violation, it had no effective means to enforce any of its decisions. It could recommend that the League refuse to issue export permits for drug shipments to offending countries, but such a prospect hardly qualified as an effective deterrent.

The Opium Convention of 1912, which Japan signed on January 23 of that year, provided that participating countries would enact laws controlling drug production, sales, and exports. In order to conform to the convention, the U.S. Congress passed the Harrison Narcotic Act of 1914. The Harrison Act not only restricted the nonmedical use of narcotics, but it also introduced tight production controls and an elaborate tax stamp system. The law also prohibited physicians from prescribing narcotic drugs to treat addiction, a situation that has only recently been partly reversed (since 2003, office-based doctors have been allowed to treat limited numbers of addicts with methadone replacement therapy).

Japanese internal regulations were simpler. Japanese narcotic manufacturers were not licensed, although permission was required annually from the Welfare Minister if they intended to remain in the business of producing drugs. Manufacturers were required to report only the amount of narcotics they produced each year, and the amount of raw material used in the production process. Manufacturers that produced narcotic medications containing less than 0.2% narcotic only had to inform the Ministry about what they were producing. No record keeping or reporting was required. Drug wholesalers did not need to be licensed. The central government did not even keep a record of the wholesalers, let alone track their sales. Retailers operated under the same rules as wholesalers. The only difference was that wholesalers had more capital, could make larger purchases, and could get better prices. Doctors could buy and sell narcotics and were required to register only once, when they first went into practice.

There was one other peculiarity about Japanese law that favored drug dealing. Laws that regulated Japanese possessions, such as Taiwan, applied only to opium. Heroin and cocaine production was not specifically mentioned. Production and sales of other narcotics came under the Home Office Ordinances, not the penal code. For all intents and purposes, regulations applicable to the production and sale of cocaine and heroin were no different than the regulations that applied to the production of sugar or tobacco.

Conviction for opium-related offenses might result in sentences of 10 years of hard labor, but cocaine and heroin dealers could be sentenced to serve no more than a 3-month term. In most cases, Japanese offenders were simply fined, and the fines were not very large. In essence, the market was entirely unregulated. Before placing too cynical an interpretation on Japan's laws or its intentions, it is important to remember that almost until the start of World War II, there were no Japanese drug abusers. Opium smoking was never native to Japan, and strict laws prohibited drug taking of any kind. Japanese lawmakers can hardly be faulted for failing to address a situation that did not exist.

During World War I, legitimate demand for narcotics increased and, in an attempt at becoming self-sufficient, the Japanese government encouraged private manufacturers to enter the field, which they did. By 1918, a handful of large pharmaceutical houses were already producing far more narcotics drugs than could be consumed locally. There were no production cutbacks at the end of World War I, leaving no place for the surpluses except for on the black market. Drugmakers continued importing opium and coca by the ton, processing the raw material into cocaine, heroin, and smoking opium, and legally selling it to a network of drug wholesalers.

The next level of transactions occurred on the world's black markets. More often than not, smugglers did not even bother to repackage drugs from the wholesalers. As a result, the brand names of the Japanese manufacturers, such as Hoshi, Dai Nippon, and Sankyo, were as well known in Calcutta as they were in Tokyo, even though legitimate cocaine exports to India were nil.

Japanese pharmaceutical houses packaged cocaine in 1 g, 5 g, and 700 g containers. Drug smugglers would repackage the smaller containers purchased from physicians and then affix their own brand names, i.e., Fujitsuru. Although no company named Fujitsuru ever existed customs inspectors around the world were all too familiar with the Fujitsuru-branded cocaine.

Drug companies in Tokyo began refining cocaine from leaves grown in Java shortly after the turn of the century. However, cocaine refining did not become a major source of revenue until Japan occupied Taiwan. Even then, it took another 20 years, and the effects of the Great Depression to be realized, before Japan became a major player in the illicit cocaine trade. The global economic downturn was so severe that Taiwan's sugar crop was impossible to sell. Some Taiwanese growers decided to explore other possibilities.

The Home Office Ordinances that governed Taiwan contained no specific provisions relating to coca production or cocaine refining, so in 1916, there was nothing to prevent farmers from experimenting with coca.

In 1916, when the medical community used cocaine, and legitimate profits were to be made in refining and selling pharmaceutical-grade cocaine, Taiwan's Governor General encouraged a plantation owner named Abe Kono-suke to try planting coca. A cocaine refinery was built, and coca seedlings were planted in different areas around the property. According to the British Consul in Taiwan, the cocaine refinery was a crude affair built a few yards away from the site of the original sugar refinery. Konosuke's efforts were not successful. Coca was not native to Taiwan and had never been grown there before; the planters knew a great deal more about growing sugar than coca.

Konosuke lost his business in 1922 and was forced to sell out to the Ensuiko Sugar Company of Formosa. Ensuiko held the monopoly to grow sugarcane and manufacture sugar in the Kagi area, which included the village of Sinei, where Ensuiko's sugar refinery was located. During the early 1900s, Ensuiko was the fourth-largest sugar producer on the island, processing nearly 10 tons of sugar each month. Ensuiko also owned large sugarcane plantations in Java, and regularly shipped large quantities of sugarcane back to Taiwan for refining. When the demand for sugar exports declined, Ensuiko's shares dropped precipitously.

Ensuiko's Chief Director, Tetsu Maki, needed a white knight to help him out of his predicament. A member of Ensuiko's Board of Directors, Norakata Takahashi, thought his father might be interested. Takahashi's father was not just any venture capitalist. He was Japan's Minister of Finance. Takahashi's father invested ¥100,000. A friend of Takahashi's, Matasakau Shiobara, invested an additional ¥150,000. After World War II, U.S. intelligence agents interviewed several sources who claimed Minister Takahashi was acting as a front man for Mitsui's trading division, Mitsui Gomei Kaisha (MGK), the same company that was supplying opium to the government monopoly.

Regardless of the source of the money, the new investors changed the name of the company from Ensuiko to Taiwan Shoyaku. They brought in new technical experts, streamlined operations, planted coca, and reversed Ensuiko's downward slide. Takahashi, as Finance Minister for the country, was certainly in a position to steer military and government purchases toward his son's company, although no evidence for that practice was produced. By the fall of 1936, shares of Taiwan Shoyaku were trading at pre-Depression levels. How much Taiwan Shoyaku's performance was bolstered by the Taka-hashi connection is difficult to say, but Matasakau Shiobara's connections probably contributed to the success of the restructured company as much as did Takahashi's connections.

Shiobara was the managing director of the Sankyo Company Limited of Tokyo. Sankyo was one of only five companies in Japan licensed to process coca and produce cocaine from leaf, regardless of where the leaf was raised: Taiwan, Okinawa, Java, or imported from South America. Sankyo also happened to be the largest pharmaceutical company in Japan. Sankyo maintained a wholesale branch office in Formosa, with gross sales of more than ¥1 million per year (roughly $1 million U.S.).

Shiobara started Sankyo in 1899 to import and sell a digestive aid invented by an expatriate pharmacist, Jokichi Takamine. Takamine was an interesting man. He owned a private research laboratory in New York City and had done contract work for Parke, Davis & Company. Along with Merck of Darmstadt, Parke, Davis & Company was one of the world's major cocaine producers. Takamine was a skilled chemist and had worked for Parke, Davis & Company, supervising the introduction of large-scale adrenalin production at their factory in Michigan, the same factory where Parke-Davis manufactured cocaine. Takamine would certainly have been familiar with the chemistry of cocaine extraction, and he would have taken that knowledge with him when he returned to Japan to become president of Sankyo.

According to the terms of a contract signed with Taiwan Shoyaku in 1928, the Sankyo factory in Tokyo was to be supplied with 22 kg per month of purified cocaine. Taiwan Shoyaku had other legitimate customers besides Sankyo, and its sales amounted to nearly 500 kg per month. Most of the semirefined cocaine went to drug companies in Japan, including Koto Pharmaceutical, Takeda Pharmaceutical Industries, Sankyo Company, The Shinonogi Pharmaceutical Company Limited of Osaka, and the Hoshi Pharmaceutical Company in Tokyo. During one 6-month period in 1928, shipments of purified cocaine to these companies alone amounted to nearly a ton.

Takamine's personal history was not all that different from Hoshi Hajime, the founder of Hoshi Pharmaceuticals. After graduating from law school in Tokyo, he traveled to New York, earned a Masters Degree from Columbia University, and started the first Japanese-language newspaper in New York (*The Japanese-American Commercial Weekly*), before returning to Japan. In 1906, he started a patent medicine company and quickly saw the commercial potential of the emerging narcotics industry. His advertising slogan was "Drugs are Hoshi."

In 1918, Hoshi Pharmaceutical, with approval of both the Japanese Home Ministry and the Ministry of Welfare and Social Affairs in Peru, purchased a 500 acre coca plantation in Peru. At almost the same time, Hoshi began growing coca leaf in the Kagi district of Taiwan Formosa. The initial plantation covered 242 acres. By 1944, Hoshi had 392 (some documents put the number at 392, others as 292) acres under cultivation in Taiwan. Coca grown in Taiwan had three important advantages over the South American variety: shipping costs were much less; it was easier to get import permits, because the Tokyo Foreign Office did everything in its power to convince Japanese manufacturers to buy Japanese; and Taiwan was a Japanese colony. But, perhaps the most important reason for using Taiwanese coca was that more cocaine could ultimately be extracted from it than from leaf grown in South America. By the mid-1920s, Hoshi's Taiwan plantation was officially producing 20 to 25 tons of coca leaf each year, but the real number was almost certainly twice as great.

The large Tokyo refiners were not, of course, totally reliant on supplies coming from Taiwan. They continued to import coca leaf from Indonesia and South America. They also began to establish their own coca plantations on the islands of Iwo Jima and Okinawa. By 1929, the plantations located in Japanese colonies were producing sufficient quantities of leaf so that Japan was able to stop issuing import licenses. The Dutch coca growers in Java were then cut out of the Japanese market. They loudly objected, but to little avail.

Once the refined cocaine reached Tokyo, Japanese law made disposing of the cocaine an easy matter. Over and above wholesale exchanges with black marketers, large quantities of cocaine and heroin, far beyond any conceivable medical needs, were sold to the Japanese armed forces. Onishi Takamatsu, an auditor with Sankyo until 1923, reported that when he was appointed director of Taiwan Shoyaku's Tokyo branch, he arranged sales of semirefined cocaine to the Japanese Army and Navy. Sankyo, he said, acted as an intermediate. In 1938, Sankyo purchased 739 kg of cocaine from Taiwan Shoyaku for direct sale to the Japanese Army. From 1940 to 1942, smaller quantities were brokered through other companies for delivery to the Japanese Navy.

At one point, the colonial government of Taiwan took over partial control of Taiwan Shoyaku's factory and even supplied special labels for the cocaine packages. During the early 1930s, customs agents in China and India regularly seized packets of cocaine marked with the label "Taiwan Governor General, Central Laboratory." The Indian government loudly complained about these irregularities to the Opium Committee at the League of Nations, specifically mentioning the "Taiwan Governor General Brand" by name. But the complaints led nowhere, and for several years "Taiwan General" cocaine almost completely replaced the Tokyo-produced "Fujitsuru" as the most popular illegal brand of cocaine in India.

The high alkaloid content of Java leaf, combined with the fact that four crops could be harvested every year, made Southeast Asian coca leaf a very desirable product. Processing the type of coca grown in Asia was tedious, but doable, and the method was no great secret. Takamine would certainly have been familiar with the process and probably helped establish the cocaine production facility at Ensuiko. Officials at Ensuiko's cocaine refinery admitted to the British consul that the yield from their crops could be as high as 1%.

(At the time, the content of leaves grown in South America was often less than 0.6%.)

Japan was required, under international treaty, to file annual reports on cocaine and narcotic production with the League of Nations. Officials at the League of Nations were apparently unaware of the differences between Southeast Asian and South American coca, and Japan was able to get away with understating its production. Between Taiwan Shoyaku and Hoshi, there were at least 684 acres under cultivation.

The average yield for prewar South American coca was generally approximated as 0.6 tons of leaf per acre per harvest, with only three harvests per year. An area of 684 acres devoted to coca production in the Andes would be expected to yield 1231 tons of leaves per year (684 acres × 0.6 tons per acre × 3 crops per year = 1231 tons), which would give a total yield of refined cocaine of approximately 6 tons (1231 × 0.5% = 6.15). The yields of today's hybrid plants are much higher.

Yet, official Japanese statistics for 1927 show total Taiwanese coca leaf production of only 204,640 kg (230 tons). That number is hardly credible, given that coca grown in Taiwan was presumably the same strain as that grown in Java, and Javanese coca was harvested four times a year. Coca leaf production in Taiwan should have been at least 25% greater than that for an equivalent area in the Andes — instead, it was reported as two thirds less. And the coca leaf that was produced in Taiwan contained twice as much cocaine as leaf grown in the Andes.

A general, and very rough, rule of thumb is that 400 lb of South American leaf will yield 1 kg of cocaine. For Southeast Asian cocaine, the number would have been closer to 200 lb. Thus, 230 tons of coca leaf grown in Taiwan should have yielded at least 2.6 tons of cocaine, even if there were only three harvests per year. A realistic estimate for Taiwanese coca production, based on production experience from Java, would be 1500 tons of leaf per year from 684 acres; that amount of Southeast Asian leaf should have yielded nearly 7 tons of purified cocaine. Whatever the real figures were, they amounted to a great deal more than could ever be accounted for by legitimate medical use. The Health Committee of the League of Nations estimated that in countries possessing sophisticated medical care systems, the average annual cocaine requirement was 7 mg per person.

As testimony given at the Tokyo War Crimes Trials subsequently revealed, Japanese bureaucrats routinely "cooked the books," adjusting production figures for opium and heroin production to agree with the permissible values set by the League of Nations. In the case of cocaine, a somewhat different approach was used. The Japanese imported coca leaf and crude cocaine not just from Taiwan, but also from coca plantations on Iwo Jima, Okinawa, and Java. During the 1920s, imports from Java averaged more than a million

Figure 15.1 Label from a 700-g container of Cocaine Hoshi Pharmaceutical. This label was used as an exhibit at the Tokyo War Crimes Trials held at the end of World War II. Japan was convicted of crimes against humanity. Among the reasons for conviction cited were black market drug sales. (From the National Archives, RG 170, Records of the DEA, Acc #71-A-3554, cartons #10–30.)

Figure 15.2 Baron Korekiyo Takahashi (1854–1936). Takahashi served as Japan's Minister of Finance during the worst years of the Great Depression and did much to speed Japan's recovery. His son, Norakata Takahashi, was on the board of Taiwan Shoyaku K.K. (The Botanical Drug Company of Formosa, which was, in fact, a large cocaine refinery.) While still Minister of Finance, Baron Takahashi invested 100,000 yen in the Taiwan cocaine factory. After World War II, U.S. intelligence agents interviewed several sources who claimed that the Minister was acting as a front man for Mitsui's trading division, Mitsui Gomei Kaisha (MGK), the same company that was supplying opium to the government opium monopoly. Right- wing extremists assassinated the Baron in 1936. This photograph appeared in a 1919 yearbook on Japanese economic development (From W. Feldwick, ed., Present day impressions of Japan, *Globe Encyclopedia*, London. With permission.)

pounds a year. The Ministry of Finance in Tokyo managed to hide all of these imports by lumping coca leaves together with other raw materials used to manufacture drugs.

When Japan's representative to the League of Nations Opium Committee stated that "The new policy of the Japanese Government would consist in reducing the output of cocaine," and that this reduction had been accomplished by "limiting the import of raw material," his claims were greeted with some skepticism. When asked by the Foreign Office for his opinion on Japan's statements, G.P. Patton, the British Consul in Taiwan, wrote "How the import of raw material is to be limited without keeping an exact record of these imports transcends one's comprehension, though possibly to the statisticians in Japan it may not be so difficult."

In 1935, Hoshi sold off its plantation in Peru, relying entirely on its Taiwan plant for raw materials. In 1944, because of the U.S. Naval blockade, Hoshi was no longer able to get coca leaf from Taiwan to Tokyo and had to

Figure 15.3   Dr. Jocichi Takamine. Takamine was recruited by Matasaku Shiobara, Managing Director of Sankyo Pharmaceutical, Japan's most important cocaine manufacturer, to be Chairmain of the Board. A trained analytical chemist, Takamine traveled to the United States in 1890 and set up his own research laboratory. In 1901, Takamine and a British scientist named Thomas Aldrich, both working independently, managed to purify and isolate a hormone that Takamine called adrenaline. When Parke, Davis & Company decided to mass produce adrenaline, they hired Takamine to supervise production. Because Parke, Davis & Company was also the largest American manufacturer of cocaine, Takamine would certainly have had ample opportunity to observe the process. This knowledge would have served him well when he took over at Sankyo.

cease production. During the 1930s, Hoshi sold the residue of its leaves, which contained large amounts of nitrogen, to farmers for fertilizer. That practice was discontinued after 10 years, because the project was not profitable enough. The extracted leaf was then used as fuel. Compared to today's clandestine cocaine manufacturers, Hoshi, at least, did its part for the environment, even if its motives were only for profit.

As the years went on, and the start of World War II approached, Japan's presentations to the League of Nations became ever more fanciful. Member countries were required to file yearly reports, detailing each country's production and sales of narcotic drugs. In 1930, Japan reported that it manufactured 320 kg of cocaine in the preceding year, claiming that only 28 kg was produced in Taiwan. Documents discovered after the war show that Taiwan's cocaine refineries were producing more than that amount each day. Of course, the other members of the Opium Committee had a fairly good idea of what was going on in Taiwan. Criticism of Japan became even more intense until Japan's representative to the League, Yosuke Matsuoka, led Japan out of the League of Nations in 1933. Surprisingly, Japanese representatives continued to attend Opium Committee meetings for another 6 years, finally dropping all pretense of cooperation, and leaving the Committee, in 1939.

The following points have been agreed upon between **Taiwan Shoyaku K.K.** (Botanical Drugs Co. in Formosa, Ltd.) (to be shortened hereinafter 'Koh') and Koto Pharmaceutical Co., Ltd., **Ch. Takeda & Co.**, Ltd., Sankyo Pharmaceutical Co., Ltd., **Shionogi Shoten,** Ltd. (shortened 'Otsu' for all the companies put together)

1. 'Koh' shall supply 'Otsu' with crude cocaine base as materials for medicine manufacture.
2. The amount for supply shall be seven hundred and fifty kilogrammes (750 kg.) and 1 per cent addition shall be made to cover the possible loss in weight.
3. Delivery shall be made in parts as per the annexed table.
4. Delivery shall be effected at each factory of 'Otsu'.
5. Price shall be fixed at ¥6.785 per 1 kilogramme of 1 per cent **refined** cocaine base.
6. **Payment shall** be made by 'Otsu' to Sankyo Pharmaceutical Co., **Ltd.**, the agent of 'Koh', as temporary payment within ten days after receipt of the goods; and full settlement shall be made within thirty days following the last delivery.

In witness of the above agreement, five copies of this shall be issued to be kept by each contracting party.

Signed by:

Korekata Takahashi
Director, President
Taiwan Shoyaku K.K.

Kenkichi Kamegawa
Executive Director
Koto Pharmaceutical Co., Ltd.

Yoshizo Takeda
Managing Director
Ch. Takeda & Co., Ltd.

Matasaku Shiobara
Managing Director
Sankyo Pharmaceutical Co., Ltd.

Gisaburo Shiono
Director
Shionogi Shoten, Ltd.

Particulars of Delivery

Month	Koto Phar. Co.	Ch. Takeda & Co.	Sankyo Phar. Co.	Shionogi	Sub-total
	kilo	kilo	kilo	kilo	kilo
July	79.333	45.787	32.413	12.467	170
August	79.334	45.787	32.413	12.467	170
September	56.000	32.320	22.880	8.800	120
October	56.000	32.320	22.880	8.800	120
November	56.000	32.320	22.880	8.800	120
December	23.333	13.466	9.534	3.667	50
Total	350.000	202.000	143.000	55.000	750

Figure 15.4 Official production reports that Japan filed with the League of Nations listed only small amounts of cocaine. Actually, very large quantities were being produced by Japan, operating in Taiwan. U.S. Army field investigators at the end of World War II discovered the contract shown here. The contract calls for the delivery of roughly 750 kg (roughly 1700 lb) over a 6-month period. A copy of the official translation was found in the old records of the U.S. Bureau of Narcotics (the predecessor of the DEA), and can be seen at the National Archives, RG 170, Records of the DEA, Acc #71- A3554, cartons #10 to 30).

In fact, so much surplus cocaine was accumulating in Taiwan that a special meeting was held at the Foreign Office in Tokyo to decide what to do with the surplus of 2500 kg that was sitting in storage. But, at the same time, Japan's reports to the League of Nation's Opium Committee put total cocaine exports at less than 10 kg per year. With so much cocaine to sell, and so little legitimate demand, sale on the black market was inevitable.

Moving so much cocaine eventually required the active participation of Japan's Army, Navy, and Foreign Office, which used the revenues generated to help pay the expense of occupying China. But their actions did not go unnoticed. Allied judges at the War Crimes Tribunal, held in Tokyo after the war, found two high-ranking government officials (Naoki Hoshino, Okinori Kaya) and one General (Teiichi Suziki) guilty, thus according the men the rare and dubious honor of being the first drug dealers ever tried and found guilty of crimes against humanity.

Cocaine Pandemic? 16

At the end of World War II there was a brief respite, but cocaine returned again in the 1980s. There is an interesting theory as to why the revival of interest occurred. Professor David Musto, of Yale University, suggested that cycles of drug abuse begin when a generation of young people no longer remembers the adverse consequences experienced by the preceding generation. Cycles end when drug users realize that other drug users they know are becoming ill. As their awareness increases, experimentation falls off, and the cycle eventually ends.

Current drug users tend to recruit new ones, so in this respect, Musto's theory treats cocaine addiction in the same way as any contagious disease is treated; victims may be affected either mildly or severely, or they may even die. Those experimenting with drugs, the "light users," will suffer few adverse consequences from their "disease" but are those most likely to recruit new users, and spread the disease to others. "Heavy users" will suffer extreme ill effects, even death, and so are unlikely to recruit any new users. Someone who dies of an acute overdose the first time they use a drug is not going to infect many others or create new recruits. If this model is correct, then the memories of those who had bad experiences with a drug will be balanced against the memories of those who did not. When there are more light users who did not have bad experiences, then the use of drugs will increase, always supposing, of course, that the drug supply is elastic — as demand increases, so does supply. But this has not always been the case.

The model seems to fit very well. By the 1920s, the initial enthusiasm for cocaine had waned, partly because of efforts by the United States to prohibit drug use and also partly because nearly everyone knew someone who had been damaged by cocaine. Although there was a great deal of cocaine available at reasonable prices, no one wanted to take it. The downside appeared to be too great. Cocaine had gone from a wonder drug to a scourge. Apart from a few show business celebrities, those who took cocaine were thought of as deviant losers. During the interwar years, another antidrug element was added — availability decreased, and prices increased. Not only did many people become ill taking the drug, it was now also expensive. The high prices and known bad effects were powerful disincentives to users. Cocaine remained available, but in the interwar years, it was an expensive indulgence and not a drug for the masses. In 1934, Cole Porter wrote about sniffing cocaine in his play *Anything Goes*; the song was by an aristocrat wearing top hat and tails. Workpeople and college students were not experimenting with cocaine. During the 1940s and 1950s, availability declined even further.

By the early 1960s, the only real problem drug was alcohol (or marijuana, if you accept the "reefer madness" of Harry Anslinger and the Bureau of Narcotics and Dangerous Drugs). World War II disrupted the traditional trade routes for heroin and cocaine, and it took years before availability returned to prewar levels. Cocaine remained an expensive indulgence — the drug of choice for the superrich. Miles Davis wrote in his autobiography that in 1972, when he was earning more than half a million dollars a year, most of the money was spent on cocaine. Prices were so high that no new users could be infected, and no new epidemic could take hold. Like polio outbreaks in Africa, only sporadic cases occurred. Spread of the disease was not possible, because there were not enough people infected.

Not only were no new users recruited, the old users, who could remember bad experiences, were dying off, or at least not using the drug anymore. An unfortunate set of circumstances led to the launch of a new pandemic. It was initiated partly by public figures like Miles Davis and other famous musicians, aided by the media and "gonzo" journalists who went out of their way to publicize drug use among the rich and famous, and abetted by misguided individuals within our own government.

By the time President Jimmy Carter took office in 1977, memories of the 1920s were obliterated by the passage of time. If this analysis does not sound credible (too simplistic), recall the comments of Peter Bourne, President Carter's Special Assistant for Health Issues. In an interview given in 1974 Bourne spoke as if the past never occurred, and he was probably telling what he thought was the truth when he said:

> ... at least as strong a case could probably be made of legalizing [cocaine] as for legalizing marijuana. Short acting — about 15 minutes — not physically addicting, and acutely pleasurable, cocaine has found increasing favor at all socioeconomic levels in the last year.

All but the barest outlines of the past were forgotten. The first half of Musto's model was in place. The only thing lacking was an expanded drug supply, and expand it did. Three factors drove the supply expansion: (1) the

Figure 16.1 Scorpion branded shipment of refined cocaine. Although this shipment amounts to only a few hundred pounds, multiton seizures have now become the norm. (From the Web site of the U.S. Drug Enforcement Administration, www.usdog.gov/dea/photo- library.html cocaine [accessed 6/18/05] With permission.]

application of new and efficient distribution practices; (2) breakthrough technology that reduced price and increased availability; and (3) loss of institutional memory by government leaders.

In the mid-1970s, Medellín cartel sales amounted to, at most, 40 kg of cocaine a week. By the end of the 1970s, the amount had grown to several hundred kilograms, and by the early 1980s, when crack made its debut, output was measured in tons per week. By the start of the 1990s, Boeing 727s, containing 5 to 7 tons of cocaine, made weekly trips across Mexico on their way to the United States. There was such a glut of cocaine available in the early 1980s that prices began to fall sometime in the early 1980s. In Medellín, in 1982, 1 kg of pure cocaine sold for $20,000, but by early 1984, the wholesale delivery price dropped to only $4000 per kilogram. Multi-ton cocaine seizures are now the rule, not the exception. In one week in June of 2004, two separate Caribbean seizures yielded 10 tons of cocaine.

Where did all the cocaine come from? South America. During the first pandemic, from the mid-1880s until the beginning of World War I, Peru was the world's cocaine supplier. Cocaine was a legitimate product, and coca production was a perfectly acceptable way to develop the local economy, especially as demand from Peru's neighbor to the north, the United States, was both strong and government sanctioned (though no longer government sanctioned, demand for cocaine imports continued to increase). Demand from European drug houses, such as Merck, was equally strong. Coca was a very good export. By the early 1900s, Huánuco emerged as the capital of Peru's cocaine trade. It remains an important, albeit illegal, growing center. Unfortunately for the Peruvians, coca lost its legitimacy almost as quickly as it was acquired. The Hague Convention of 1911, antidrug legislation in the United States, and a simple shift in people's perceptions combined to put an end to the industry. The Peruvian industry dried up.

The demise of the Peruvian industry did nothing to diminish supplies in the Far East. As the Peruvian industry contracted, the Southeast Asian industry expanded. The only difference was that output from the Javanese and Taiwanese plantations went directly to Japanese pharmaceutical houses, which then sold their product on the Indian and Chinese black markets. Only an occasional odd packet made its way to the United States, usually in the trunk of a merchant seaman returning from the Far East. Even the Asian connections were disrupted by the beginning of World War I. From the end of the war until the early 1970s, only insignificant amounts (seizures were then measured in ounces, not tons) of cocaine made their way to Europe or the United States.

When the coca business in the Huallaga valley died out, it caused great hardship for the indigenous peoples living there. The United States, in return for Peruvian support in its antidrug campaign, sent Peru development funds. The money went to building roads in the jungle and to encouraging a shift from planting coca to planting coffee and tea. With U.S. sponsorship, the Tingo Maria Tropical Agricultural Station was established in 1943, on a large tract of land that was originally owned by Japanese coca growers. For a time, the efforts appeared to be successful. Many landless peasants migrated there. But the project was underfunded from the beginning, and undersupported by a Peruvian central government that remained perpetually in turmoil for more than 20 years.

Ultimately, development efforts failed, but not before thousands of people resettled around the Tingo Maria estate, only to find themselves again deprived of any viable source of income, and the result was predictable. The people of Huallaga went back to growing coca, the one product they were sure they could sell. When the rock stars and journalists started to experiment with drugs in the 1970s, and demand for cocaine slowly reemerged, growers were there to meet the demand. At first, coca leaves were smuggled from Peru to Bolivia for refining and transshipment to the United States. But, Colombia was even more poorly governed and more prone to civil strife than Peru, and it quickly emerged as the refining and shipping center of choice. Entrepreneurs in Medellín had a long tradition of smuggling marijuana into the United States, and cocaine is much easier to transport than marijuana.

Medellín's transition from marijuana way station, to cocaine capital, began with the efforts of Fabio Ochoa Restrepo, who first established the Caribbean as Medellín's forward base and major transshipment depot. Fabio Ochoa's private Caribbean ranch contained not only indulgences like a zoo and bullring — it also boasted a private airport. Pablo Escobar, who rose from street thief to international most-wanted status, had a vision that was more far-reaching than Fabio Ochoa's. Like Angelo Mariani, Escobar created a completely new business model: the first vertically integrated cocaine conglomerate. Were it not for his trade, he would certainly have been honored by many major business schools.

Escobar's agents bought leaves directly from farmers, shipped them directly to Escobar's own laboratories for refining, and placed the finished product in planes and boats for delivery to contracting gangs in the United States. In order to expedite shipping (and minimize risk), Escobar built his own airstrip in the Bahamas. Escobar bought off government officials and executed those who would not cooperate with him. Escobar's way of keeping subordinates and his associates under control was known as "*plata o plomo*" (silver or lead): you took his money or you died. He was the prime suspect in the killing of three presidential candidates in Colombia, including one aboard an Avianca jet in 1989.

Escobar also built hospitals and housing for the poor, which put him in good graces with the local bishop, Dario Castillón of Pereira. It is possible, though unlikely, that the Bishop actually believed what he was saying when he argued that the Church had done nothing wrong in taking the money, because it kept Escobar from investing in brothels. Escobar's drug network, El Cartel de Medellín, eventually controlled a huge portion of South American cocaine production and, by extension, the U.S. cocaine supply. In 1993, at the age of 44, Escobar was killed by Colombian police, allegedly as he and his bodyguards tried to escape by climbing to the rooftop of the safe house where they were hiding.

His death mattered very little. The Medellín Cartel was involved in a deadly drug war with Colombia's other main drug cartel, Cartel de Cali. Allies during the later 1970s and early 1980s, at the time of Escobar's death, the two cartels were at each other's throats. With the death of Escobar in 1993, the Cali group came to dominate the market. Their market dominance was, however, short lived. By 1996, most of the important Cali Cartel members had either been killed or were in jail.

The "geopolitics" of coca cultivation and cocaine production continue to evolve. Colombia eclipsed the other Andean cocaine producers and now accounts for more than 80% of the world's supply of finished cocaine and 90%

of the refined cocaine reaching the United States. This is a substantial change. As recently as 1995, Colombia was dependent on Peruvian and Bolivian suppliers of coca leaf, and Colombia accounted for only 25% of the world's total. Net coca cultivation in Colombia more than tripled since the dissolution of the old Cali Cartel, increasing from 50,000 hectares in 1995 to 169,800 hectares in 2001.

In 2000, the magnitude of these increases led the United States to formulate Plan Colombia, originally priced at US$1.3 billion. Plan Colombia was an aid package designed to help the Colombian government eradicate coca, largely by aerial spraying of pesticides on the growing coca crops, but also by supplying manpower to fight rebel insurgencies, especially the Revolutionary Armed Forces of Colombia, better known as the FARC. The program has not been without some success.

According to a report released by the United Nations in June 2004, coca cultivation decreased by 30% from 1999 to 2003. In 2003, Colombia produced 86,000 hectares of coca, a decrease of 16% compared to 2002, the third consecutive annual decrease since 2000. In Peru, the total numbers in 2003 were estimated at 44,200 hectares, a 5.4% decline from the previous year. But in Peru, there were worrisome signs that farmers were making up for the decline in acreage by hybridizing the plants to increase per-acre yield.

In 2003, coca was a problem in two separate regions in Bolivia, with a total of 23,600 hectares of coca under cultivation, sufficient leaf to produce at least 60 metric tons of cocaine. According to past intelligence estimates, the total area under coca cultivation in the Andean region declined by 11% in 2003 compared to 2002, an impressive decline of 30% since 2000.

The worrisome signs have now proven correct. On June 14, 2005, the United Nations Office on Drugs and Crime (UNDOC) released its annual report on cocaine production. The U.N. estimates that South America's cocaine output rose 2% last year, reversing 5 years of declines in Peru and Bolivia, and more than compensating for decreases in Colombian cultivation. From 2003 to 2004, cocaine production rose 35% in Bolivia and 23% in Peru, but fell only 11% in Colombia.

While defoliation efforts decreased Colombian acreage under production, Peruvian production rose. In a replay of events that occurred in Tingo Maria in the early 1940s, the United States has been supplying funds to help grow alternative crops and to build new roads and bridges so that those crops can be brought to market. As in the 1940s, the impoverished farmers find they can make more money by growing coca. The new bridges and roads make it easier to get their coca to market. Large-scale coca cultivation is also now occurring in Ecuador for the first time. As the Second Spanish Viceroy discovered, nearly 500 years ago, replacing coca with food crops is a good idea, but a hard one to implement. Any successful program requires continued effort and a continued infusion of cash. Otherwise, the situation will only get worse. The Tingo Maria disaster is repeating itself.

Events mirroring the Tingo Maria experience of the 1940s are also occurring now in Bolivia. The United States has also been supplying funds to the Bolivian government under a program called Plan Dignity. The goal is to eradicate coca growing almost entirely. From 1998 to 2002, the U.S. government budgeted nearly a billion dollars for the project. The funds were to be spent on eradication in the Chapare region (about $180 million), with the balance going toward the introduction of alternate crops. Unfortunately, most of the development funds never arrived, and in October 2003, the indigenous peoples rebelled, though not so much over the sorry plight of the coca growers, but because of violent objections to the development of natural gas reserves that are to be shipped to the United States via a Chilean port. Production increases reported by the U.N. document the failure of this effort.

The one factor Professor Musto's model does not account for is the technology of drug abuse — the invention of crack. Crack changes the course of drug abuse in much the same way that the invention of the hypodermic syringe, during the Civil War, changed the course of medicine and addiction. Smoking crack makes it possible to get more cocaine into the bloodstream (and to the brain), more quickly. The introduction of crack was an important turning point in the history of cocaine, not so much because cocaine had become more addictive than the sort of cocaine snorted and smoked by movie stars of the 1970s and early 1980s, but because, on a unit dose basis, crack is so affordable. Affordability assures wide use and greater exposure, thereby reinitiating the disease cycle.

It is not clear who deserves credit for this innovation. Conspiracy theorists maintain that crack was invented and introduced by the U.S. Central Intelligence Agency (CIA). While there can be no doubt that some CIA agents were, in fact, deeply involved with Central American *narcotraficantes* operating in Los Angeles, allegations of a plot give the CIA both too much and too little credit. These allegations also ignore a good deal that is known about the history of cocaine, including the fact that freebase cocaine, or something very much like it, was, as we saw in Chapter 7, first discovered in the late 19th century by Henry H. Rusby. His same technique is still used by clandestine drug laboratories today.

During the early 1980s, teenagers in Brazil and Bolivia began smoking a mixture of marijuana and semirefined cocaine, eventually just leaving the marijuana out of the mix. Smoked in this way, semirefined cocaine is, for all intents and purposes, the same thing as crack. The practice slowly began moving northwards, and this may explain its arrival in the United States in the mid-1980s. However, it would not account for the arrival of crack on the East Coast, and in the Caribbean, at almost the same time.

The Bahamas have always been an important transshipment point for cocaine on its way to the United States, and cocaine was available there from the early 1970s, though only among the very rich. Levels of consumption were sufficiently low that use of the drug was not considered a real public health problem. But something happened in 1984. The Sandilands Rehabilitation Hospital, in Nassau, on New Providence, where most of the Bahamians live, reported that while it had no cocaine-related admissions in 1982, admissions climbed to 69 in 1983 and 523 in 1984, and almost all these patients were smoking crack. Visitors and migrants from the Caribbean took their newly acquired habits with them when they arrived in New York and Miami.

Thus, by the mid-1980s, all of the three elements required for a new cocaine pandemic were in place: (1) few people, if any, could remember ever knowing someone who had a bad experience with cocaine; (2) cocaine was readily available, abundant, and cheap; and (3) governments had forgotten that the traditional approaches to drug control had all been tested and been found wanting.

Proposed solutions to the cocaine problem generally consist of four elements: (1) aggressive local policing with crop eradication, (2) crop substitution, (3) international cooperation, and (4) establishment of tighter border controls. The rationale for these proposals appears to be that once the total output of coca leaf is decreased, there will be less cocaine produced, and interdiction of the remainder will be more feasible. This line of thinking equates solving the cocaine problem with solving the coca cultivation problem.

The Second Marqués de Cañete, the Spanish viceroy in Peru from 1555 to 1560, was the first to pass laws requiring crop substitution. His attempts at limiting coca production were as ineffectual then, as they appear to be now. Current leaders might be forgiven for not knowing about the Marqués de Cañete, but it is hard to excuse their fixation on controlling coca production in South America, when, at one time, more coca leaf was exported from Indonesia than from Peru. It could happen again.

Coca leaf was grown commercially in Nigeria, Sri Lanka, Malaysia, Indonesia, Taiwan, and Iwo Jima. If, as it seems, no one knows that the Southeast Asian cocaine industry ever existed, then it is even less likely anyone would know that the varieties of coca grown in Taiwan and Java contained more than twice as much cocaine as the varieties grown in the Andes. If planners did know, they might wonder whether, given sufficient financial incentive, these areas could again become coca producers. Indonesia, after all, has nearly 14,000 islands spread over 3200 miles. A prohibition on coca growing would be impossible to enforce, even if there was a will to do so.

The cocaine problem in the United States appears to be improving. Fewer people are experimenting with the drug. Application of Musto's disease model suggests that things will continue to get better. But there is always a delicate equilibrium. What if the supply was to surge again, and cocaine prices were to drop precipitously? Would that not initiate a new pandemic? Almost certainly it would. Optimists might point to the significant reductions achieved by Plan Colombia. Pessimists might wonder how long it will be until cocaine producers move to another weak state on another continent. Will the United States also have to defoliate Indonesia or Nigeria? This may happen, but only if we refuse to learn from past experience.

Afterword

In 1910, Sir Edward Grey, the British Foreign Minister, wrote to the American Ambassador in London, warning that the "spread of morphia and the cocaine habit, is becoming an evil more serious and more deadly than opium smoking, and this evil is certain to increase." Grey's warning was certainly prophetic, though it is unlikely that even Grey could have conceived just how bad the situation would become.

In 1930, the total population of Europe was less than 360 million, with only 122 million living in Northern and Western Europe, areas where cocaine was widely used. At the same time, 135 million people were living in North America, and another 75 million were living in South America. The population of Southeast Asia was approximately the same as that of Europe. Thus, the total number of people who could have potentially used cocaine during these years was less than 500 million.

League of Nations experts estimated that during the years 1934 to 1937, the average total world cocaine production amounted to less than 5 tons per year. Allowing for Japanese clandestine production, the total output could not have been more than 10 tons a year for 500 million potential users, amounting to roughly 20 mg per year for every man, woman, and child in Western Europe, the Americas, and Southeast Asia. That figure agrees surprisingly well with estimates from the League of Nations. The League maintained that legitimate medical cocaine use amounted to 7 mg per year.

The situation has changed drastically since the end of World War II. The cocaine content of the South American coca leaf has increased substantially. Leaves grown in Bolivia now contain, on average, nearly three-quarters of a percent of cocaine. Given current refining techniques, half of the cocaine contained in the leaves can eventually be converted to cocaine. These advances, particularly in the plants hybridizing process, explain why the U.S. government's Plan Colombia has proved to be such a dismal failure. Leaves grown today in South America contain nearly as much cocaine as did the old leaves from Java.

The total amount of cocaine produced today is not known with any certainty. In the 1920s, the League of Nations could make reasonably accurate production estimates. The process was simple, because all production was legal and in the open. There was no clandestine industry. Today, virtually all cocaine production is clandestine, and production estimates are a matter of guesswork. Several variables, each very difficult to quantitate, are involved. Infrared satellite mapping can be used to estimate the number of acres under cultivation, but yield per acre is another matter. Yield depends on the strain and age of the plants, the rainfall, and the cocaine content of the leaves. All of these factors vary from region to region and can only be established by direct inspection, on the ground. The chemical process used to extract the cocaine is also important, but unpredictable. The percentage of cocaine finally extracted depends on the skill of the chemists and the availability of appropriate chemicals. The only way to assess any of these variables is by inspecting the laboratories, or at least inspecting samples taken directly from the laboratories.

The U.S. Drug Enforcement Administration (DEA) production estimates for Bolivia, which were based on direct observations and measurements, illustrate how widely divergent these figures may be. For example, the average annual yield in the Chapare region of Bolivia is 2.7 tons of leaves per hectare, while the yield in Yungas, the other prime Bolivian growing area, is only 1.8 tons. If the figures from Chapare were used as a basis for estimating total South American production, values would be overstated by at least one third. If the Yungas yield was used as the standard, the opposite would be true. Then, of course, there is the inherent bias of the estimators. A number of authors have noted that because U.S. foreign aid to coca-producing countries is often keyed to production levels, U.S. government officials tend to underestimate coca production, while Bolivian officials tend to overestimate it.

More than 48 tons of cocaine was confiscated in Colombia in 2003, compared with just 8 tons in 1999. The area of land devoted to cocaine cultivation fell to 280,000 acres in 2003, down from 420,000 acres in 2001, nearly a 33% drop. And, yet, street prices are stable, and cocaine is as easy to get as ever. To avoid having their crops sprayed with pesticides, coca farmers have begun sowing in environmentally sensitive national parks, where aircraft are prohibited from fumigating. They cover their plants with protective chemicals and plant smaller, more widely dispersed plots. Most importantly, they developed pesticide-resistant plants that contain more cocaine. The body count (or at least the number of dead cocaine plants) has increased, but we are not winning the war.

Using the most conservative estimates, South American cocaine production probably amounts to more than 500 tons of refined cocaine per year. Using less conservative assumptions, the number could well amount to more than 1000 tons per year. A case could be made for the less conservative scenario, since, in 1994, the U.S. government confiscated more than 220 tons of refined cocaine. Not even the most optimistic experts suggest that anything close to one-half of the drugs smuggled into the United States are detected and, in fact, the U.S. government has all but admitted that Plan Colombia is a failure. During a tour of Colombia's coca growing regions, the White House drug czar conceded that spending $3.3 billion (the estimated cost of Plan Colombia through mid-2004), seizing tons of raw cocaine, destroying coca crops, and locking up thousands of drug traffickers in Colombia and the United States has had little impact on the flow of cocaine on American streets.

The populations of the United States and Europe are nearly twice what they were at the start of World War II. The population of Southeast Asia increased by even more. Assuming that 1.5 billion people now live in those same areas, and the total refined cocaine output is 1000 tons, then at least 300 mg of cocaine are produced each year for every man, woman, and child in Western Europe, America, and Southeast Asia. The 20 mg per person available in the 1930s would not have been a large enough quantity to produce measurable physiologic changes in the population, but the 300 mg per person available today could. In some situations, 300 mg would be sufficient to cause toxicity. This increase in quantity available occurred despite four different international treaties, and the expenditure of countless billions of dollars on interdiction and policing. If Sir Edward Gray, the British Foreign Secretary, thought that a worldwide production of less than 10 tons was a threat to public health, how would he have reacted to a worldwide supply of 1000 tons?

There is no evidence today that coca is being grown in Southeast Asia. If production was to resume there, however, the total world supply could easily double, and probably triple. But a worse scenario can be envisioned. Cocaine is a relatively small molecule. It should not be that difficult to decipher the DNA codes for its production, manufacture copies of the DNA instructions, and insert them in some innocuous plant such as corn or soybean. The genetic manipulations necessary to produce spoilage-resistant tomatoes were probably more difficult. So far as anyone knows, this process has not yet occurred. The explanation is simple. Naturally grown cocaine is so cheap, and so abundant, why spend the money on genetic engineering?

Japan entered the drug trade because the time and circumstances were right. There were plenty of well-heeled investors with few moral qualms, there was a xenophobic government with few scruples, and the army had a pressing need for cash. In this new millennium, xenophobic governments with few scruples are not in short supply. Some may consider drug dealing an attractive option.

Further Reading

Chapter 1
The Inca and Spanish Conquests

There are several useful books that deal with this historical period. Joseph Gagliano wrote an excellent textbook based upon the original documents produced during the Spanish Colonial Administration. The account presented here draws heavily on Gagliano's book, *Coca Prohibition in Peru*, from University of Arizona Press. Another favorite that covers much of the same material in a far less academic fashion is Golden Mortimer's *Peru History of Coca, the Devine Plant of the Incas, with an Introductory Account of the Incas and the Andean Indians of Today*. The book was first printed in 1901 but was reprinted in the 1980s, and modestly priced used copies can be found in the bookshops of most college towns. Cieza de Leon's *The Inca*, translated by Harriet de Onis, and published by the University of Oklahoma, is interesting reading, and so are the standard histories by Cespedes and Harin, both of which are highly readable and authoritative.

Chapter 2
"Joyfulle News"

Of course, the best place to start is with Monardes' own writings (*Joyfulle Newes Out of the Newe Found Worlde*), or at least the English translation by John Frampton, with an introduction by Stephen Gaselee, published in 1925 by Constable and Company, reissued in a facsimile edition in 1925 as a Tudor Translation, 2nd series, IX. There are also the general histories and biographies of Kew Gardens, but most of the information contained in this chapter is taken from medical journals, including *Lancet* and the *British Medical Journal* from the end of the 19th to the beginning of the 20th century. All of the former are available online through Elsevier's ScienceDirect service.

Chapter 3
Botanists, Naturalists, and Pedestrians

For a general account of the Amazon and its exploration, read von Tschudi's *Travels in Peru during the Years 1838–1842*. Wiley and Putnam published an English translation in 1847. Otherwise, no single book covers all of this material. As in Chapter 2, useful information is to be found in the various books about the Hookers of Kew. A review paper by Bo Holmsted was published more than 20 years ago in the *Journal of Ethnopharmacology* but remains useful. Sadly, Holmsted has since died. For a very good account of the hunt for quinine (which more or less determined the hunt for coca), consult the long out-of-print book entitled *Science and Scientists in the Netherlands Indies*. This book was edited by Pieter Honig and Frans Verdoorn and was published, during World War II, by the Board for the Netherlands Indies, Surinam, and Curacao. For the rest, you will have to go to the primary literature. The *British Medical Journal*, in particular, covered Weston's foot race in great detail.

Chapter 4
Celebrity Endorsements

This chapter is really about Angelo Mariani, and that presents a problem, because it would probably be a mistake to take too seriously anything Mariani has to say about himself, and there is no good biography. For good insight into the business of making coca-based wines, read *Coca Java* by Emma Reen, published in 1919 by the University of Paris. Reen's book (really her doctoral thesis) is included with two other cocaine monographs in my book, *A History of Cocaine, the Mystery of Coca Java and the Kew Plant*, published by the Royal Society of Medicine Press in 2003.

Chapter 5
A Cholo of Huarai

Karl Fredrich Philip von Martius (1794–1868) and Johan Baptist von Spix (1781–1826) both wrote accounts of their adventures, and both were translated, but copies are only likely to be found in major libraries. Very little has been written about Rossbach and Aschenbrandt. Books about George Davis come mostly from the company he helped found, Parke, Davis & Co., and read more like corporate reports than insightful biographies.

Chapter 6
Genies and Furies

The best general book is Hans Maier's monograph, *Der Kokainismus*. Parts of this book were translated into English and published under the title *Maier's Cocaine Addiction*, by Canadian pharmacologist Oriana Josseau Kalant in 1987. The Addiction Research Foundation translated the book, and it appears to still be in print. To learn more about Freud and Koller, read the medical literature published at that time. There is no substitute for the primary literature. Most of the important papers are in German and were not translated. But, many of Freud's cocaine papers were collected and published. The most useful collection is *The Cocaine Papers and Sigmund Freud*, edited by Robert Byck. Another useful collection of papers was published by George Andrews and David Solomon, called *The Coca Leaf and Cocaine Papers*. According to Amazon.com, both of these last two titles are still in print, and used copies are available.

Chapter 7
Death by Misadventure

All of the early Amazon explorers, especially Johan von Tschudi, expressed concerns about the apparent dangers of coca chewing, but others, like Sigmund Freud and Paolo Mantegazza, ignored what they did not want to hear. Clear explanations of cocaine toxicity are to be found in my textbook, *The Pathology of Drug Abuse*, 3rd ed. (CRC Press, 2001). Freud's accounts of what transpired are mainly self-serving, but the books critical of Freud's work with cocaine are so strident, they are probably not worth reading.

Chapter 8
A New Disease Emerges

For an introduction and general overview of this disorder, see my *Pathology of Drug Abuse*, 3rd ed. (CRC Press, 2001). All of the relevant primary literature can be found in the reference section of that book, or through MedLine. The *New York Times* piece by Dr. Edward Williams really should be read. It can be downloaded from the *New York Times* Web site at a nominal cost.

Chapter 9
Coca Java

Extensive details about the Indonesian cocaine industry are to be found in
Emma Reen's *Coca Java*, which was translated and reprinted in *A History of
Cocaine, the Mystery of Coca Java and the Kew Plant*, published by the Royal
Society of Medicine Press in 2003. This book also contains two other, never
previously translated, monographs on the cocaine trade, and several papers
from the Dutch literature.

Chapter 10
A Beautiful White Powder

There are no general books on this topic. The two anthologies recommended
in Chapter 6 may be helpful. The material describing Sigmund Freud's
relationship to Merck and Parke, Davis & Company is based on a paper by
A.E. Hirshmüller (*Gesnerus*, 52, 116–132, 1995).

Chapter 11
The First Cocaine Cartels

Since the first edition of this book was published, an excellent book on the
topic was written by William B. McAllister (*Drug Diplomacy in the Twentieth
Century: An International History*, Routledge, 1999). The files of the British
Foreign Office offer a goldmine of information about how international drug
regulations were finally implemented. All British Foreign Office correspondence regarding the drug trade was published as a six-volume set, usually
available at large reference libraries. The standard text on narcotics control
is David Musto's *American Disease* (Yale University Press, 1973).

Chapter 12
Risky Business

Mark Pendergrast's book on Coca-Cola remains the definitive work on the
subject, although it is fascinating to read about the case from the other side.
When Harvey Wiley left government service, he became an editor of *Good
Housekeeping*, where he often editorialized under the guise of reporting.
Several issues are worth retrieving from the library: "*The Coca Cola Contro-
versy*" and his "*Soft Drinks and Dopes*," were both published in 1912 (*Good

Housekeeping, 55, 242–256, and 386–392). Wiley's *The Cocain (sic) Crime*, published in a 1914 issue (Vol. 58, 393–399), is also worth a read.

Chapter 13
The "Legitimate Business of Poisoning Hindoos"

These are essentially the same references as those cited for Chapter 11.

Chapter 14
Harpies in the West End

Mark Kohn's *Dope Girls: The Birth of the British Drug Underground* (Granda Books, 1993) gives a good overall view of what was happening in Europe and on the Continent. Perhaps the best way to learn more about this period is to read one, or more, of the novels published at the time. The connection between drugs and racism is clearly evident in Sax Rohmer's Fu Manchu creations. Aleister Crowley's (1875–1946), *Diary of a Drug Fiend* (1922; reprinted by Weiser Books in 1977) was set within Mayfair's café society and, again, some of the settings and incidents almost sounded like testimony at the Carleton inquest.

Chapter 15
Japan's Adventures in the Cocaine Trade

Japan's cocaine and drug trafficking is described, though not in sufficient detail, in the trial transcripts from the Tokyo War Crimes Trials. The best source, though, is the recently declassified material from Henry Anslinger's old Bureau of Narcotics. Anslinger supplied drug intelligence officers to MacArthur's occupation forces and kept copies of the reports for his own files. Bureau of Narcotics records from the 1930s were taken over by the U.S. Drug Enforcement Administration (DEA) and were still classified when we filed Freedom of Information requests in 1993. The documents of most interest are contained in RG 170 — Records of the DEA, Acc #71-A 3554, cartons #10 through 30. Interesting information is also to be found in the "SCAP" records (Supreme Commander Allied Pacific). The Public Health section deals with drug-related problems. However, some of the files remain classified. These records, along with Anslinger's papers, are now located in the new Archives Center in suburban Maryland. Also, since the first edition of this book, John Jennings published his study of Japanese cocaine and opium production. Jennings' book is based upon Japanese sources and sheds considerable light on many drug-related issues and leading players (*Opium Empire*, Praeger Publishers, 1997).

Chapter 16
Cocaine Pandemic?

Elaine Shannon's book, *Desperados*, published in 1988 by Viking Books, is still available, and highly recommended. The desperados in question were U.S. Drug Enforcement Administration (DEA) agents, not the cocaine dealers they were pursuing, but the book provides a clear insight into the drug wars of the late 1980s. The theories on what drives the recurrent epidemics are based upon mathematical models derived from David Musto's original writings. See Caulkins, J.P., Behrens, D.A., Knoll, C., Tragler, G., and Zuba, D., Markov chain modeling of initiation and demand: the case of the U.S. cocaine epidemic, *Health Care Manage. Sci.*, 7 (4), 319–329, 2004.

Index